RADICAL
REPARATIONS

RADICAL REPARATIONS

Healing the Soul of a Nation

Marcus Anthony Hunter

AMISTAD

An Imprint of HarperCollinsPublishers

FIRST EDITION

Designed by Nancy Singer

Library of Congress Cataloging-in-Publication Data is available upon request.

ISBN 978-0-06-300472-6

23 24 25 26 27 LBC 5 4 3 2 1

CONTENTS

1

SAMBO'S SMILE

Hidden from the sun with limited air supply. Deep beneath the sugar, rice, and freshwater. Underneath the gold, silver, copper, and diamonds. Well below the coal, ivory, and barrels of rum. A young West African boy lay deep within the ship's bowels, separated from everything he knew. He was unsure how long he had been in the dark, encased as he was in an endless loop of confusion, pain, death, suffering, tears, and unanswered prayers. When the ocean current settled enough for the swaying and rocking to stop, he allowed his mind to wander. He would try and estimate how long he had been engulfed in darkness. He figured it had been at least a month and some weeks, if not longer, since he last saw his mother, father, sister, grandmother, friends, and village. There was no way that he could be sure of the elapse of time, unable to see the sun or the moon nor the height of the tide—the tools he had been taught to measure time. All that he could recall was the long line leading onto the ship, the taste of iron from the bit implanted in his mouth, and the stench of rotten yams and okra meshed into the woven fibers of the sack the kidnappers pulled over his head. As the image of the African shoreline disappeared into the recesses of his mind, he felt his memory of home and what he looked and sounded like fade.

When the boy could conjure memories of his mother's smile, a small comfort would come over him. It was always short-lived, however, disturbed as he was by the sounds of someone's soul and spirit finally escaping their sick and sorrowful body. Even when interrupted, the boy would still try to smile back at his mother behind his tightly shut eyes. Each time was more unsuccessful than the first, her face and bright white teeth moving further and further out of the range of the boy's imagination. The overwhelming darkness changed his vision and ate away at the boy's hope for rescue or return. He could feel in his stomach the sensation that the ship was sailing farther and farther from home.

Sometimes he would muster just enough energy that he would try and live on his own smile. But even then, the grip of the bit in his mouth was too much to overcome. The punishing taste of the blood of his gums tickled his tongue and rolled back onto his parched throat—a painful reminder that Africa was gone. With each attempt came the penalty of rust, blood, iron, and the jarring flavors of unfamiliar metals and minerals. And so it came to pass that somewhere between months and weeks on the journey, there at the very bottom of the ship, the boy stopped smiling altogether. It simply hurt too much to smile, to remember, to think.

Unable to see his own reflection, the boy became convinced that his smile was gone anyway, useless if ever returned. What would he need a smile for if his mother, village, sister, and Africa had left him? Was a smile real if there was no reflection to confirm its existence? He asked himself these questions and others like them over and over, hoping that a voice inside would rise and give some insight, a sign, or some affirmation. But absolutely nothing and no one came.

The boy knew that while he was by himself, he was certainly not alone. Despite the darkness that engulfed all in the boat's bottom, he knew he was in a tightly packed container of Black suffering. He knew there were other boys aboard the vessel. He heard their cries for their fathers and mothers, grandmothers and chiefs, teachers and preachers.

But like his cries and pleas, theirs too would go unanswered. Eventually, a great silence came upon all below, swallowing up all the sound. The crippling silence was a sign to him that all the other children had given up hope too; they too had lost their smiles to the tortuous bit. The adults lying at their feet, with their legs on the left and their heads on the right, were so deep in their suffering and sadness that they appeared utterly still.

If not for the subtle sounds of life and the smell of death, the boy would have been unable to gauge his surroundings and those who were surviving the voyage with him. Though he was not sure how many would join him when and if they were allowed to leave their chamber of hell on the sea, he was determined that he would again see the sun. He wiggled his toes as affirmation, promising himself that his feet would again touch the earth.

A sudden cold sensation came upon the boy. Startled, the boy was unaware of the sensation's source, but as his shivers shook off some of the wetness, he smelled a familiar aroma. It was water. Fresh water. He cracked his mouth wide enough at each end to allow some of the drips inside. The tiny droplets rolled behind the bit to wash away the bloody drought that had made a home at the back of his tongue. He could hear the water splashing about, buckets falling to the floor, and men and children waking from their sleep and stillness. Others were unresponsive— dead and gone, perishing in the darkness somewhere in between the boat's rise and fall across the choppy Atlantic waters. A voice, speaking in a language he had only heard once before when the ship first set to sea, roared with the fearsome command: "That's right. Up and at 'em, fellas." The sounds of chains in motion clanked with a sliding boom. Then, before the boy knew it, there was a tug, and he was upright for the first time since the voyage began.

A line formed, and knapsacks were placed again on his head. He tried to bob and weave away from the knapsack, for it reminded him of the origin of his living nightmare. His efforts were met with a hard blow across his face. He could feel a tooth fall onto his tongue behind the bit.

Right then, the boy was sure what was left of his perfect smile was officially destroyed. He relented and felt tears stream from his eyes as the bag went over his head.

Counting in his head as he walked, he noticed a change in the air around step fifty. Then around step one hundred, he felt the heat of the sun for the first time. Then the same voice shouted: "Lift on my count! On three. One! Two! Three! LIFT!" And with that, the bags were removed, and for the first time, he saw colors again. Not just one color, but every color with blinding intensity. Red was deep and swirled into orange, colliding with yellow and opening into a blue-green blend. The ship was mahogany with salty white lines cracking along the floor like his grandmother's forehead when it caught a slight chill. The sky was a mix of turquoise and gray, and the smell of salt was everywhere, seeming to jump off everything; it was as if the boy was swimming inside one of his uncle's ceremonial salt dishes.

Remembering the promise he made to himself, he looked above his head and saw the sun. Blurry and thick at first, he began to feel its caressing warmth. The sun saw him too. He was sure of it. He hoped that a wave might get the sun's attention, and that the sun might send a signal back home that he was alive, and that it might even convey his actual location and aid a potential rescue. He felt the smile coming, and before his face could fight the bit, he cast his eyes to the salt-strewn deck floor. The blood from his broken loose tooth fell upon his tongue, a painful reminder that he'd lost control over his body when they kidnapped him. Lifting his head, he scanned the ship. It was large and looked like one of those trading boats he once saw when his father approached the shoreline to exchange silver for food during the drought. As he peered around, he counted at least two hundred men and boys, some from his village, others from neighboring villages. Some were the Big Men he recalled from the battles and mini wars that had occurred over his short life back home.

Many of the children began to sob and scream for help as one of the shackled men attempted to run. The boy knew the man, for he was known throughout many villages as "Kojo, the fastest man alive." Back home, Kojo would be seen every Monday wearing his many medals from the racing events he handily won. As Kojo ran, his chains followed him and revealed the horrifying system that linked each of them to one another in sets of ten. The chains made it so Kojo's running meant he was also dragging children behind him. The kidnappers or the ship crew or whoever designed these chains had already anticipated running might be a response once exposed to the sun or given any space, air, or light. Therefore, every grown man was linked to eight children and one adult man like bookends.

As Kojo sprinted toward the edge of the ship, he was shot in the back shoulder. He paused for a moment and hunched over as though he was about to fall down. Then, when he believed no one would notice, the boy raised his hand to grab a little of the sun for himself, pulling the light into his heart. After a few beats, Kojo lunged forward, jumping off the boat into the great sea.

Kojo and three children attached to him had disappeared into the dense steel blue of the sea by the time the four white men ordered to fetch him got to the edge of the boat. The remaining children held on tightly as an older man at the opposite end of Kojo's chains held onto the links with all the power he could muster to avoid going overboard. The chain splintered the boat's edge and began ripping at the man's hand. The children pushed their feet against the short wall to avoid being pulled over, and piercing screams reverberated as the chain started crushing and bruising their ankles. One boy dangled just over the edge of the boat, just a foot or so shy of the water. After a bit of stumbling and pulling, the white men were able to cut the link, remove the boy dangling for his life, and place him back onto the deck. One boy's ankle looked broken in the ordeal, but they all embraced each other nonetheless. The children crowded around the older man who had refused to let the chain pull them all under. For a moment, they'd forgotten where they were. They felt alive.

Meanwhile, the man in charge of the ship and crew, or "the commander" as he was called by the white men, shot his gun into the air. The booming bullet made a sharp noise, and the boy could feel the heat of the gun near his cheek, as he was standing so close to the commander.

"Well, that's it! You can't do anything nice for these animals!" the commander yelled aloud, followed by a complex and noticeable hacking cough.

No one spoke. Those in chains continued covering their ears and kneeling to the ground. Several men even began to pray loudly, calling upon God, Jesus, and Olodumare to swoop down, save them, and deliver them home to Africa. The answer they got was a good pound upside their skulls from the white men as they coerced them all back below.

Feeling the tug on the chains at his foot, the boy knew it was time to proceed. If he refused, he'd learned from Kojo's jump that he'd be dragged below by those in front of him. It was not until then that he noticed he was at the end of the chain, unlike the other children. Unlike the others, there was no adult behind him. Just as he came to this observation, the commander put his hand upon his shoulder and smiled. "No Fenton Plantation for you, Sambo," the commander's rigid face gave way to a wide-eyed smile. While the boy was relieved to see a smile, the commander's was not nearly as lovely and inviting as his mother's. In addition to having wooden teeth at the front, the commander's smile was menacing and nefarious.

"Don't you worry," he coughed. "You are special," the commander whisper-smile spoke to the boy. The commander was sure that the young child had no clue what was said and spoke no English from the befuddled expression on the boy's face. "This is my little Sambo, fellas!" he announced with a seriousness that made everyone pause and stop in their tracks. "Take a good look at 'em! And whoever hit him across the face will be paying me back from their share! You hear me! Hell has nothing on me when someone is on my bad side! You hear! Now back down into the pit they go! Next stop for this lot—Barbados!" A hacking cough followed and echoed behind as the captives stepped closer and closer back to the bottom of the boat.

For the boy, time atop the boat's deck was so many thoughts, feelings, and things all at once. The boy was scared, confused, shocked, curious, and intrigued. "Where are we going? What is 'Barbados'? Is it in Africa? Why am I special? And what was that name I was called? Saaaaaaam . . . Samm . . . Samboo, Samboo . . . Sambo, Sambo?"

"It means he owns you," he heard a decisive and clear response in Twi, his native language. So used to talking to himself, bouncing around thoughts inside his head, he had not realized he had uttered those questions aloud.

"Owns me? Owns me . . . Owns me!" His eyes shot all the way open, sharply cutting through the darkness. It was then that he knew he was never going home; now, the boy could see light in and between the dark.

As he began weeping, he could feel the little piece of the sun he captured on the deck rolling around inside his breaking heart. As he cried, he heard others near and far away from him let out their sadness too. It was a collective realization all at once: none of them were going home or would ever see Africa again. Afraid that the sadness would overtake everyone, the boy thought of a simple beat of music his parents would play as the sun rose above their home. The boy began knocking a familiar drum beat with his right hand, drawing out the sunlight he'd captured until it appeared in his left hand. His knocks were soon joined by others familiar with the rhythm. The men and boys cried. They knocked until, after a full ten beats, the boy opened his left hand, and a revelation of sunlight burst from his palm and lit the bottom of the ship from end to end.

Beholding the wonder of the light of the sun from the little boy's left palm, for the first time, they all saw each other. No sounds were made. There was not much motion, save for their eyes meeting one another for as long as the light flourished. And for those set of seconds, they felt heard and seen and believed. Maybe, just maybe, they would survive. The beating stopped, and the light left the boy's hand as it rose a few inches before fading into the thick, pungent air as quickly as it had arrived. He closed his eyes and fell asleep.

The remainder of the voyage was a fog—subsumed in an ugly routine of throwing the dead overboard, being splashed with water, and, occasionally, getting a smattering of an oatmeal paste mixed with some sort of spinach-and-algae-tasting green soup. As disgusting as the pasty soup was, it was the only time the bit was removed, which offered slight relief, lost tooth and all. By the time the ship arrived at Barbados, more than half of the men and boys had perished from depression, malnourishment, and sheer sorrow. The white men gathered the remaining captives, pushing them down the plank and off the boat.

Making his way toward the plank, the boy and his chains moved in rhythm with those in front. Then, abruptly, the commander cut his link and stood before him. "You stay!" The commander saw the boy's eyes fill with numbing confusion and pointed him to a door at the back of the deck.

As the boy walked, he was amazed by how similar this new place, "Barbados," looked from the sea to Africa. The palm trees were a bit wilder and untamed but familiar. Maybe they were still in Africa, and the white men made them stay on the boat for a long time to fool and disorient them. When he saw the white men come from the jungle and meet the chained men and boys at the dock, he knew it was not Africa.

Continuing the walk down the deck to the room, he then heard a familiar voice calling, "Kwame! Kwame!" Though his back was turned, he knew exactly who it was. It was Ami, his little sister. The boy was both astonished and horrified to discover that Ami had been on the boat all along. He realized Ami too must have been taken that night by the fire after grandmother bid them good night after story time. Shaken and surprised, the boy's head spun with the newfound awareness that there were women and girls aboard as well. The women and girls had successfully been kept hidden from the men and boys and stored opposite them. *A cruel trick indeed*, the boy thought.

He immediately pivoted and attempted to race to Ami, but the commander grabbed him and held him so tight he couldn't breathe. There was nothing he could do as he watched Ami walk down the plank, yelling and crying his name. He tried to be strong, but he screamed when he saw the white men take her and disappear into the jungle. The commander put his hand over his mouth and nose, his other arm pressing even harder against his lungs. Unable to breathe and helpless, the boy fell unconscious.

When the boy awoke, he found himself at the foot of the commander's bed. Moonlight drenched his face as its glow emanated from the window across the room. The boat rocked, and the sound of the sea all around him was a reminder that he had not dreamt of Ami; it had all really happened, and now she was gone from him forever. Maybe he might make it back to the place they call Barbados and find Ami one day.

Sensing that the boy was awake, the commander stood from his bed and sat before him. "You will be safe with me." The boy turned his face away from the commander. The commander grabbed his face and looked him square in the eye. "You will be better off. You may not believe me—" A hard cough interrupted his words. The commander wiped the phlegm that had flown from his mouth with a handkerchief from his back pocket, continuing as if nothing had happened. "You will be better off with me. You will find being my right hand is better than being on that wretched island." Convinced that the boy could not understand what he was saying, the commander paused, looking the boy up and down. "Poor Sambo. Sambo, I will teach you English, and you will help me. I didn't pay that wretched chief to have a hapless mute." Unexpectedly, the commander removed the bit from the boy's mouth. He then cut away the chains from the boy's wrists and ankles. He gave the boy a potato sack to use as a blanket and another as a pillow. The boy didn't know what was happening; he could only think about Ami and his parents and how sad they all must be. There on the floor of the commander's bedroom, the boy cried for the last time. He decided underneath and atop potato sacks that there would be no more smiling and no more tears until he was reunited with Ami or returned home.

Over the next ten months of the voyage, the boy learned that English breakfast was both a type of meal and a tea, that the commander needed his feet rubbed for at least an hour before he could sleep, and that the crew was terrible at math, quickly losing count of the inventory of their shipment. So the boy became the commander's chief of merchandise. He counted all the rice, ivory, minerals, coal, the dead, and the alive using a system of check-marks that he would later furnish for the commander in return for a light pat on the head and a hot plate of the commander's leftovers.

Finally, when the boat pulled to the shore, the commander awoke with a glee the boy had never witnessed. "We are home!" the commander said as he pointed at the cottage-lined coast.

"Home?" the boy repeated back with an air of disbelief.

"Yes, Sambo. This is England, my home."

As the boat anchored along Morecambe Bay, the commander became giddy like a mischievous Catholic schoolgirl hiding something from the nuns. He ran back and forth across his chamber, brushing his hair here, combing his beard there, checking the mirror to make sure not a hair was out of place. The boy was astonished by the rapid cleanliness, as he had only seen the commander disheveled for the entirety of the time he had known him.

"Welcome to Sunderland Point, Sambo." The commander bowed before the boy as if he were local hospitality. The boy laughed, even though he really didn't mean to; he just found the whole performance ridiculous. Feeling foolish and self-conscious, the commander shot back at the boy harshly, "You know you can tell you're missing that tooth when you laugh!" The commander laughed heartily at the boy's expense. "Now Sambo, you will stay here at this pub while I head to take care of the business of reporting our inventory with the magistrate at Lancaster Castle." He pointed his finger east just beyond the horizon. "Then I will be off to see my wife and children. The crew will be unloading the cargo."

Fearing that the boy's scanning of the area might encourage an escape attempt, the commander continued, "And don't you get any ideas, Sambo. Just so you know, in about an hour, the tide will rise so high you can drown if you are not indoors. When the tide rises, there is no escape, and I would hate to see you end up like crazy Kojo."

The boy nodded in agreement and headed inside the pub to his quarters.

"That's all you have to say, Sambo?" the commander inquired impatiently.

"Yes, sir, I under—" A slight cough interrupted him. The boy cleared his throat and continued. "I understand. Wait here until you return, sir."

"That's a good boy, Sambo." The commander smiled, patted the boy's head, and turned toward the castle in the distance.

Here lies

Poor SAMBOO

A faithful NEGRO

Who

(Attending his Master from the West Indies)

DIED on his Arrival at SUNDERLAND.

Full sixty Years the angry Winter's Wave

Has thundering daſhd this bleak & barren Shore

Since SAMBO'S Head laid in this lonely GRAVE.

Lies still & ne'er will hear their turmoil more.

Full many a Sandbird chips upon the Sod

And many a Moonlight Elfin round him trips

Full many a Summer's Sunbeam warms the Clod

And many a teeming cloud upon him drips.

But still he sleeps__till the awakening Sounds

Of the Archangel's Trump new Life impart

Then the GREAT JUDGE his Approbation founds

Not on Man's Color but his __WORTH of HEART

James Watson Scr.   H. Bell del.

1796

There, one hundred yards from the pub, reads the inscription atop the boy's grave. Adorned with fresh daisies, roses, peonies, and daffodils, the boy's body lay thousands of miles away from his village in Africa.

I arrived at Sunderland Point on a sunny day in May 2018 at the invitation of noted Black British poet extraordinaire SuAndi. During the drive from Manchester, I played DJ, spinning through Earth, Wind & Fire; Stevie Wonder; and Chaka Khan—in that order. SuAndi told me of the small town where we were headed. Though I did not speak it aloud, upon hearing the name "Sunderland," an ominous feeling came upon me. We were heading to where an enslaved Black boy went *asunder*, never to be seen again. Asunder land. I found it curious that a white town had memorialized an enslaved Black person. And with that curiosity swirling inside, I quelled my ambivalence, determined to fully experience the unfolding day. Intrigued, I took a deep breath and looked at the trees until the soft and then sharp scent of the bay wafted through the air.

The pathway to Sunderland Point was quite the maze of winding roads, high brush, and then a short stone bridge of two lanes—one to arrive and the other to leave—that carried us over Morecambe Bay into Sunderland Point. Sunderland Point is a small town with old-world cottages and some new builds scattered alongside the shoreline. During the triangle slave trade, the Point served as the port for Lancaster. Bells and painted lines are about a foot or two high at the corners of each structure to indicate the rising tide that separates it from the mainland. Without speaking, SuAndi and I looked at each other after parking the car, an unspoken agreement that we would make sure we got our Black selves out of Dodge before the water rose. While leaving the parking area, I noticed a gang of cockles along the stone bridge and a small memorial.

"Is this the marker?" I asked SuAndi.

"Oh no. It's inset some yards into the town just near the salt marsh."

"Ahhh, I see. But then, what is that for?" I responded with an even more profound inquisitiveness.

"A year or so ago, twenty-five or more Chinese migrants drowned at this point while collecting cockles to sell at the market for money to take care of themselves," she said, her words rising and falling with a sadness that I too felt while listening.

For several minutes we didn't speak; we stood and gazed at the marker. I took another deep breath. Asunder land, indeed.

We were soon greeted by an associate producer for the BBC and then the whole team. SuAndi had been invited to participate in the filming of an episode of *Great Canal Journeys*. Aired on BBC Channel 4, the show follows legendary British couple Timothy Lancaster West and Prunella Margaret Rumney West Scales as they explore the United Kingdom on a canal barge and narrowboat trips. West, known for his classical theatre performances, and Scales, known best for her role as Sybil in the long-running BBC comedy *Faulty Towers*, were kind and lovely to both me and SuAndi. They offered tea, coffee, and a small bite as they readied themselves for filming.

During our brief discussion, the couple emphasized that they chose Sunderland Point because they believed it essential to cover the role and presence of slavery in Britain and the use of the canals to facilitate its horrors. The show for them was not merely a recording of the magisterial scenery of the UK waterways. Instead, they both felt a duty to inform and educate BBC watchers of the stories and histories—good, bad, and ugly—that these waters hold. Like Scales's forthcomingness about her battle with Alzheimer's and the dementia it caused, the couple was invested in the program as a meditative truth serum for BBC viewers.

After some touch-ups, filming began with SuAndi taking West and Scales on a tour of the town, highlighting its role and place in the British slave trade. Next, she took them around the pub where the young, enslaved boy was believed to have stayed. The couple was attentive, even scholarly, in their questions for SuAndi. After some questions and answers, the crew cut and directed everyone to the next scene, which would be at the gravesite near the salt marsh.

As I walked with a few crew members to the burial grounds, we talked about the grave and how the boy might have wound up dead so far away from his quarters in the pub. A few paused and reflected; others answered mostly that he likely died from an illness. I confessed I found it odd and suspicious. I presumed that he may have been killed, dragged in the dark, or even attempted to run and got stuck in the darkness, his feet sticking into the salty marsh. With no help and no one to hear him, he sank and died at the spot where he was stuck. All this imagery and possibility played through my mind like a movie. As filming at the gravesite resumed, I imagined the grueling voyage, the losses, loneliness, and cruelty of what this little Black boy endured.

The producers staged the scene and called "Action!" I sat several feet away from the scene, visible only to the small rabbit huddled in the borough to my right. As it turns out, no one really knows how the young boy wound up one hundred yards from the pub nor the cause of his sudden death. What is known is that he was left behind while the ship's captain headed to nearby Lancaster Castle to meet with various aristocrats and dignitaries. Perhaps the tide rose before he was able to return. Maybe the Captain imbibed too heartily and needed to sleep off a night of drinking and intended to retrieve the boy and his boat after the hangover subsided. Whatever the case may have been, the result was a dead Black child alone where a pasture meets a salt marsh as the tide rose at the other side, cutting him off from the rest of the world.

Meanwhile, SuAndi was being filmed alongside West and Scales, reading the inscription on the gravesite. Then, she consecrated the area just above the plaque where an additional statement resides, set in place after the original gravestone had been desecrated:

> Thoughtless and irreverent people having
> damaged & defaced the plate, this replica was
> affixed. RESPECT THIS LONELY GRAVE

Reciting and heeding the warning atop the grave, SuAndi completed the ancestral ritual by pouring out a bit of libation. She passed around a bottle of red wine, and the couple followed her lead. She followed it by reciting an original poem.

Her brown skin and long black hair grew with a glowing majesty as she read aloud in honor of what the boy had lost. Then, recalling his loss of home, she ended by calling forth an imagined end to his suffering where his spirit ascended and traveled home to Africa. Upon reaching home, he sees his mother again, and she smiles, and he returns with the smile he had lost along the way.

It was a moving scene to behold.

As the scene came to an end, a calming breeze passed by my right shoulder. I closed my eyes. When I opened them, I realized that perhaps SuAndi's efforts had released his spirit from Asunder Land. Her poetic phrasing about smiling and returning home also made me reflect on the sheer loss of humanity that slavery authorized, permitted, and perpetuated. And while many freedoms were taken from Black African people in the practice and legally sanctioned operation known as enslavement and the slave trade, the boy buried before us also demonstrated that freedom varies.

Freedom is both large and small. Large freedoms lost like language, family, autonomy, and land are undoubtedly important. But so too are the small freedoms lost like the ability to smile. Unfortunately, these small freedoms are often eclipsed to repair and retrieve the bigger ones. As the breeze swirled around me, a new awareness unlocked. I realized that any idea of repair and restoration from slavery must recognize all the freedoms lost, especially the small ones, because as the wisdom of the elders holds: "Little things add up to big things."

As small of a loss as a smile may seem, a person's smile is the biological and anatomical anchor of their thymus gland, which boosts, determines, and organizes a healthy immune system. By stealing the joy smiling brings, the bit also destroys the body from the inside out. The bit and the ship ensured that many Black women, men, girls, and boys perished from disease and illness. Therefore, those alive today are the descendants of those who survived despite the bit's attempt to block their smile and access to their birthright of happiness it affords. It is here, within this truth, when smiles and joy and home and family and labor were stolen and lost, where the premise of radical reparations resides. *Radical Reparations* seeks to identify, retrieve, and acknowledge the freedoms lost to light the way to how and why we must heal the lives, cultures, families, and people harmed, maimed, killed, and devastated by and through enslavement.

This book is based on more than a decade of research and travel across the United States, the Caribbean, Europe, and Africa. As I retraced and studied the steps of the slave trade and enslavement, on every plane ride back to my home in the United States of America, I came to recognize that all the horrors and losses that occurred were unimaginable.

Our minds and hearts are not prepared to take in the sheer volume of the terror, yet they must. If we desire a world, or even a nation, better and more humane than the one we inherited, we must confront and understand the past. Not so that we get lost under its weight. Instead, so we may heal and see that humanity is something shared and that slavery did not happen simply on plantations. Slave ships were provided through loans and credit, underwritten like home mortgages are today. Slavery was a global enterprise, thus there are no clean hands.

What started off as an academic research project transformed into something more. Conveying what I have learned in my journey required that I write from the center of my heart's brain to connect with your heart and imagination; for that is where actual change is possible. If anything about slavery is true, then anything is possible. All we genuinely live are stories—the ones we create, the ones created for us, and the ones kept secret. America is not just a set of states, cities, territories, laws, cultures, and customs. America is first and foremost a story, a collection of ideas and imagination. When and where you enter the American story does not preclude the narrative that has already taken shape. All points of entry are built atop the existing premise of America: enslavement and land dispossession.

America is a beautiful mansion with many rooms on a beautiful block. A gleaming beauty from the outside, America on the inside reveals a different story. So thoroughly impressed with America's exterior, those who enter inside are often aghast. Across its many rooms are piles of wall-to-wall dirty, filthy laundry. Piles on piles. Flies swirl above and below the piles. The stench and filth surround you until you no longer notice it, and though there seems to be no room, more piles emerge as you find your spot inside.

Piles everywhere: 1) *political reparations*: restorative and reparative historically informed advocacy transforming government and political representation and participation; 2) *intellectual reparations*: the purposeful and public recognition and acknowledgment of the creations, inventions, and ideas of formerly enslaved people and their descendants; 3) *legal reparations*: restorative justice, and racial equity established and authorized in laws and policies; 4) *economic reparations*: pecuniary and/or monetary assistance, subsidy, restitution, and debt relief; 5) *social reparations*: restoration and repair of the social contract to end racism and mindsets premised on racial and ethnic hierarchy, thus affirming the dignity of human beings; 6) *spatial reparations*: a restorative and reparative geography of socioeconomic and political opportunity, and land healing, particularly for those displaced and dispossessed by American slavery and their descendants; and 7) *spiritual reparations*: the purposeful and intentional recognition, representation, and recovery of the religious and spiritual cosmologies, practices, and beliefs harmed and lost in the triangle slave trade and American slavery. Within these seven forms of reparations, or P.I.L.E.S., we can unlock a new foundation and pathway to truth, love, justice, racial healing, and freedom in America and everywhere Black people are, heretofore, *radical reparations*.

Our divinely manifested and shared humanity has been the original promise and bond that enslavement and land dispossession disfigured.

We can and must heed the domestic and global calls for comprehensive repair, racial healing, equity, and truth. As challenging as the work ahead may appear, it is nowhere near what our ancestors endured. If we can begin to acknowledge and unlearn the false premise that diminishes reparations simply as a racial problem, then we achieve the new untapped radical awareness of it as what it truly is: a fundamental, urgent human crisis in need of redress.

When Black people were chained, held captive, tortured, kidnapped, raped, bought, and sold, our collective humanity was too. Slavery is not just an aspect of American and global history; it is a founding premise of the current human condition. Therefore, a radical reparative justice frame is always already based on rescuing and restoring the soul of humanity. For if there is such a thing as race, then the human race is its truest form.

Europeans imported and exported a global distortion of the ancient system of primary colors to subjugate African and Indigenous people. Black, as a color, was perverted into something other than the powerful foundational hue that manages to absorb all other colors while maintaining its integrity. White juxtaposed with black; the color white then elevated at the expense of red, yellow, and blue, and their purple, green, and orange children.

Once upon a time, not long ago, there was no such thing as white people. Domination over other humans, nations, and continents is why systemic racism exists. And while this distorted color system has organized our ideas of race, value, and a hierarchy of humanity, we can opt into something healthier, something more authentic. We can return the system to balance. What is distorted can always be healed, for it is an underlying pain that hides and controls our sense of the future, revealing only unverified and useless fears of one another.

May the truth and possibility serve as a new lighthouse to guide us into the purposeful and collective work needed to build the world we know is possible. A world where we embrace and accept the harms of the past, leaning into such not to blame or shame, but rather to build and heal. This work will produce a new infrastructure of love and freedom that balances and replaces the old and existing systems of racism and human hierarchy with systemic equity and humanity, continuously working to repair and reconcile the sins of a system, country, and people who, while long gone, are still with us.

Let us begin.

2

THE PARABLE OF JUBILEE,
SOUTH CAROLINA

Anticipation filled the air everywhere. However, when cameras and reporters first arrived, folks were skeptical. Residents were suspicious that recording or discussing the result would jinx the whole enterprise.

Jubilee had been one hundred years in the making, and with the stroke of a pen, President Lyndon Baines Johnson could advance or destroy all they had accomplished. "Jubilee is a testament to the tenacity and fortitude of African American people!" Ruby smiled confidently as the camera zoomed in on her face, centering on her chocolate brown irises. She had been on a whirlwind tour, traveling to nearly every corner of the United States campaigning to ensure Jubilee's longevity. Along the way, Ruby experienced a combination of fear and joy each time she stood before an audience to educate people about Jubilee's origin and growth. She was both afraid and happy to expose the existence and history of Jubilee. Time and again, she told the powerful and nearly mythological history of how a small sustaining Black village had blossomed into a full third of the entire state of South Carolina. Some were dubious of her stories about Jubilee, summarily dismissing it as a scam meant to disrupt the hundred-year solace brought about by the end of the Civil War. Others believed Jubilee was paradise, an African American Jerusalem, often informing Ruby of their plans to move to the area as soon as possible. Both reactions caused her stomach to tighten, for her mission was only to inform and not to convince or recruit.

During her missions, Ruby was always accompanied by Jubilee's trusted advocate, Geneva Crenshaw, Esquire, senior partner of Crenshaw & Associates. Geneva had been selected by the Council of Elders, a group of eighteen members from the nine founding families, based upon her expertise and success in winning civil rights lawsuits. Geneva's approach fascinated the elders; her approach was premised on the idea of using Jim Crow and racism to Jubilee's advantage. Geneva was persuasive in reframing segregation, arguing that the same Jim Crow laws permitting discrimination by white people against Black people could be used to authorize an exclusively African American territory recognized as a legal entity by the federal government.

During her presentation before the council, Geneva shared all of the legal battles Black families and individuals lost in favor of racial segregation. From the Dred Scott decision forward, she demonstrated the federal government's pattern of protecting racial segregation and white property ownership. When the two issues were combined, the case in favor of the status quo was quite tricky to win. Then, of course, the landmark 1954 *Brown v. Board of Education* Supreme Court decision ended racial segregation in schools and universities. Still, according to Geneva, that was an outlier. The council was especially taken with Geneva's evidence of the poor treatment of Black students made to be the great integrators.

"Racism is hardly based on logic. We need to fight racism the way a forest ranger fights fire with fire." Geneva's metaphor was compelling. "Civil rights advocates must first see the racial world as it is, determined by the need to maintain economic stability. And then, in the light of that reality, they must try to structure both initiatives and responses. We need, for example, to push for more money and more effective plans for curriculum in all-Black schools rather than exhaust ourselves and our resources on ethereal integration in mainly white suburbs."

The council all nodded in agreement.

"And now for the pièce de résistance." Geneva was not finished just yet. She put up a large poster that had a concept in the middle—*Racial Preference Licensing Act*. Underneath the concept were three bullet points and a large arrow inscribed with the word "outcome" pointing to the words "Jubilee is Free." After securing the poster to the wall and making sure that all were able to view it, Geneva began speaking and explaining again.

"Racism is more than a group of bad white folks whose discriminatory predilections can be controlled by well-formed laws vigorously enforced. Traditional civil rights laws tend to be ineffective because they are built on a law enforcement model. They assume that most citizens will obey the law; and when lawbreakers are held liable, a strong warning goes out that will discourage violators and encourage compliance."[1]

"Yes, this sounds like the goal of *Brown v. Board*," said one of the elders, interrupting Geneva's flow.

"But the law enforcement model for civil rights breaks down when a great number of whites are willing—because of convenience, habit, distaste, fear, or simple preference—to violate the law. It then becomes almost impossible to enforce because so many whites, though not discriminating themselves, identify more easily with those who do than with their victims."[2]

Geneva paused to observe the group and make sure everyone was still following her. Not only were the elders following her, but they were also captivated. Each looked to be hanging on to Geneva's every word.

"Given the way things have gone historically, as all existing civil rights laws were invalidated, legislation like the Racial Preference Licensing Act might be all African Americans can expect. And it could prove no less—and perhaps more—effective than those laws that now provide us the promise of protection without either the will or the resources to honor that promise."[3] Geneva was on a roll and took a swig of water. "The question is whether the activity reflects and is intended to challenge the actual barriers we face rather than those that seem a threat to the integration ideology."[4] Geneva took another gulp of water. "We might begin by considering the advantages of such a radical measure as the Radical Preference Licensing Act. First, by authorizing racial discrimination, such a law would, as I suggested earlier, remove the long-argued concern that civil rights laws deny anyone the right of nonassociation. With the compulsive element removed, people who discriminate against Blacks without getting the license authorized by law may not retain the unspoken but real public sympathy they now enjoy. They may be viewed as what they are: lawbreakers who deserve punishment."[5]

Geneva's logic piqued the council's interests even more. They sat at the edge of their chairs as she continued. "Second, by requiring the discriminator both to publicize and to pay all Blacks a price for the 'right,' the law may dilute both the financial and the psychological benefits of racism. Today, even the worst racist denies being racist. Most whites pay a tremendous price for their reflexive and often unconscious racism, but few are ready to post their racial preferences on a public license and even less ready to make direct payments for the privilege of practicing racism. Paradoxically, gaining the right to practice openly what people now enthusiastically practice covertly will take a lot of the joy out of discrimination and replace that joy with some costly pain."[6]

Some of the council members clapped heartily, moved just by Geneva's sheer gumption alone. Unsure if a law of this nature was possible was irrelevant. What was important was Geneva's compelling perspective about how to exploit the tendency and predictability of white racism and discrimination.

Geneva took a final sip of water. "Third, Black people will no longer have to divine—as we have regularly to do in this antidiscrimination era—whether an employer, a Realtor, or a proprietor wants to exclude them. The license will give them—and the world—ample notice. Those who seek to discriminate without a license will place their businesses at risk of serious, even ruinous, penalties."[7] Geneva let her points sink in with the council. She enjoyed the sound of quiet when thoughts and words were penetrating the listener.

"We must learn to examine every racial policy, including those that seem most hostile to Blacks, and determine whether there is unintended potential African Americans can exploit. Think about it! Rather than assimilate Jubilee into South Carolina, why not make Jubilee its own state or territory?"[8] she implored the council. No other candidate for legal representation had dared to directly pose a question or challenge the elders, nor had they posed the idea that Jubilee become its own state. This impressed the council greatly, as it was a vision of Black longevity and Black political power; it allowed them to use racial segregation to their advantage.

The council's search for legal counsel had been based upon the need to have an in-house legal team to defend them against white claims of property owned before the Civil War's conclusion. However, as Jubilee grew from the original forty acres that each of the original nine families acquired through General Sherman's Special Field Order No. 15, white antagonism grew. Many white families started investigating their family lineage to find even the tiniest sliver of familial ties to plantation owners to spite Jubilee.

These ties would then be used to wage litigation and lawsuits against the property ownership rights of Black families in Jubilee. Instead of leaning away from claims of participation in slavery, white families across South Carolina were lining up and carrying portraits of slave owners who were so-called relatives to stake a claim on the land that had been settled as Jubilee. In the beginning, Jubilee was initially constituted of an area of South Carolina thought of as wasteland. During slavery, no plantation owner wanted the land; it was part landfill, part manure farm, part marshy swamp, and part scorched earth from cannon and gunpowder blasts during the Civil War battles.

Embarrassed by the South's loss, many whites initially did not bat an eye at the Black settlement, for it was "the blood-soaked earth of the losers," as white South Carolinians called it. But when forty acres became four thousand, and four thousand transformed into forty thousand and counting, the legal battles ensued and threatened to financially ruin Jubilee. This, the Council of Elders would not, could not, allow. If Jubilee were going to fail, it would be based upon its people's lack of need and interests. They refused to be run out of their homes, refused to be pushed out of the land they had alchemized into the most fertile soil east of the Mississippi River.

After a brief discussion amongst themselves, the elders unanimously selected Crenshaw & Associates as their legal team with the caveat that Geneva Crenshaw agree to accompany Ruby during her missions of informing the public of Jubilee's existence and need to survive. Geneva not only agreed, but she also did them one better. She promised to utilize the full range of her connections within the Civil Rights Movement and get federal legislation to authorize it as an independent territory or even a state with voting rights. Geneva's undeniable confidence was infectious, and the elders were convinced.

That was ten years ago.

By the time 1965 had come, Geneva's promise had been well kept. Jubilee's independence was a line item in the second set of civil rights legislation, the Voting Rights Act of 1965, which sat on President Johnson's desk for signing by that July. But, of course, there were still debates and vicious racists attempting to defeat the legislation on all fronts. And so, it was essential and urgent that Ruby kept a full schedule of missions, traveling everywhere she could to ensure there were more allies than enemies. Ruby had strict instructions to always be disarmingly beautiful and speak in soothing tones. Ruby was never to wear all black, as it might trigger white fears of an all-Black militia—like the ones that handily and triumphantly defeated the planter class's Confederate soldiers all up and through the South.

Therefore, Ruby made sure to never wear the same outfit twice; most were white and yellow, sometimes blue; she always wore a smile and kept her hair neat, tidy, and as perfectly coifed as possible. Her hair must never be too short, and her clothes needed to be fashionable but modest. On rare occasions, Ruby wore her hair in its natural state as an Afro. Even then, she only wore it briefly and exclusively in a chocolate city like Detroit, Harlem, Philly, or Washington, DC; and even then, the Afro was a perfectly round circle, not a hair out of place. Together, her clothes and hair, especially when she wore it pressed and shoulder-length as the council preferred, gave her an undeniable halo effect.

Ruby was "the archangel that had been selected by God to tell of the wonders of Jubilee," her father, Reverend Dr. Ronald Calhoun, would exalt as a reminder. "And it was her mission to spread the good news and to secure that Jubilee would endure into the future," Reverend Calhoun restated to her every time she reported feeling weary, frustrated, bored, annoyed, or defeated. When her father sensed that Ruby was exhausted or harbored any bad feelings that might upend her participation, he would impress upon her the urgency and dramatic impacts of her missions. He would hug her with comforting warmth and then sit her down and recall the story of how she and her brother were conceived. The story always began and ended the same, with a patterned and moving rhythm, tone, and rise and fall in plot and climax. It always began with the thesis that she and her brother were a miracle, especially after her mother, Lucy, had been unable to sustain a pregnancy after the couple's many unsuccessful attempts to become parents.

According to the reverend, Ruby and her brother Reginald, or "Reggie" as her brother preferred, came from forty days and forty nights of intense fasting and prayer. Lucy had suffered eight miscarriages over five years, some a few months, and the most painful being miscarrying just as she neared the third trimester. Lucy was heartbroken by the idea that she might not ever be a mother. Not one to cry, however, Lucy woke up one Sunday morning with a message received in her dream from her Lord, Jesus Christ. Lucy informed the reverend that she saw herself sitting before the great throne in Heaven. Taken with its beautiful and gleaming gold and diamonds, Lucy bowed before the throne. She saw no figure upon it at first, and then she looked up, and Black Jesus appeared, sitting.

Lucy was mesmerized. Black Jesus was solemn at first, then grinning, and then a smile rose from his face as bright as the sun. Finally, Black Jesus reached out to her and pulled her hands together in a praying position. When she went to clasp her hands together and close her eyes to pray, she looked down at her knees, and there was a baby basket. Lucy could hear the sounds of babies cooing underneath the white cloth that covered the basket. So moved, Lucy closed her eyes to pray, and when she opened them, she was lying in bed next to her husband.

Compelled by this vision, she directed the reverend that they needed to pray to God not with sorrow or confusion over their losses but with gratitude before they headed to church. They needed to thank God and his son Black Jesus. They must express gratitude for the eight losses they'd endured, as it was their great trial as a couple, and they'd survived together. And for that, they would be blessed. So right there, at the foot of their bed, the couple prayed aloud and thanked God and Black Jesus for their suffering. Together they offered their lives and continued faith, exclaiming their shared awareness that the eight losses were meant to assure their victory and triumph as a couple and soon as parents.

After that, Lucy firmly held the belief that the miscarriages were a test. Ever since her vision, Lucy no longer held sadness. She knew deep inside that being childless was not a destiny but a temporary condition that would be the basis of her testimony. This testimony would reside on their tongues to encourage and restore hope and faith for those in need.

After some praying of his own and two weeks after their shared prayer, the reverend told Lucy that he was visited by the Holy Spirit. The Holy Spirit had come to him during prayer and reminded him of Jesus's time in the desert; the focus was not the suffering so much as the process and length of time—forty days and forty nights.

"Divine math," he explained to Lucy. "Eight miscarriages by five years equals forty." He wrote on paper as he broke down the mathematics and numerological wisdom the Spirit had educated him of their struggle to birth children. And so, he instructed Lucy that they must fast and pray for forty days and forty nights. On night forty-one, they conceived Ruby and Reginald.

God blessed them with two children at once—a girl and a boy. Ruby and Reginald were testaments to his glory and mercy and to the obedience of their beliefs. At the same time, the children's birth ensured their legacy as one of the founding families of Jubilee. As much as the reverend wanted to be a father, he also craved to be Jubilee's supreme leader, with the baton staying within the bloodline. Indeed, his great-grandfather Reverend Calvin John Calhoun received the vision of the scorched pasture and led his then small group of congregants to the forty acres he received using General Sherman's order. Those forty acres had been the sacred ground upon which Jubilee had begun.

Because Ruby was born first, just by ninety-nine seconds, she was chosen to lead her family and the people of Jubilee into the future. Her name was chosen as Ruby because she was "the crowning jewel that emerged from the blood of the family." The name "Reginald" was made from a combination of the word "regal" and his name "Ronald"—Reg-i-nald. He was his father's "royal heir." Also, Reginald was what her father called "family assurance, family insurance," as he ensured that it was "the Calhoun family that remained at the helm, come hell or high water."

A passionate and persuasive speaker, Ruby's father's retelling of the story always brought her to tears. Each time Ruby's father recounted the story, she knew that her powers of persuasion and her extreme gift of gab were inherited from her father. Reggie was more reserved, like her mother. Never one to add needless sentences to a discussion or state something just to be heard, Reggie was far more careful with his words and more secure in the power of silence than Ruby.

Ruby and Reginald were nearly identical, the complexion of bittersweet chocolate; their eyes pointed at the ends with short eyelashes. Both Ruby's and Reggie's eyebrows were thick and bushy, their noses slender, their lips full, and their body frames long and slender from head to foot—two giraffes sprouting from the ground of Jubilee, able to see the path ahead with renewed clarity and vision. Despite being fraternal twins, their identicalness was for their parents yet another piece of evidence of the miracles God will do when you keep your faith and obedience high.

While Ruby did all the talking, Geneva stayed pretty quiet in the forums. Geneva would sit at the back of the room and take notes. For example, Geneva would record how many people were in attendance and how many questions were asked, familiar and new. In addition, Geneva would write down rough estimates and compositions of the attendees, their race, sex, and, if she could glean it, their age as well. Geneva believed all this information was essential to track if any politicians attempted to thwart their forward momentum by mischaracterizing what was said, by whom, and for what purpose.

Whenever Ruby felt nervous or lost, she would look to the back of the room, no matter the size, for Geneva, who wasn't hard to spot. Geneva's strawberry-blond locks would shine, glossy from the coconut and jojoba oil combination she used to keep her hair hydrated. With sharp blue-black skin, her hair was a striking balance of contrast and harmony. Wearing her hair in a styled updo, Geneva's hair was a buoyant crown even when her head was down. "Look for the crown," Ruby would say to herself when she felt unsure, frustrated, or even pleased with how the event was going.

Although Ruby was only two years younger than Geneva, she looked at Geneva as a mother figure. Ruby saw Geneva this way, not because she was warm or exceptionally loving; rather, Geneva reminded her of her mother, Lucy, back home in Jubilee, who too was stoic, steadfast, intense, full of belief, and not easily intimidated or impressed. Together, Ruby and Geneva were a powerful force—Jubilee's dynamic duo. While everyone back home continued growing and building Jubilee, the duo trekked the country, going hither and thither.

When the crowd was all Black, Ruby enjoyed herself the most, especially in the North. Since General Sherman's order did not pertain to the North, Black folks up there were usually some combination of awe-inspired and surprised. With the idea of a sustaining Black region with coastal locations, farmland, and urban areas, some would come up to Ruby immediately following the question-and-answer segment to inquire about how they could move there. Ruby especially enjoyed when Black Northerners would say, "Forget Atlanta. Jubilee, here I come!" While Ruby didn't hold anything against Atlanta, it did tickle her to think of how her efforts might reroute the flock to South Carolina rather than Georgia. Others offered up a surprise in the good-bad-and-ugly kinda way. "I ain't nevah going back South! I don't care if they allow Negroes to have their own planes and trains. You hear me! The South is hell on earth," an older Black man living in Harlem had once confronted her. While he had been the one to make the statement, he was not alone in his opinion.

Applause and "Right on!" accompanied statements like the one the man had made. Ruby couldn't get angry, not only because any upset could upend the purpose of her mission, but also because she understood the source of the discontent, disbelief, and discomfort Jubilee triggered. Millions of Black people had left the South and were leaving the South for cities like Philly, Chicago, and San Francisco. "Great Migrants," as they were known, had numerous testimonials of escaping lynching or watching a relative, spouse, loved one, or even a Black child be lynched. They recalled the mobs of Ku Klux Klan members who terrorized any Black person or Black family who attempted to build a remarkable life or home for themselves.

Having witnessed her fair share of KKK terrorism, Ruby knew these were not made-up stories or false fears. She would, however, remind them that Jubilee was real and had managed to not only survive but to thrive in those white supremacist conditions. Then, taking it a step further, she would adjust her shoulders forward and, with the most soothingly subtle tone shift, restate the lynching numbers across northern locations. "Fifteen in Chicago. Twenty in Philly. Twenty-nine in California. Now, I wouldn't call that safe either. Do you?" That response tended to disarm people, a well-disguised hard left jab to the gut of Great Migrants. A pause would usually follow, and then a slow-moving clapping vibration in affirmation.

"Sista, you are right!" the older man responded, lessening his confrontational tone into one of openheartedness. "When you put it like that, Negroes ain't safe nowhere. So what makes Jubilee different?" This time his question was not antagonistic. Instead, it sounded like a young student seeking guidance from his well-accomplished teacher.

"It's different because it was, is, and has been all Black. You see, we took those forty acres and combined them with other Black families' forty until before you knew it, we were an entire third of the state of South Carolina. It wasn't our intention, but it was our outcome." Nods and eyes bobbed as Ruby continued. "We have our own police, banks, stores, beaches, schools, parks, and markets. We have alchemized Jim Crow. So if white people wanna be separate from us, we said, 'Hey, let them!'"

A woman stood up and shouted, "Hallelujah. I know that's right!"

Ruby was now in full command of the audience. "In Jubilee, we don't believe you need to wait on white people to stop being racist to thrive while being African American in America. In fact, more than believe it," she said, passing around the unofficial map of Jubilee, "we have proven IT!"

Then, looking over the map, two young Black men said in unexpected unison, "Well, I'll be damned. This is REAL!"

More discussion would follow, but that was pretty much how the mission went in Black communities.

Now, white audiences were an entirely different bag. White people tended to be more reserved and more surveillant. Ruby tended not to pass around the map, though some white people seemed to have one already, which she found scary and suspicious. More often than Ruby and Geneva cared to remember, white audiences would try and pit Jubilee against the broader Civil Rights Movement.

"What does Dr. Martin Luther King Jr. have to say about this Jubilee situation?" a white man would commonly ask with an air of superiority ringing underneath his tone. "Yeah, yeah, what does Dr. King say about

Jubilee?" voices from white audiences would follow in what had become, over the years, a very predictable rhythm. So it was on those occasions when Geneva would rise ever so quietly from the back of the room and pass around her own sheets of paper.

Without a word, she would sit back down, and you would hear and see the ripple effect of her leaflet come over the room. Before their very eyes, in print was a paper full of endorsements for Jubilee that included Dr. Martin Luther King Jr., Malcolm X, Ms. Rosa Parks, Dr. W. E. B. Du Bois, Queen Mother Audley Moore, former presidents Woodrow Wilson and John F. Kennedy, and a host of others. None were more shocking to white audiences than the one that Geneva intentionally placed at the very end, FBI Director J. Edgar Hoover, whose endorsement stated: "Jubilee is an example of solving the problems of American race relations. We needn't force integration when we can support the grassroots efforts of sustainable all-Negro communities such as Jubilee, South Carolina."

Ruby could always tell when White audiences had reached the end of the page because large uncontrollable gasps and gags would echo through the room. Finally, Geneva would look up at Ruby, and they would exchange a smile. Then, as Ruby stood before the white audience with a smile, the shift would take hold. A now confused and discombobulated white audience was in the palm of Ruby's hand, unsure why they were opposed. To begin with, white audiences would look up from that page of endorsements and offer suggestions of whom to contact or mobilize to ensure Jubilee's independence survived as a line item in the bill.

Ruby recalled all of these occasions and the long journey to 1965 as the camera angled back from her kind eyes. The room went quiet after she captured her affirmative opening statement. The camera crew organized themselves. A matching cherrywood chair for the interviewer was placed a few feet across from Ruby. A crew member called out that the preparations were complete, the setup looked good, and the angles were suitable for the three cameras to capture and record the conversation.

"That's a wrap for today. We are all set up for tomorrow, Ms. Calhoun," the lead cameraman, Tom Chewey, looked though his spectacles and informed Ruby. Everything was set for their live interview tomorrow, and she was okay to leave for the evening. He thanked her for her time.

While Ruby thought it was odd that the interviewer wasn't present to greet her during the setup and that they filmed her by herself saying that one statement, watching the cameras and lights go up gave her an unexpected joy. For the first time, Ruby could finally see and feel how successful she had been. As she stood, Geneva walked up from the back of the room with notes for her to consider. Ruby had only made one statement, and Geneva still had a page full of notes for her. As the dynamic duo headed out, Geneva could be overheard giving her some soundbites and tricks to handle the lighting.

"Tomorrow will be glorious," Ruby said to Geneva.

Geneva responded in kind. "Yes, it surely will be one for the books."

22 JULY 1965

"Greetings from Mustardseed Baptist Church here in Jubilee City, South Carolina. This is Bill Plante here in Jubilee. I am joined by Ms. Ruby Calhoun, Jubilee's leading spokeswoman. Thank you, Ms. Calhoun, for joining us today." The interviewer's eyes blinked steadily as the camera shot panned to Ruby.

"A pleasure to be here and welcome you and your viewers to Jubilee, Mr. Plante. And please call me Ruby." She half smiled back, her mouth extended just enough to show the white tops of her front teeth just behind her lips. Her blue dress sparkled as it increased her posture, sculpted by her mother Lucy to be a sophisticated, regal, subtly luxurious garment that required her to sit upright, composed, and strong while wearing it. Lucy had sourced the fabric from Paris, France, and spent a year making the dress in anticipation of a national interview.

The embroidered blue pearls that covered the top half took Lucy four months alone, each one stitched into place by hand one at a time. Ruby looked marvelous, like a Queen sitting upon a throne before an adoring court to issue decrees and rules by which all would abide. The dress was by no means comfortable, nor was it constructed to allow or provide comfort. Locating some ounce of relief within the constraints of the dress, Ruby crossed her ankles and folded her hands in the cherrywood chair.

The rising sun hit the orange-yellow-red stained glass of the chapel, bathing the interview space in an undeniable glow as Ruby adjusted her shoulders. She could feel the pressure of the dress on her stomach and remembered her mother's last words in the dressing room after she was zipped up. "Ruby, what the dress lacks in comfort it more than makes up for in being convincing. We need you to look and sound the part, so we can all be comfortable after the president signs the bill."

"As you know," said the interviewer, jumping right into the questions, "President Johnson appears poised to sign the Voting Rights Act of 1965, which would, among other things entailed, authorize Jubilee to become an independent territory with some state-level powers. This would be the first ever for African Americans in the history of the United States of America. How does that make you feel?"

"We, in Jubilee, feel confident that President Johnson will do what is right. But as the old saying goes, 'Best not to count your chickens before they are hatched.'" Ruby let out a soft, kind sigh.

"So are you saying that you believe the president might renege?" Plante's response was abrupt and less friendly than his opening.

"I am not saying that at all," Ruby shot back, her fingers tightening in their fold. "Look, I have traveled to almost every part of the country to bring awareness and support for Jubilee's independence. Therefore, I am acutely aware of the delicate balance that has been required to make it this far. We thought that we would make it into the Civil Rights Act of 1964. When that did not happen, we were disappointed and realized we needed to keep our faith high and our eyes on the prize. So until he signs—President Johnson, that is—nothing is official."

"I see. That had to be pretty disappointing to not make it in 1964. How did you and Jubilee manage to carry on with hope afterward?"

"Well, we in Jubilee are a faithful and hopeful people. We gathered in chapels and temples across our community, like the one we are seated in today, and we prayed. Today, the blue dress I wear before you, my mother, Mrs. Lucy Calhoun, designed to reflect the hope that kept us going. We in Jubilee understand that spatial reparations, or any reparations for that matter, can be divisive among the American people. But we certainly haven't made it one hundred years without keeping hopeful and most certainly without the occasional disappointments."

"I know that the whole *60 Minutes* team and I can certainly vouch for how peaceable and kind everyone in Jubilee City has been during our time here. This is simply a miracle of a place!"

"Thank you, sir. That is high praise, and we will certainly take it!"

The two chuckled together.

"Okay, so let's get back to the serious business at hand."

"Yes, okay."

"You mentioned reparations or spatial reparations? If I heard you correctly?"

"Yes, I did."

"Okay, that's what I thought you said. But, unfortunately, as you are probably aware, the topic and issues are not very supported in white or Negro communities. So why do you think it is working in this case?"

"First, we prefer the terms 'African American' or 'Black' persons. We do not subscribe to the term 'Negro' in Jubilee."

"My apologies. I meant no offense, as I was under the impression that the term 'Negro' is the acceptable term."

"Apology accepted, and great question!"

"Thank you. You know that's why they pay me the small bucks." Plante let out a hearty belly chuckle of relief.

"Well, here's the thing about reparations. They are repayment for slavery's outstanding debts to African Americans. This country has a hard time accepting responsibility and properly acknowledging slavery as what it truly is—an evil and terrible crime against humanity. The authorization of land and space is but one provision for repairing the harms of slavery and is far less complicated in our case because we are already here. We only followed the provision of General Sherman's Special Field Order Number 15. In fact, we did it without the mule! As you may be aware, we only got forty acres."

"I was not aware. No mules ever arrived?" Plante was puzzled, having seen so much livestock about the farms in Jubilee.

"The mules never arrived. But we count our blessings and never cry over spilled milk. For example, we have been more fortunate concerning acquiring the forty acres compared to African Americans in Georgia, Alabama, Tennessee, Mississippi, and Louisiana, just to name a few."

"So are you saying that Jubilee is reparations for slavery?"

"No. What I am saying is that the Voting Rights Act of 1965 would merely reenforce an existing promise made to African Americans during the Civil War by one of its most famous and powerful military leaders. And keeping that promise is a critically important sign to African Americans not just in Jubilee but across the United States. Because, unfortunately, we have been made to feel as though no promise made to Black people in this country has ever been kept."

"Does that make you angry?"

"Angry, no." She laughed dismissively. "Committed would be more accurate. Suppose there are ever to be any true reparations or civil rights, for that matter. In that case, Jubilee must be protected especially from frivolous claims that only seek to harm it or upend our tremendous progress."

"Speaking of progress, how did Jubilee become what it is today? During my ride throughout the area, I saw churches and temples of all kinds, banks, farms, marketplaces. There are even two universities! I must admit—my team and I were deeply impressed."

"Thank you. Jubilee, as you see it today, did not happen overnight. My grandfather, Reverend Calvin John Calhoun, began Jubilee with his small congregation in 1865 using the provision of forty acres. The other congregants were afraid to go into town and make the request, so he, being the reverend, was compelled to make the request. So one day, he went ahead and did it. Per Sherman's order, and much to his surprise, the forty acres were awarded to him. Soon after, the remaining congregants, comprised of the eight other families, eventually conquered their fears and requested their forty-acre allotments. That developed into the 360 acres that formed the original land that is now called Jubilee City. Over the years, many families within the surrounding areas felt it safer to have their allotted forty acres in proximity to Jubilee. And something really surprised my grandfather and my father after him. Those who were from other states that had seen their forty acres taken during Reconstruction came to Jubilee, became residents, and then successfully refiled for their forty acres."

"That is a pretty incredible story."

"Indeed it is. We often refer to Jubilee City as 'Miracletown.' We say this not just because of its origins but also because the land it was built upon was literally burned, scorched, and considered wasteland. No one wanted this land, which is most of the reason why our ancestors were able to get it so quickly and easily."

"I can't imagine a wasteland ever existed here."

"It most certainly did. This was the area historically used by the plantation owners as a landfill for the dead livestock and slaves, garbage and refuse, unwanted and broken furniture, etc. When Civil War battles were fought upon it, and nearby, the area was revealed to be highly flammable. Gunpowder and cannon explosions only worsened the quality of the land. By the time the war ended, the land was literally blackened and scorched. No one wanted it."

"I see. How very fascinating that is. So was that the case for all of the land provided by the state or just the initial acres?"

"Primarily, it was the condition of the initial one thousand acres or so provided. The remaining acres extended out and surrounded that area. Jubilee wouldn't be the size it is today if not also for the gift of segregation."

"The gi-giff . . . gift of segregation," he stuttered with confusion. "I do not believe I have ever heard a Negro—Black or African American person, excuse me—frame segregation as a gift."

"By gift, I only mean to suggest that Jim Crow laws and practices made it so that each family awarded the forty acres were only given land that was adjacent to the existing settlement because white people did not want and do not want to live with Black people."

"I think I understand now. Segregation has inadvertently helped in the growth of Jubilee." Plante was wide-eyed, as he was having an ah-ha moment of his own. He continued, "So you are saying that Jim Crow laws helped make Jubilee what it is today?"

"The residents and families of Jubilee made it what it is today. I am saying that rather than battle with segregation, we accepted it and used it to our advantage. Some estimate that we saved South Carolina money on building Black-only facilities because we had our own, and Black visitors to South Carolina preferred to visit and live in Jubilee. Now that said, it is important that people also understand that the awarding of acres was stopped at the beginning of World War I."

"But isn't the bill set to dismantle Jim Crow and segregation laws and practices like it throughout the Union, including here in South Carolina?"

"Yes, you are correct. And that is exactly why our independence is so urgent. We do not want former segregationists using the Civil Rights Act of 1964 and the Voting Rights Act of 1965 against Jubilee."

"How so?"

"You may not see this. But there is a dangerous and persistent vengeance bubbling underneath the fragile veil of white Southern hospitality and charm you and your crew have probably experienced and received during your time in South Carolina. It would give many white Americans in South Carolina and across the country, especially the Ku Klux Klan, no greater pleasure than to use the rewards of the Civil Rights Movement against Jubilee."

"Ahhhhhh, how interesting."

"With all due respect, Mr. Plante, what you call 'interesting' we in Jubilee call scary dangerous."

"I am sorry, again. I meant no offense."

"None taken. I just believe it important that your viewers understand that we in Jubilee are not segregationists, which is why we are supported from all corners of the Civil Rights Movement. In fact, Dr. King and my father are dear friends, and the Reverend C. L. Franklin was just here preaching in the pulpit behind us Sunday before last."

"Those are some great friends and supporters to have. I imagine their championing Jubilee has been an indispensable resource."

"We are truly fortunate and grateful for their support and the support of Mrs. Coretta Scott King and Ms. Ella Baker, among many others. My point, however, is that we in Jubilee understood that racism and segregation are deeply ingrained in the psyche of white America and will certainly not change overnight. You can tear down signs and buildings, but beliefs lodged in the heart are a whole other matter unto themselves. Hundreds of years of racism, segregation, racial terror, and white supremacy will not disappear just because the president signs a new law."

"That sounds a bit like backhanded praise and cynicism for the very legislation you have lobbied for, for so many years. The Voting Rights Act of 1965 would facilitate some needed change around race in this country, given all the turmoil we have witnessed, from Selma to the Freedom Rides to the Montgomery Bus Boycotts to the horrific bombing of the 16th Street Baptist Church in Birmingham. But it sounds as though you are saying nothing will ever change?"

"Thank you for saying and asking what you just did because I get some form of this sentiment and question a lot, particularly in white communities and amongst white allies. Put simply, laws cannot change what resides in the heart. In fact, that is not the function or purpose of the law. Instead, laws protect, enforce, restrict, reframe . . ."

"I think I see where you are going."

"Okay, so you see, the legislation is certainly important and vital to moving the country forward. But we would be fools, especially those of us who live in the South, to think that we will see hearts and minds change overnight the moment that bill is signed. Just look at what happened to the Little Rock Nine. They were spat upon, harassed, belittled, bullied, and all in public. National news cameras were rolling, and white people, young and old, male and female, were all in defiant resistance to President Eisenhower's enforcement of the Supreme Court ruling."

"I remember. I was there myself, covering that historic occasion, and found the entire treatment of those brilliant Negro—I am sorry—African American students unsettling and highly disappointing."

"And at the same time, it is quintessential America. That is this country. We do ourselves a great disservice when we do not accept the reality of racism as a founding principle of the United States. Can it be changed? Yes. But will it happen overnight or because a president and Congress say so? No."

"That is a sobering analysis and take on the United States. I don't know if I have quite accepted that, and I would be lying if I didn't confess that as I sit before you now, there is some piece of me that both agrees and disagrees with you."

"And that is fine as well. Because another founding principle of the United States is the freedom of opinion, the freedom of speech."

Plante paused slightly, taking in her words at first with a grimace he did not want to be recorded. He looked to Tom, the lead cameraman, and winked, an inside understanding that this part would be clipped. Ruby, curious about how the crew and Plante would communicate with each other during filming, observed the production's pause and took mental note of Plante's wink as an editorial command.

"Sir. Mr. Plante, is everything okay?" Ruby reached her arm across the invisible line that separated them, asking half curious and partly invested in marking the pause herself.

"Yes. We often do that in our interviews before we begin a hard pivot switching into other topics or lines of discussion. That way, our team has places to edit without the flow appearing disrupted when televised. Which reminds me—I don't know if I said this, but please call me Bill."

"Sounds good, Bill." Ruby nodded with affirmation.

"I noticed that there are a variety of places of worship across Jubilee. I believe I saw a mosque, a temple, and a variety of Protestant and Catholic churches. As I know that this is sort of the capital of a broader area, might you tell me how this came to be, and is it true outside of Jubilee City?"

"Oh yes, the spiritual reparations of Jubilee." Ruby realized she had said "reparations" a few times now and was coming up against Geneva's advised allotment of no more than five times during the interview. She paused slightly and then continued on. "Jubilee is religiously diverse. Although we began with Christian ministers, over time, many of our residents rediscovered and reclaimed other spiritual practices, some of which were from West African countries such as Ghana, Benin, and Nigeria."

"Now, did I hear you say spiritual reparations?" Plante was swift with this question as he sensed he may have caught Ruby in one of those savvy traps that interviewers felt might land them a Pulitzer or Primetime Emmy.

"What is vital to hear is that Jubilee is comprised of a diversity of religions. We welcome all African American belief systems and practices rooted in obedience to faith and love of God. For example, some of our temples are actually for practitioners of the Yoruba faith, most prominently followed today in Nigeria and many other places in the Caribbean and South America. In that belief system, they call upon and venerate orishas while worshipping and being in gratitude for God and his divine creation of the world. Others are Catholic, Baptist, Seventh-day Adventist, Jehovah's Witnesses, Episcopalian, Lutheran, and Muslim. A small and growing population of Buddhists has also sprouted in the last decade or so. We saw a significant rise in our residents' conversions to Islam when our dear brother Malcolm X was the international spokesperson for the Nation. His combination of love of

Black people and of Islam was quite compelling for many in Jubilee. And they have rightfully formed a dynamic and sustaining community of worship."

"That sounds quite open and lovely, I must say."

"Like my father, Reverend Calhoun, often says: 'There is perhaps nothing more dangerous than a non-God-fearing person.'"

"I believe I've heard a similar refrain growing up from my grandfather, and I cannot say I disagree."

"Faith and belief are important here in Jubilee. But so too is it that Black people have the freedom to recover and explore the worship practices, spirituality, and beliefs that enslavement stripped away. We do not want people just being Christian or Muslim or Jewish or Yoruba because that is all that has been made available. We want people, especially those who managed to survive the horror of slavery and continue to endure the terror that is racism, to be allowed to explore and restore the belief systems that ring true for them in their souls."

"How powerful! I see what you mean. Growing up with Catholic, Protestant, and Jewish people was very informative for me over my life. I imagine it must be the same for you and the residents of Jubilee."

"Now, don't get me wrong. I love Jesus and am an 'every Sunday Southern Baptist Church and every Wednesday Bible study' Christian woman myself, but I do not believe that people should be forced to do the same. After having so many things thrust and forced upon us, African Americans are entitled to arrive at their own sense of spiritual awareness and purpose. And what you find is that when people have that religious and spiritual freedom restored, they find a community of existing belief that fulfills them and only adds to the beauty of what we have here in Jubilee."

"Let's pivot our discussion to talk about the geography of Jubilee, which I have found quite fascinating. In the map we received from you ahead of this interview, Jubilee comprises five major areas. Is that correct, and if so, what can you tell our viewers about those areas?"

"Sure. We are currently in Jubilee City, which is the capital. West of the capital are two areas, Westmoreland and Borderton. East of the capital are two areas, Eastland and Oceanair. Westmoreland is a combination of rural and suburban, beginning at the outer western edge of Jubilee City. Adjacent to Westmoreland is what we term Borderton, primarily because it sits at the boundary of South Carolina and Georgia. It's comprised of flatlands and roads that lead directly into Atlanta, Georgia, because many of the residents who settled fled Georgia to reclaim their forty acres. Eastland begins at the outer eastern edge of Jubilee and resembles Westmoreland in that it is relatively rural and suburban. Oceanair is comprised of our coastal shoreline communities and beaches. As you will see, it is primarily the area along the Atlantic Ocean. Oceanair is a favorite summer destination for many of the families in Jubilee and is quite a sight to behold. It's our Inkwell-meets-the-Hamptons relaxation landing place."

"Sounds divine. We are planning to make that the last stop on our tour of collecting footage and short sound bites from residents."

"I am sure you and your team will love it." Ruby's smile widened.

"We have heard so many wonderful things about Jubilee, but any person watching might be reasonably skeptical about issues of safety. So would you say Jubilee is safe? What about violent crimes and the community's relationship with the police? Do people go to prison? And as I ask, I don't recall seeing a prison."

"Whoa. Those are some loaded and broad questions!" Ruby shot back.

"Oh yes, please take a moment to process them. As you know, we are recording this and will edit it later for the segment that will air."

Ruby took a deep breath, affording her some breathing room inside her dress and an opportunity to gather her thoughts and recall best practices she cultivated on the road to answer such questions. Memories of Geneva's many notes and suggestions came into her mind as she pulled air into her nostrils and released it through her pursed lips.

"Is Jubilee safe? It is undoubtedly safer for African Americans here than anywhere else in the nation. Over the years, there have been several surveys conducted regarding this issue. For example, in a survey of the country conducted by the NAACP, the National Association for Advancement of Colored People, Jubilee residents reported higher levels of safety and happiness than any other place, including Harlem, Watts, San Francisco, Chicago, Kansas City, St. Louis, and Oakland, to name a few. And it was not even close. Reported levels in Jubilee were higher by a wide margin."

"Okay, so people in Jubilee feel safe and happy. But are you saying there are no crimes ever committed? No robberies, burglaries, or murders happen?"

"My gosh, Bill. You sound as if you expect because it is all Black that there would be violent crime."

"Ohhh, that's not . . ."

"Well, I am sorry to disappoint, but violent crimes are rare in Jubilee. There are occasional thefts and misdemeanors like shoplifting here and there but nothing outrageous. In fact, we have a police force sanctioned by the state of South Carolina. In addition to training at the police academy, our officers also receive mandatory training in nonviolent conflict resolution. We invited leaders like Bayard Rustin and even some practitioners from India to instruct and educate officers on enforcement through nonviolent means. We take seriously the idea that our police should first and foremost operate as peacekeepers, then law enforcement. And to put it simply, it has worked."

"And prisons—do they exist?"

"No, they do not. Instead of prisons and jails, we have rehabilitation facilities where people receive additional education, counseling, and recertification to reenter society. It has proven quite the success, and in fact, there is some discussion in California of wanting to replicate our approach."

"I understand. Please note that before I was interrupted, I attempted to say that I do not think or believe that Negroes—again, apologies— African Americans are somehow inherently violent people. I only ask the questions that I know viewers will want to be answered, and we have a large audience hailing from all over the country, and we want them to watch the program and leave informed and educated about Jubilee in all aspects."

"I understand as well."

"Good. Glad we have that shared understanding." Plante's grimace reappeared.

Ruby looked up at the lead cameraman, catching his left eye glance just above his spectacles as he winked to signal that they might want to edit Plante's reaction there.

The cameraman nodded, and Plante continued. "As we are reaching the end of our time, Ruby, I would like to ask the question that probably everyone wants to know. And that is, what is the first thing you plan to do when the bill is signed?"

"Celebrate! And celebrate some more. And then from there, we shall see." Ruby's words were happier sounding than she appeared to be while speaking the answers.

"I can imagine contagious happiness will be all around the people of Jubilee. I have noticed what looks like the beginning of a large stage and possible festival being constructed at the city's center. Is that where the festivities will happen?"

"Oh yes. My brother Reggie is the coordinator of the annual summer Jubilee Festival. He has been hard at work to make this year's extra special. We think it is no accident that the schedule of the bill's signing should occur at the same time as our annual Jubilee Festival. He has promised that the festival will be legendary." Ruby then knocked on the wooden arm of the chair. "Knock on wood, we have South Carolina's own Mr. James Brown headlining the festival and a special appearance from Motown prodigy, the amazing Stevie Wonder. There will be local acts and food and more. Reggie had kept it somewhat top secret, as everyone wants to avoid anything close to the disappointment we felt last year when Jubilee's independence didn't make it into the Civil Rights Act of 1964. And you know we have survived our share of disappointments. For example, many of our residents lost their savings when the Freedman's Bank collapsed in 1874. The assurances this time around, however, and this interview affirm that it will happen this time, but as I said earlier"—both she and Bill unexpectedly said it in unison—"Don't count your chickens before they have hatched," to which they both grinned and nodded in agreement.

"And what is next for you after Jubilee's independence? Any plans for a family or marriage?"

"Well, Bill, they say when you make plans, watch how God will laugh. So though I do not know what is next, I am sure it will be glorious. Amen!"

"Needless to say, any man would be lucky to have you as his wife, and I am sure you have a line of suitors and gentlemen callers a mile long." His smile was wide and self-assured.

Ruby was profoundly uncomfortable and hoped that this time it was not *her* face grimacing. Just in case, Ruby looked up at the lead cameraman and winked. Bill noticed her wink, and unaware of its intended direction and purpose, he winked back at Ruby.

"So now we get to the last part of our interview." He paused and reviewed a cue card, put it down, and returned to Ruby. "This all sounds like, basically, Jubilee is a utopia of sorts. A self-sustaining Aaaa-African American . . . wait, let me do that again, guys." Plante cleared his throat and began again. "All of this gives the impression that Jubilee is a utopia of sorts—an African American self-sustaining, peaceful, religiously diverse community in the South. What's there not to like. Right?"

"No. Jubilee is not a utopia. Jubilee is a Black masterpiece in progress." Ruby felt pride exude from her body outward as she spoke those words.

"I like that. A Black masterpiece in progress," Plante restated with a sense of personal joy and pride.

"And now we have reached the last question. I must confess I could talk with you all day. This has been quite enlightening." Bill's voice filled with the incredible pleasure he had found interviewing Ruby.

"My pleasure," Ruby replied confidently.

"In your view, what is the take-home message here? What should Americans watching this interview and hearing the story of Jubilee for the first time take away from this?"

"Wonderful question. The message is quite simple. African Americans are patient and loving people. Despite what folks in the media—not you, Bill." Ruby grinned. "But despite the many negative images and stories people read and see about African Americans, we are patient and loving people. After hundreds of years of forced and legalized enslavement and bondage, we have chosen to stay in the United States and live with and alongside white Americans. Many who have survived our condition may have taken a route including that of violence, killing their oppressors. African Americans, however, have proven that we see the humanity in all people, and all we have requested is mutual respect, dignity, equal protection, repair, and restoration. And I believe Jubilee represents all of that and more." Although Ruby knew she had gone a bit off-script, she was shining and shimmering as she finished answering the final question.

"I think that is a good place to conclude."

"Thank you, Bill."

"Thank you, Ruby." With that, Bill waved his hand, a signal that the recording was finished. The lights turned off within seconds of his wave, and the cameramen stopped recording. Ruby took a deep breath and attempted to relax her shoulders even though the dress wouldn't budge. Both Ruby and Bill stood from their chairs. Bill then reached his hand out to Ruby. She reached back, and they shook hands. Ruby noticed how sweaty Bill's palms were. She was somewhat surprised as Bill seemed cool as a cucumber for most of their interview. Ruby had assumed that she was the one who had been processing any nervousness or anxiety during their long discussion.

"Ruby, I must say that was probably one of the best interviews I have ever done. You most certainly kept me on my toes." His eyes scanned the full size and shape of Ruby for the first time.

Noticing Bill's increased fascination with her figure, Ruby stepped back and released the handshake. "Bill, it was certainly a pleasure. The segment will air this Sunday, correct?"

"Yes, that is correct. And my team and I have a bit more work ahead of us. We have gone through four areas and taken some passing shots that will overlay during the segment. We also had an opportunity to speak with of few of the members of . . . What is it called again?"

The lead cameraman, overhearing this discussion, yelled out, "The Council of Elders!"

"Oh yes. Thank you! The Council of Elders. Yes, we spoke with a few members. Also, as I mentioned during our discussion this afternoon, we head to the Oceanair area from here. There we will record some scenic shots, potential sound bites, and panning footage. After that, we head to our CBS field office in Charleston. We will spend the full day in the Charleston office editing and polishing the footage. That will pretty much take the entire Saturday. Then, once it's approved by the higher-ups, we head back to New York. The segment will air in the feature slot during the last third of the program. Tom, our lead cameraman, is a huge James Brown fan and plans to attend the festival before heading to Atlanta for our next story. You may not know, but Tom's family has roots here."

"Thank you again, Bill. Sounds great. Look forward to seeing you, Tom, at the festival." Ruby grabbed her personal items.

"I am looking forward to it, and a few friends are planning to join as well." Tom wiped the fatigue from his eyes and did his very best James Brown glide.

Ruby gave Tom a thumbs-up and turned to the pew where she placed her handbag and a small notebook that contained all of the producer's and Geneva's pre-interview instructions. Ruby quickly scanned the notebook to review Geneva's advisement. She also quickly scanned the remarks she had prepared and memorized ahead of time, relieved that she had managed to restate most, if not all, of them during the interview.

After grabbing her personal items, Ruby adjusted her dress slightly, as it had pulled a little at her waist. Ruby then headed back toward the dressing room where her mother and Geneva awaited. No one had been allowed to be on set during the recording. They had been instructed that sound equipment is susceptible to picking up even the smallest of noises. To avoid any disruption, everyone had agreed that Ruby would sit alone for the interview.

As Ruby exited the room, she could feel Bill's eyes following her down the aisle and out of the door. Grateful that the interview was over and relatively uneventful, when she sensed she was finally out of earshot, Ruby let out a deep, audible, relief-filled breath. Nearing the dressing room, Ruby replayed the interview and her answers, anticipating Lucy's and Geneva's awaiting replay and recall requests. As her mind raced, she was sure of one thing, and that was she was proud of herself and her performance. She was confident that everyone would feel the same as well.

24 JULY 1965

Ruby spent the day in bed. She was exhausted. She hadn't realized she'd slept the entire day until she went outside to fetch the mail and noticed the sun setting instead of rising. Her hair was wrapped, and she waved hello to her neighbors across the street.

As she headed into her yellow-and-white house past the palmettos that adorned its entrance, she scanned the mail. Most of the mail was unimportant. As Ruby ripped up the useless mail, she remembered that she forgot to collect and read her mail before heading to meet Bill and the 60 Minutes team. By the time Ruby returned home, she was so exhausted from wearing that uptight dress and answering and recounting all the sordid details for her mother and Geneva, it was all she could do to put on her evening robe, get the silk wrap onto her head, and go straight to bed.

The interview was the culmination of a decade-long journey replete with travel, questions, and answers all to represent Jubilee in the very best light. Ruby was proud. Ruby was tired. But as Ruby neared the end of the pile of mail, she noticed one letter that gave her excitement and made her anxious. Next, Ruby grabbed her keys, closed the front door, walked along the wraparound porch to the back, and took a seat in the rocking chair for reading and meditation. As she reviewed the envelope, she felt a big smile in her heart emerging, filling her body with great warmth.

> PJ Washington
> 1312 Auburn Ave
> Atlanta, Georgia

A few tears of joy unexpectedly welled up and fell upon the envelope, smearing the front script a bit. She turned the envelope around, and when she went to lift it, the seal opened with ease. Ruby's face exuded the elation of a child at Christmas.

19 July 1965

My beloved Ruby,

I write to you on the occasion of your upcoming interview with the good white people over at *60 Minutes*. Oh my, how my Ruby has shined so brightly over these years. Now the whole world will be able to bask in your glow. A glow that has warmed my heart since I first saw your face, eyes, warming smile; heard your biting humor; and smelled your ever-present sweet fragrance. Oh, how I have missed you over this year. I know that we agreed that after the fiasco of the legislation in '64, we would wait until after you finished your missions for the year to resume our romance. But it has been a hard one for me. It has taken everything in me, my mind, body, and soul, to not write you over this year. I understand that when you are away, your mail may be intercepted. So when I learned of the nationally televised interview and segment on Jubilee on *60 Minutes*, I knew you would surely be home, and that you would find this. And I would again have your full attention.

I sent this hoping that you might receive it before your interview to offer my loving encouragement and help ease your nervous anxiety that you confess others don't notice or don't seem caring enough to tend to. If it is the case, which is likely, that you should find this letter after your interview, then take its arrival as a sign confirming that you are everything! Even in my disciplined waiting and agreed radio silence between us, I have fallen asleep every night with your picture atop the pillow beside me. Do you remember the one of you in the red dress, red lips, and Afro and red hibiscus in your hair? Well, that's the one. My very favorite. Knowing I was behind the camera and how free you felt with me is reflected back every time I lie next to it.

I often fall asleep with my hand holding onto the ends of the photograph. How beautiful you are. Your parents certainly got it right when they named you Ruby because a precious bold gem you are. My gem in the storms of life. My gem when my spirit grows weary and sad because of our long time apart. But I take solace in knowing we shall be together again, and that the work you are doing for your people, all Black people, is historic. I hope you know that. You are not only making history, but you are also HISTORIC, Ruby Calhoun. A once-in-a-lifetime, one-in-a-million rare treasure. The right time we planned is just ahead. Our time is fast approaching, for which I am grateful to God, the sun, the moon, and the stars above. Please don't be too mad at me for writing. I just couldn't contain the love and words any longer.

Until soon. Know that among your many admirers, I shall be glued to my television on Sunday beholding the wonder that is you, Ruby. May our future together be glorious.

Yours forevermore,

PJ

B. A. R.

Ruby held the letter tightly to her heart and watched the sun go down over Jubilee.

25 JULY 1965

"And let us turn our eyes and rest them upon the great prayer of Ezra. Ezra, a chief priest and descendant of Aaron, was ordered by the king to teach the ways and knowledge of God.

"After years in Babylon, Ezra sought to bring the light back to Jerusalem. Under the orders of the king, he was accompanied by a large group of exiled Hebrews. Soon after Ezra's return to Jerusalem, he offered and scribed a prescient prayer. This Sunday, we will turn our attention to an essential portion of that prayer for our time together. Saints, please join me as I read from the Old Testament, the holy book of Ezra, chapter nine, verses eight and nine.

"And now for a little space grace hath been shewed from the Lord our God, to leave us a remnant to escape, and to give us a nail in his holy place, that our God may lighten our eyes and give us a little reviving in our bondage." The reverend's solemn tone shifted up a few gears to reach a booming resound by the end of reading the next verse.

"For we were slaves; yet our God hath not forsaken us in our bondage but hath extended mercy unto us in the sight of the kings of Persia to give us a reviving, to set up the house of our God, and to repair the desolations thereof, and to give us a wall in Judah and in Jerusalem."

Many of the devout men stood, as they traditionally did, as the reverend read the scriptures from Ezra. Others raised and waved their hands and recited the verse aloud with the reverend. After reading the scripture, the reverend looked out into the eyes of each of the congregants. He wanted them to feel the message was meaningful and for each person.

After the brief pause and his eyes having visited with the packed church, the reverend's voice was measured, mild, and matter-of-fact. "Jubilee is the wall. Jubilee is Jerusalem. Jubilee is the wall. Jubilee is Jerusalem."

"Amen!" rang out from several congregants.

"Turn to your neighbor and say, 'Neighbor, did you know Jubilee is the wall? That Jubilee is Jerusalem?'"

Congregants turned to one another, asking and answering the question amongst themselves.

Following the neighbor-affirmation call-and-response, the reverend pulled everyone's attention back to him by raising his left hand. By the time the reverend concluded his rebrand of the Ezra scriptures and remarks, some congregants were in full praise mode.

"Amen. Amen," congregants spoke aloud, some closing their Bibles, others underlining the passages read by the reverend.

Reverend Calhoun seemed larger and taller that Sunday. As he stood in the pulpit, Bible in hand, he appeared to grow taller with every impassioned word. The pride of the national interview on the horizon had enveloped him the entire service. A typically gleeful and stocky figure during church service, this Sunday, he moved and stood like a lion claiming victory upon the mountain.

"Some may wonder why I would choose this scripture on this day. The answer would be the Holy Spirit came to me in prayer, reminding me as it had all those years ago about the power of divine math. Eight is the number of transformations. Nine is the number of completion. And so, Ezra is speaking and praying at a grand moment of completing transformation completely. I will say that again. Ezra is speaking and praying at a grand moment of completing transformation completely.

"Ezra and his people had endured the wilderness that is bondage. Slavery is an intense form of wilderness, separated as you are from your own freedom, your own body, your own mind, your own spiritual purpose. WE were enslaved, suffering in the wilderness of the Atlantic Ocean, stripped from our homes and villages and families in Africa.

WE were made to find and make a home and refuge in the wilderness of America. And guess what, saints—WE were delivered because we delivered ourselves through faith and obedience to God! America is Babylon, and Jubilee is Jerusalem. Amen!"

"Amen! Amen!"

"As everyone here is aware, we are set to be revealed to the whole world later this evening on CBS's *60 Minutes*. Who knew that something built by a small collection of Black families in South Carolina would feature on national news? God! Who knew that Jubilee would be the size it is today? According to recent estimates, approximately a third of South Carolina is comprised of Jubilee residents. Who knew? God!

"This is what Ezra's prayer is aware of—the mighty power of the living God! There is not anything that he cannot and will not do for the betterment of his people. Jubilee is the space of grace and new mercy; it is the wall. And Jubilee has grown because of your fortitude and courage. Jubilee still stands because of all the people fighting for equal rights for Black people in the United States! We don't call this place the *Mustardseed Baptist Church* for nothing. Amen!"

"Amen! Hallelujahhhhhh!"

"On tonight, we will see my daughter, Jubilee's daughter, Ruby . . . Ruby, stand up. Stand up now!"

Ruby, like a soldier, stood with immediacy upon her father's command. Upon her rising, the church burst with rolling, roaring applause inside and outside. Lasting for several minutes, Ruby could see the walls rumble with reverberations of this rousing appreciation. She turned for all of the church to see, her face adorned with a profound expression of humility and gratitude.

"Now," the reverend continued after the applause dissipated, "as any builder or carpenter knows and will tell you, walls are important; for they reinforce, uplift, and protect the people inside and the structure itself. Walls provide and support the integrity and security of a place. And isn't that what we have built in the Babylon of America? A wall of blackness that provides sanctuary and refuge, a place of protection? It has proven that it can keep the white supremacists and racists at bay, at a distance, even while we on the other side work together with God's grace and new mercies every day! Amen."

"Amen! Amen! Hallelujah!" some congregants stood and shouted aloud, affirming the reverend's message.

"We must remember and never forget that as we pulled ourselves from the brutal bondage of slavery, God and his son Jesus were by our side. From the first cannon blast to the last one, God was there guiding and protecting us. And then came the wall that would help us erect a Jerusalem amidst the Babylon of America. Upon scorched earth, God ensured we would not only survive, but that we would THRIVE! Give praise unto God in this place if you understand, if you appreciate his foresight in hiding our abundance underneath land the white folks had shunned. Land the white people shunned! Glory! Some days . . . I must confess to you all today. Some days, I have been weary and thought I would lose my faith, wondering would Jubilee survive, could we make it as the lawsuits and litigation mounted. And I would pray, and you know what God said? He said YES!" The reverend raised and shook his right hand as a sign of the glory and mystery of God.

"Yes! God said YES!" the church reflected emphatically in reaction.

"And he delivered Ms. Geneva Crenshaw right to our doorstep. Ms. Crenshaw, please stand so that we may give you praise and love on this Sunday here on the eve of the revelation of Jubilee." As he spoke, he scanned the room and located Geneva's strawberry-blond crown of locks at the back of the room where she preferred to sit.

Unlike Ruby, Geneva did not like to be commanded. She at first hesitated, her automatic and natural response to resist orders.

"Come on, dear Sister Geneva. Please rise. Now, everyone, she will be mightily upset with me after this because anyone who knows her knows that she does not do her work for Black people for the attention. She prefers to go about her work with a quiet power. But on today, I feel it is only right for all of us to applaud her for her tireless work. Without this brilliant woman, we would not have a bill in Congress ready to be signed by the president of the United States. We would not have a bill enforcing and authorizing the independence of Jubilee!"

Excited as he was, the reverend modulated his tone to one of warmth and deference—a sign that eased Geneva considerably. And with that, she stood briefly.

The church went crazy. Many had seen Geneva running around here and there, but others had never quite realized that this dark-skinned Black woman with this crown of reddish-tinted blond locks was the legal mastermind that the council had raved about and put their trust in a decade ago. The congregants were honored to knowingly be in her presence. The reverend continued as Geneva sat back down.

"Ms. Crenshaw, Sister Geneva, you are a true visionary. When we all thought that all we had was land, you helped us see that we were the wall. We are Jerusalem. May God continue to bless and keep you, my dear sister." The reverend paused to pivot.

"So do you all see now? We are the former exiles turned children of the light! Jubilee is the refuge from Babylon! Jubilee is the wall and Jerusalem! And here's the thing about God—he does not bring you far to turn you back. He brings you far so that you may go further. In this land, where the earth was bloody and burnt, I declare us victorious! I declare Jubilee is the little space grace hath been shewed from the Lord our God to leave us a remnant to escape, and to give us a nail in his holy place, that our God may lighten our eyes, and give us a little reviving in our bondage. For we were slaves; yet our God hath not forsaken us in our bondage but hath extended mercy unto us to give us a reviving, to set up the house of our God, and to repair us a wall, Jerusalem, Jubilee! Now oh yea, people, please rise and let us praise the Lord! Make a noise unto him to express your gratitude. Make a noise in this place here so that he may know that you were present and accounted for on this revelation Sunday! Amen. Asé. Inshallah. Namasté. Shalom. Amen."

As the church joined the choir in a rousing rendition of "Go Tell It on the Mountain," the reverend was in full shout mode. He praised the name of Jesus repeatedly, chanting the name in rising and falling crescendos of admiration. "Hallelujah!" rang out from every side of the church. The sound reverberated from the stained glass. First, the praise spread across the congregants' sweaty palms as they waved in affirmation. Then, as their voices swirled, they echoed out into the streets where an overflow of a thousand or more listened from a speaker.

By the time Reggie finished his solo, the reverend, his father, was speaking with the fullness of the Holy Spirit. Many congregants went quiet, mesmerized by the rapture that had come over the Reverend, the choir, and Reggie. They just watched and lifted their eyes to the sky with tremendous gratitude. More than witnesses of Jubilee's success, they had all realized at that very moment that they had been chosen to shepherd it into future prosperity and stability. Tears rolled down the eyes of every man, woman, and child, and soon across several pews at the front and back, congregants lay prostrate.

The Reverend reapproached the pulpit, wiping his forehead with a white cloth. The reverend directed all to stand to their feet with a powerful aura that enraptured everyone on the stage. The reverend, overwhelmed with pride and joy, wept. He wept not with sorrow, but a joyous surrender to the history that was sure to unfold on his watch.

"The Spirit, the Holy Spirit is dwelling in this place. Divine confirmation! Hallelujah!" The reverend's eyes returned forward as he affirmed the energy moving the congregation.

It took a few minutes for the church to quiet. And even when it did simmer down, shouts and tongues and praises echoed from outside—folks feeling the Spirit as it traveled through the church, outside, and all through the streets of Jubilee City. As the sun shone through the colorful glass, an orange glow adorned and glistened along with the deepest dark chocolate hues of the reverend's skin.

"Amen!" rang out in unison.

It was a sight to behold. As the service concluded, the joy of those in attendance was contagious and boisterous. Individuals and families could be heard sharing their plans to watch the *60 Minutes* special. Others were discussing what food they planned to prepare as they watched. Everyone exuded a love that had been hidden. Yet even those who had been long-time residents or who were members of founding families maintained a reserve of cynicism. Though none of them spoke it aloud, the service had provided a significant release of the fears many held that one day Jubilee would be taken. After the failed attempt in 1964, some had lost hope. That Sunday, however, no matter the direction they walked or drove or carpooled to get to Mustardseed Baptist that Sunday, no matter how long they had lived in Jubilee or the surrounding areas, all were full of love and emptied of fear.

As everyone headed home, their thoughts raced. Their hearts were full. After one hundred years of praying and hoping, their work had finally paid off.

26 JULY 1965

Ruby awoke with a splitting headache. Her face was covered in a white residue from uncontrollably sobbing. She couldn't remember when she fell asleep or how long she had been asleep at all. Everything was a blur. Her house was in disarray. The television lay busted on the floor, the bat still atop the dented exterior. The dishes were still in the sink, and her bike was lying on her front lawn. She couldn't recall the exact order of events and, for the time being, was more focused on finding the letter from PJ she received a few days earlier. In a hazy, dizzy fog, Ruby searched and searched, looking in her bedroom dresser, her nightstand, in the kitchen cabinets, underneath and near the rocking chair, and still nothing. Finally, unable to handle the frustration, she burst into tears. Ruby fell to the floor, her knee nearly grazing the broken television glass.

As she wept wildly, memories of the night before flooded her mind. She tried to recall where she had placed the letter, but all she could remember was racing out on her bicycle to Reggie's house after watching the *60 Minutes* segment. She pedaled her bike with fury and rage, sadness and shock. Closing in on Reggie's house just a few minutes from her own, Ruby was furious that she allowed herself to be played by the white people.

How had she been so trusting, and how could those people betray her so? She asked herself these questions over and again until she reached Reggie's house. She knew her parents were probably furious and disappointed, so she left her house as soon as she could to avoid their wrath. Those editors had made her look like an angry rabble-rouser and Black segregationist who was self-interested and not at all caring or supportive of the struggle of all African Americans.

When she arrived, Reggie was out back entertaining friends, drinking and smoking from his marijuana garden. Sensing the distress in her eyes, Reggie immediately disbanded the small gathering. Most everyone was from the artist community that Reggie led. Over the last five years, Reggie had transformed the few blocks between where he and Ruby lived into a Black artist commune of sorts. While Ruby traveled spreading the word of Jubilee for political reasons, Reggie operated as an informal cultural ambassador. He spent most of his time meeting with Black painters, musicians, and writers in the various chocolate cities across the country. More often than not, he was racing between Atlanta and Jubilee City, transporting local artists for gatherings and small shows to encourage folks to think about headquartering themselves in Jubilee.

Reggie thoroughly believed that, in terms of sheer musical talent, Jubilee already rivaled Memphis's Stax Records, Detroit's Motown Records, and Philadelphia International Records. In his vision, Reggie saw that Jubilee would emerge as more than just a collection of Black towns in South Carolina with a critical mass of Black artists. He believed that Jubilee could become the new Renaissance destination.

As a child, Reggie had been deeply influenced by the great poets and writers of the Harlem Renaissance. He especially loved Langston Hughes's poetry. Unfortunately, he didn't have the penchant for poetry himself, though he tried over the years. He fared better when he sang, and so his first songs were compositions he developed by putting some of his favorite Hughes poems to music. None of them proved to be a hit, but they taught him how to properly control his voice, use distinctive phraseology, and maintain his buttery tone.

When Ruby arrived, Reggie was smoking and singing one of his Langston tunes, as he affectionately called them. Because they shared so many features, he could see the red line forming around the edges of her almond eyes, and he knew it was time to clear everyone out. Ruby was in deep distress and needed a safe space to be with her brother. Over the years, they had developed a way of communicating without speaking. As children with parents whose hearing abilities were near superhuman, they learned how to have full discussions just using gestures and cues to avoid their parents' gazes. That they were near-identical twins helped a great deal in the process because their eyes, nose, and mouth were the same, making it easy to implement and sustain their code language and communication.

In a matter of minutes, Reggie's house was clear. And no sooner than the last person's foot hit the sidewalk and turned the corner of the house's perimeter did Ruby burst into tears. There was no sound initially, but then he could see that Ruby was about to scream. He grabbed her and pulled her inside.

Reggie went into his bathroom and closed the window. He pushed Ruby inside and closed the door. When the door closed, Ruby let out a howl of a scream. For nearly a minute, she screamed at the moon until she was breathless.

Sensing that Ruby had screamed enough, Reggie knocked on the door. "You ready to talk, Ruby?" His voice was gentle and soothing. Ruby did not respond. "Come on out, Rubes, and let's figure this out," Reggie softly spoke, hoping to coax Ruby from the bathroom. There was a pause. After a few beats, Ruby emerged from the bathroom, tears strewed across her face. Ruby's hair and clothes were uncharacteristically disheveled; it appeared that she had not only been screaming in the bathroom but also pulling at her hair and clothes at the same time.

Although Reggie hadn't watched the segment, he suspected something must have gone terribly wrong for Ruby to be in such duress. Given how prone Ruby was to maintaining composure, Reggie was immediately concerned at the sight of his visibly distraught sister. Reggie would tease her as a kid because she even slept composed. Unlike him, Ruby slept with her hands neatly folded across her chest and made little noise.

When they were around eight or so, Reggie snuck into her room to talk. When he entered her room late that night, he saw her asleep for the first time. With her hands folded and barely looking like she was breathing, Reggie thought she was dead. His rising surprise turned into fear, and his automatic response was to quietly shake her a little. However, she was still warm, and soon her eyes opened, just popped open, causing Reggie to jump back. Reggie was unaware of Ruby's sleeping form because they'd always had separate bedrooms.

As the shock wore off, Reggie realized that, of course, Ruby slept perfectly. Such was the case with everything she did. Ruby had, since they were children, maintained a strong perfectionist streak.

It was in that dynamic where they were not identical. Reggie was a wild sleeper who often awoke upside down, right side up, on the floor, or tangled between the bedspread and fitted sheet. He wasn't nearly as manicured and curated as Ruby and tended to look the part of the town's local Bohemian. Though he tended to be relatively quiet when he was in public or at family gatherings, when Reggie was in his element, he was the life of the party with a distinctive, angelic singing voice. On the other hand, Ruby seemed social, as she was quite the gabber at gatherings and parties, but when she was home, Ruby preferred solitude and quiet and didn't have any friends—just Reggie and sometimes Geneva.

"I take it you didn't see *60 Minutes*," Ruby finally spoke. Her tone was sharp and pointed.

"You know me. I am not so much into television. And besides, it was you, Ruby, which means it was perfect. Like always, right?"

Ruby's head sunk and fell into her lap.

"Come on, Rubes. What is it? You know I don't like guessing games!" Reggie's tone, while still mild, was more direct and commanding.

"They played me. Those *60 Minutes* people played me badly," Ruby responded, her voice muffled by her dress.

"How is that possible? You told everyone almost verbatim what was said." Reggie was dubious, with his initial thought being that Ruby had been overreacting or giving herself a hard time. "Are you sure? I haven't heard anything . . . though. Then again, the crew and I weren't watching. But Mama and Daddy haven't called me." As soon as Reggie spoke those words, his phone rang.

Ruby shot him a look. "See, I am not making it up."

They both knew it was their parents. He let the phone ring and did not answer.

"Reggie, answer the phone! They are gonna keep calling, or even worse, they will come here looking for me, and I cannot be around them right now. I don't need any more ridicule in my life at this moment!"

As Ruby predicted, the phone rang again. Reggie rubbed her back and answered the phone. To make sure that Ruby would overhear the conversation, Reggie spoke loudly enough so she could hear.

"Hi, Mama . . . No, Mama. I haven't seen Ruby . . . No, Mama, I didn't watch . . . You know that I don't watch . . . Okay, Mama . . . I will, Mama . . . Good night, Mama . . . Okay, I will be there tomorrow . . . Love you too, Mama . . . Good night." Reggie hung up the phone. After hearing how upset and mad his mother sounded, he knew Ruby's suspicions were correct.

"You are right, Rubes. Mama is fish-grease mad! What in the world happened during that interview?"

"First, the white people made Jubilee look kind of scary! All of their shots, angles, and tints were distorted. Second, it made everyone, no matter what shade of brown they really are, look really dark. And I mean super dark." Ruby pointed to their shadows on the wall cast by the light overhead. Ruby continued, "We, and I mean, every person including me during the interview, looked like dark shadowy figures running around talking about getting reparations in South Carolina."

"Well, that just confirms how they see us anyway. And from what

I remember in your recounting of the interview, you didn't go over Geneva's 'no more than four reparations mentioned' allotment. That's not on you, Rubes. That's not on you." Reggie held her hand, attempting to console her.

Ruby was not buying it. "I don't know how they did it, but everyone, and I mean everyone, looked like menacing shadowy figures. And you know how easily rattled white folks are by Black people already, let alone if our skin colors are all distorted, so we just look like one menacing hue."

"Well, maybe that's how everyone looked. Right? . . . Never mind, I don't even know why I just said that." Reggie shrugged. "Okay, so that's the first thing, which means there is a second and third thing. What else? Mama and Daddy can't be mad at you because the white people messed with the color."

"Second, they edited me so that it had me saying, 'No, Jubilee is not a utopia. It is reparations. Spiritual reparations. Spatial reparations' . . . and some version of me saying something like, 'African Americans having the option of killing white people because of slavery' without any context or the setup of the question. It made me come off as a critic of Jubilee instead of a supporter. It also took a series of comments made separately and poured them all into one remark. So even if I did follow Geneva's advice, the comment is like a sandwich of reparations. They had it like I just said that on my own and suggested that something was wrong with Jubilee. And even worse, they didn't even give people a sense that the kinds of reparations I was talking about wouldn't cost anybody anything more than maybe the pride of some of these racist white people."

"Well, there are things wrong with Jubilee. You and I both know that! It is certainly not a utopia, and I am glad that you said it. Unfortunately, they have tried to beat it into our brains that we live in some kind of utopia when that is not the case. Don't get me wrong—when it is beautiful here, it is wonderful. But then there are those ugly ways, ugly opinions that surface, and it makes me sad that we are not living up to our full potential. We should make ALL Black people feel welcome, not just the ones the church deems as righteous and virtuous." Reggie found pleasure in the idea that Ruby had offered any ounce of criticism for Jubilee. Reggie appreciated Ruby's impromptu honesty, given his struggles with the rigid culture and perspectives of the older folks and many residents.

"That's not the point, Reggie! The point is that it misrepresented my response and makes me out to look like I lied to everyone when I recounted what transpired during the interview." Ruby's concern for herself shifted to concern about Reggie following the line of logic she clearly understood.

"And that's not all, Reggie." Ruby looked right into Reggie's eyes. "They had two residents saying that they planned to cash in their land and leave after President Johnson signs the bill. And they used that as a way to question if Jubilee would survive and if everyone is happy, or is Jubilee just a scam? Can you imagine? They actually aired that for the nation to hear . . ."

Ruby ran into the kitchen and grabbed a wooden spoon. She pulled air into her chest and imitated the formal white voice of Bill Plante. "Perhaps Jubilee is a land scam. Perhaps it's a utopia. Although no one seems to know which it is, after the president signs the Voting Rights Act of 1965, it shall be an independent territory within the United States with voting powers . . . *dun dun*. Can you believe it?!?"

Reggie was now officially shocked. He didn't know what to think.

"Woah, a 'scam'! That's no good. That is some defamation! Maybe Geneva and her firm will have some ways to navigate this so that we can come out as unscathed as possible."

"Look here. In all my thirty-one years of life and all my missions, I have learned that the easiest way to destroy something Black in America is two-pronged: one, scare the bejesus out of white folks, and two, make Black people paranoid. And from where I am sitting, *60 Minutes* did both. They did both! Bastards!" Ruby had moved from one extreme of overwhelming sadness to now righteous rage.

"So you know this means that Mama and Daddy will want to meet, and I am sure that the council will want to have a meeting. What should we do?" Reggie asked, looking for Ruby to offer some direction.

"What do you mean? I don't know! It's done!" Ruby shouted at Reggie.

"Hey! I am on your side! I am always on your side. If we need to leave, I am leaving with you. If we need to fight, then I am fighting with you. We were created together, came into this world together, and if we must leave Jubilee, we will make our way together. My life is your life. Your life is my life," Reggie responded with their blood oath to each other.

"You're right. I am sorry. I shouldn't be taking out my anger and frustrations on you. I am just . . . just . . . feeling blindsided and lost," Ruby confessed and hugged Reggie.

They hugged each other tightly, and Ruby rested her head on Reggie's shoulder. Reggie patted her hair, rubbing the frayed edges.

"I got it. I will call Uncle Martin. He will surely have the words. He will know what to do. And I will just take my licks. I refuse to believe that God has brought us this close for it all to fall apart because of one, ONE INTERVIEW!" Ruby exhaled.

"Yes! Great idea, Ruby. Uncle Martin always knows what the right play is, and there isn't anything he hasn't seen white people try. You want to call him now?" Excited by Ruby's stroke of genius, Reggie reached for the phone and began dialing the number, which they both knew by heart.

"No, not yet," Ruby responded, and Reggie hung up the phone.

Ruby pointed to the clock, and then Reggie noticed that it was already after 2:00 a.m.

"It's late," Ruby confirmed, "and I don't want to wake up Auntie Retta and the babies. But I am sure they watched, and I can call tomorrow and get advice. Like we learned in Bible study, new mornings equal brand-new mercies." Ruby smiled.

"Amen." Reggie smiled back, affirming he was down with the plan. "Okay, so that's it!"

"Well, that's not everything. Remember, there was a third thing," Ruby reminded him.

"Oh right. So what's the third thing? Given how much your attitude has shifted, I assumed that was everything and you forgot the third."

"I get the sense that someone has been through my things. There is an item, a personal item, that has gone missing. After church, I looked everywhere but couldn't find it. It wouldn't bother me too much, but it's personal."

"Huh? Ruby Calhoun, what are you trying to say? Someone is watching you?!? The Feds are here?" Reggie ran to the window and pulled back the curtain, anxious that his carefree marijuana use and the small farm were being watched or photographed.

"No, not like that. I don't think it was any Fed, though you can never know. I don't put anything past that Hoover guy, and he has been known to recruit his fair share of Black moles. But no, I mean like it is just one item, and I just received it a few days ago. A letter. And, like, why would someone take just the letter? It's weird and unnerving."

"Well, what does the letter say? Is it saying that you hate Jubilee or that white people are the devil? What is it?"

"No, it doesn't say those things. It was just . . . just . . . personal, okay?" Ruby was becoming flustered, and her comments were only piquing Reggie's curiosity.

"Sounds like a love letter to me." Reggie smirked and laughed. "Let me find out, Rubes, you got you a secret lover! But then, the plot thickens . . . *dun*."

"Never mind. I knew I shouldn't have told you. You love to tease me at the most inopportune times."

"I am sorry, Rubes. Let me know what I can do."

"I am not sure what can be done. I just need to look again."

"Yes, look again. Are there others? Maybe you put it with other letters." Seeing that Ruby was getting upset at the insinuation that there were stacks of love letters, Reggie pivoted. "Not saying that you are hiding bunches of them, just saying that maybe you put it with your other mail."

"Maybe. I haven't looked at all of the mail. The thing is, and please do not say anything or react after I say this." Ruby's eyes were demanding as she looked at her brother.

Reggie nodded.

"I have received just a few of these letters over the last few years, and I burn them shortly afterward so that folks can't get into my business or go looky-loo through my things when I am away on my missions."

"I see. Well, it is nice to hear that there is a human in there with some love in her life. I like this Ruby way more than the Ruby that is always dutiful and perfect. I will keep your secret, and I am also happy you shared it with me. I will also let go of the fact that I am just learning about this when I tell you EVERYTHING!" Reggie laughed, and Ruby laughed too. They embraced again.

Ruby ended the hug. "Let me go home and see if I just misplaced it or put it with the junk mail. I will call Uncle Martin in the morning and let you know what he says."

"Great plan as always, Rubes. As always."

"I love you, Reggie. We were created together, born together. My life is your life. Your life is my life."

Then in unison, they restated their love credo again. "We were created together, born together. My life is your life. Your life is my life."

"I love you too, Ruby." Reggie kissed Ruby's cheek before she headed back to her home.

As the moon disappeared behind the rising Monday morning sun, Ruby called Uncle Martin to seek his advice. She grabbed her phone and dialed the number, which she knew by heart. While the phone rang, Ruby rehearsed what she planned to say and also cleared her throat.

After three rings, a tenderhearted voice answered.

"Hello, Auntie Retta, it's . . ."

"Oh, my darling Ruby! How lovely it is to hear from you! We were so upset last night by how those *60 Minutes* folks tried to sabotage all of your good work. You know how we love Jubilee so."

"Thank you so much, Auntie. You don't know how much that means to me."

"You are welcome, my darling . . . Yeah, I am on the phone with Ruby. Yeah, it's her. She's on the line now."

Ruby could hear a familiar voice in the background saying, "Great. I was hoping I could speak with her."

"Your uncle is coming to the phone now. Meantime, you keep your head up and know that we all love and cherish you and Jubilee. So pay them white folks no never mind. You hear me?"

"Yes, Auntie Retta. I love you too."

"Okay, here comes your uncle."

As Ruby awaited his voice, she saw a note slid under the door. She grabbed the base of the phone and walked the long cord toward the front door. She picked up the folded parchment. Her name was on the front. She opened it, and it read:

Emergency family meeting tomorrow morning, Tuesday, 27 July, at 8:00 a.m. sharp.

Do not be late. Do not be cross.

Mama & Daddy

Ruby was shaking. She had never had her parents slide a note under her door. She was also unsure when it arrived because she had been sleeping most of the day.

"HEY THERE, OUR GEM OF the ocean. Uncle Martin here."

When Ruby heard his voice, her body immediately stopped shaking. She always felt so soothed when he spoke, especially when he called her his favorite nickname, "gem of the ocean." Although she didn't know what would come of the conversation, she was glad to have trusted her intuition and called.

She was even happier that she got to hear from Auntie Retta as well. Auntie Retta was always like talking directly with sunshine on a cloudy day.

After letting the soothing sensation wash over her like a freshwater bath, Ruby walked the long-cord phone into the kitchen, sat at the table, and placed the note into the trash.

"Hey, Uncle, I really need your help," Ruby disclosed, her tone reminiscent of a lost child seeking refuge from a swirling storm overhead.

"I suspected as much. Now, go on ahead and tell your uncle Martin what's going on. I'm here now."

27 JULY 1965

An hour into the family meeting, no one had yet spoken. Instead, they just sat in silence, looking at one another, eating eggs and bacon and grits. There had been no speaking. The only sounds were the forks hitting the plates and the swallowing of orange juice and coffee. Ruby's father began with a short grace before they ate, but even that was a bit stale and curt. Usually, he was verbose and booming during even the shortest of prayers, but this day he was not—a sure signal to Ruby that the waters were troubled.

As she sat moving her food around the plate more than she was eating it, Ruby couldn't remember the last time she felt such silence in her family home. The home which her grandfather had built and left to her father was always full of life, music, and people. People looking for advice. Women looking for Lucy's insights about dreams and visions and designs. Families looking for the reverend to baptize, christen, marry, or preside over the funeral of a loved one. Reggie at the piano, tickling the ivories with his signature flair and chord progressions. And Ruby running from room to room, playing hostess, guest, and speaker all simultaneously.

Any suspicion Ruby held that the interview had gone terribly wrong was all confirmed as soon as she entered her family's home. She was not greeted. She had been the last to arrive, and her parents and brother were already seated at the dining room table awaiting her arrival. When she sat, they each grabbed hands as their father offered grace. But that had been an hour ago, and Ruby could no longer stand the thick silence. And so, she was determined to slice through it and end her suffering.

"I know you are both mad with me. So can we please just get to it?" Ruby demanded.

"Listen here, little girl, you will not and shall not demand anything of us in our home!" her mother admonished her swiftly. "Eat your food, and then we will talk, no sooner and no later."

Ruby always hated when her mother called her "little girl," not just because she was nearly thirty years old but also because the older she got, the more she felt the gumption to just get up and leave. She did not need any more upset and hassle than what she had already endured.

"You hear your mother, young lady. Eat your food. We want to make sure we are of full stomach and sound mind when we talk about difficulties," her father consolidated Lucy's disposition.

After an hour of pushing the food around, it had gotten cold and even less appetizing. Nonetheless, if the condition was going to be that no discussion happened without food being eaten, then Ruby would eat the food, and fast. In a few minutes, Ruby's plate was cleared, and she drank her juice.

Turning back to her parents, Ruby retorted, "Okay, so now that I've eaten, let's get to it."

Reggie was stunned by Ruby's sudden defiance. In all the years they had been alive, he had never seen Ruby challenge or command their parents, ever. Stuck somewhere between laughter and shock, Reggie let out an awkward chuckle. Reggie's laughter seemed to tip the scales, though unintentional, adding to Ruby's words. Then, finally, Ronald broke the ice and began to speak.

"I know I speak for your mom when I say how disappointed we are in not just the interview, but in you as well, Ruby. White people are gon' do as they do. This we know. But that you would give them such fodder is beyond me. What were you thinking when you corrected the man when he used 'Negro'?!? And then saying that Jubilee was not a utopia?!? I mean, child, what has gotten into you?"

As Ronald spoke, Lucy shot Ruby a look worse than any whooping she had ever received. Her mother looked at her like she would wring her neck if she could. Ruby could see that the hostility was real and that nothing could be said that could change their feelings. Even still, she loved her parents tremendously and still wanted to try and rectify the situation.

"And Reggie, this is not a time for laughter! Son, I mean, really, do you plan to grow up at some point?" Ronald shifted his gaze from Ruby just slightly to admonish Reggie, who thought he would escape the firing squad that morning.

"What does that mean?" Reggie was insulted. "This whole thing is uncomfortable to sit in. I didn't even see this God-forsaken interview. Ruby has worked too hard for so long to be expected to be perfect all the time! And just so you know, I've *been* grown." Reggie glanced up and saw his mother's sadness at the tone he was taking with his father and took a slight pause. "Sir."

Ruby took a few deep breaths and began to answer or, at the very least, provide some clarity. "You both know I love this family, and I love Jubilee. I have spent ten years on these missions, and there is nothing I would like to see more than for Jubilee to receive its independence. That said, I refuse to accept blame for the things that I said. They were all true and, in one form or another, are things I have said publicly in forums across the country. They just edited me to look a certain way. That's how I see it." Ruby was passionate but firm.

"That may well be the case, but this interview was not a time to be caught slipping, and it's a bit immature to be blaming 'editing.'" Ronald used air quotes to also demonstrate he was not buying what Ruby was selling.

"Well, 'editing'"—Ruby sarcastically reflected back the air quotes— "Is a real thing. A real issue. In fact, when I spoke with Uncle Martin, he said . . ."

"Lord have mercy, the child has spoken to Dr. King about this fiasco, Ronald!" Lucy was even more upset.

"I did. Uncle Martin said, 'If I had a dollar for every time white folks in the news and media misrepresented me and our cause, I would be a millionaire!' He said that this is what these news people do. They are not interested in Black stories. He said they like to make us look like antagonists not because we are but because it makes their audience think they are impartial. It helps them maintain their 'journalistic integrity.'" Ruby used her air quotes again.

"Well, that might be fine and well for Dr. King to say, but it is not his home that is on the chopping block every day!" Ronald shot back, joining in upset with Lucy. "And if you think that he can save you in this room with us right now, then Ruby, you are sadly mistaken."

"None of this would have happened if everyone didn't put so much pressure on Ruby all the time. Somebody should have sat up there with her. Instead, she was there with some notes and no support!" Reggie was now also distraught for Ruby. He took no pleasure in hearing her be diminished and dismissed, especially after the sacrifice he knew she had made over the last ten years. "Ruby has sacrificed so much for all of us. She doesn't even really have friends because she is on the road all the time. After finishing college early, Ruby could have gone to law school like she wanted. But no, Ruby put that on hold for the greater good. She could be dating or married, but she put that on hold for the greater good. Shame on you, Mom and Dad, for not embracing her and lifting her up." Reggie looked both his parents square in the eye as he squeezed and held Ruby's trembling left hand under the table.

"Hmmmphhh, has she really?" Lucy let out a big sigh of disbelief and looked at Ruby with an expression that suggested that she knew something.

"Yes, she has." Reggie was matter-of-fact in his response.

"ENOUGH!" Ronald decried. "Here's where we are. The council wants to meet with the family tomorrow morning. They plan to recommend that you take a vow of silence until the bill is passed. Many elders have assessed the fallout and response after discussions with folks across the country, getting the major papers and seeing how the interview has been rehashed. Geneva spoke with her connections in Washington, DC, and they confirmed that the bill is still scheduled to be signed by the president in ten days. The council feels what is done is done, and we do not need any more unnecessary attention."

Ruby was relieved to hear that she wouldn't have to speak, though she could tell that her parents believed they were issuing some sort of punishment. After years of being on the circuit, Ruby was tired of talking, and to hear that she would be able to keep to herself was a genuine silver lining amidst all the madness of the last few days. Even still, she knew her parents needed to think that she was disappointed, so she played the part.

"That doesn't seem fair. Why wouldn't the council at least hear me out first? Besides, I am due to join the council after the bill is signed anyway since you agreed to step away once Jubilee received independence," Ruby responded, pretending to be upset by the news.

"Well, there's been a change in that plan as well. I will leave the council to inform you about those changes. But for now, let's just say after our independence is authorized, you will begin a new assignment, and I will stay on in my capacity as an elder." Ronald was genuinely hurt to share this with Ruby, especially in this context. "What's done is done. All we can do is move forward."

"That's right," Lucy chimed in. "And we certainly will not be moving forward with any PJ Bar."

Reggie and Ronald looked at both Lucy and Ruby, confused. Lucy pulled a folded letter from under her placemat.

"PJ Bar," Reggie and Ronald repeated aloud in a staccato-near-unison voice.

Ruby was furious and knew precisely what her mother had done. Her letter had not been lost. Instead, her mother had found it and searched through her belongings. Before she could let out any statement of upset, Lucy continued.

"Yes, Ruby. I did look through your things at your house. I found it in that rocking chair you love—the one my mother gave to you before she died—and there it was. In the seat, there was a letter." Lucy looked at each person at the table. "A love letter. From a PJ Bar in Atlanta."

"How dare you go through my things, Mama! How dare you!" Ruby was outraged and furiously snatched the letter from her mother, who dared not attempt to take it back.

"Do not speak to your mother that way, young lady," Ronald admonished Ruby. "And who is this PJ Bar? I don't recall there being a Bar family in Jubilee. And Atlanta? What is this all about?"

"Well," Ruby tried to calm herself down. "Well . . ."

As Ruby searched for words and explanations, a light bulb went off in Reggie's mind. Reggie knew who it was. Reggie recalled meeting a Freedom Rider and activist during a small conference that Ruby and Reggie attended in Detroit. There was a small house party later, and he remembered a short, stocky, dark-skinned Black woman named Patricia Jo, who preferred that she be called PJ, who had attended the forum on Jubilee earlier. She and Reggie had a drink and a good conversation where she told him all about the artist community in Atlanta and invited him to visit. The thing was that Ruby didn't attend the party, but there was no way that was a coincidence. Reggie kept his mouth closed and held tightly to Ruby's hand as she searched for her words.

"Well what, young lady?" Lucy beseeched Ruby for answers.

"People write me all the time. There is nothing to talk about there. I just wish that you wouldn't have gone through my things is all." Ruby was soft and repentant in her tone.

"If you say so. I'll leave it at that and remind you that you are already set to get engaged to Michael Richardson, a nice young military man and firstborn son of the Richardson family. He has been patient and waiting for you to finish your missions. Ruby, you always knew this was on the horizon, and you said you were agreeable. As you know, the Richardsons hold a crucial place on the council," Lucy reminded Ruby.

"I know. But Mama, what if I don't like him? What if I don't like . . ."

Lucy interrupted Ruby. "Who said anything about liking? This is the plan. And we are obedient in the household. Right?" Lucy looked at both Ruby and Reggie for their responses.

"Right," Reggie and Ruby repeated, sounding like young teenagers who hoped to escape further punishment.

"Now that we have gotten all of this on the table, and you know about the council meeting tomorrow, why don't you and Reggie go on home and get yourselves prepared? Your mama and I will clean up here."

"Okay," Ruby and Reggie said as they pushed their chairs back and placed their napkins on the table.

"And I know it may not always feel or seem like it, but your mother and I love you both very much. Our expectations are high not to punish but to prepare you. You must always remember that. Nothing great ever was achieved without preparation. Strategy is the mother of victory. So the greater the outcome, the greater the preparation."

Ronald hugged Ruby and Reggie. Lucy, following suit, hugged them both.

28 JULY 1965

When Ruby entered the room, the Council of Elders was unmoved. For over ten years, the elders had always greeted Ruby with unmistakable excitement and encouragement, but this day was clearly different. Unwilling and unable to endure the mysterious and ominous meeting alone, Ruby requested that Reggie be allowed to sit alongside her for support.

The council accommodated the request and insisted that Reggie's proposal and progress on the annual Jubilee Festival be discussed before issuing their disposition on Ruby. Both Reggie and Ruby agreed. While Ruby had no clue about Reggie's proposal, she was grateful that he would be by her side. Ruby really could use the support, especially given that both her parents were on the council and had made their stance painfully clear over breakfast the day prior. Usually, Ruby felt a sense of calming peace in the council's headquarters. It was only a ten-minute walk from her home, and she enjoyed strolling through Jubilee Square Park to get there.

Located at the center of Jubilee City and next to Jubilee Central

Train Station, the council building was patterned after a West African stool. The architects who designed and constructed the building had been deeply influenced by books and images of the Ashanti Kingdom in Ghana. Because the stool represented political power, bloodline, and chieftains, the building was constructed to look like a larger-than-life stool; brass and copper were laced and intertwined across the roof. Although the building was only four stories tall, the beautiful metal atop gave a grand feel and made the building appear as though it was twice its actual height and size. When Ruby was younger, her father told her that the Black Jesus of Lucy's vision would walk down Heaven's stairway out of the sky one day. He'd look upon the great stool of Jubilee and take his rightful seat. Anyone who walked out of the park and stood in front of the council building couldn't help but be taken with the building's sheer beauty, majesty, and imposing stature.

However, Ruby was not happy to see or be inside the council building on this day and under these circumstances. When she and Reggie entered the room, all eighteen elders were present, including her mother and father. Geneva was at the back of the room as usual. The council's meeting room was shaped in a large oval. Their table was made of the wood from the former slave quarters they retrieved after the Calhoun plantation had been ransacked by the mercenaries hired by the Union Army. At first, there wasn't a clear idea of what they would do with the wood. However, the builders had a sense that they wanted to put it to good use. They determined the wood would be used to remember what they had survived and as a symbol of their collective courage to forge a new path for them and their families. As the stool was being constructed to adorn the rooftop, the elders had determined that they needed a unique table for their meeting room.

The table, shaped in the form of a massive key, was pressed and polished from the old oak wood of the slave quarters; it was lacquered with a reddish-orange color and then buffed and polished. The oversize custom table took seven months to make. When it was completed, it became a great source of pride, especially for the elders. Guests sat along the long end of the table. The eighteen elders sat around the half circle at the top of the table. The key-shaped table had ridges with seating for visitors and speakers. When seated, the elders could see and hear what was going on and what was said.

When Ruby and Reggie entered, they greeted the council. Their greeting was met with an unusual silence. She and Reggie took their seats, and even then, none of the elders greeted them or smiled, not even her parents.

As Ruby sat down, she felt Geneva's extended hand rub her back and then grasp her right hand. Then, just as the proceedings got underway and Ruby took her seat, Geneva kneeled forward. She whispered into Ruby's ear: "You did good work, my dear sister. Do not let them or anyone steal your joy."

Geneva's words provided a healing solace. This was the first time Ruby had seen Geneva since Sunday service. It had been even longer since anyone had spoken any kindness or support. For Ruby, the past three days felt more extended than the last ten years of mission work and forums. Ruby let the warmth of Geneva's words provide much-needed grace.

As Geneva's words comforted her, Reggie held Ruby's hand. It was there, then, and in that split moment that Ruby sensed a significant change was coming. There was something new on the horizon. What it was, she was not sure of at the time. Ruby did, however, arrive at a more profound realization. Ruby was sure that if she was ever going to have the life she desired, no approval mattered other than the permission she would give herself.

If the council could be so cold to her after all that she had done, then she knew the road to pleasing the elders was not a pathway. Instead, it was a rabbit hole—one she could spend her whole life toiling in unsuccessfully. Upon her realization, she felt an ease come about, a new feeling of possibility. Affirming the sensational awareness, Ruby felt compelled to acknowledge this personal revelation with prayer. And so she folded her hands in prayer, making sure it was visible to the Council of Elders. Ruby then began softly reciting the serenity prayer. Reggie, always a prayer partner for Ruby in a time of need, heard the familiar words and quietly joined her. Together they chanted the short prayer. "God, grant me the serenity to accept the things I cannot change, the courage to change the things I can, and the wisdom to know the difference. Amen." Geneva, overhearing the quiet prayer, added a soft "Amen," as well. No sooner than Ruby finished the words of the serenity prayer and unclasped her hands did the council turn their attention to her and Reggie.

Fully adorned in their ceremonial all-white regalia, the elders were all straight-faced. Comprised of two members of the nine founding families, each elder's white attire featured an embroidered crest specific to the family from which they descended. The elders sat according to last names in alphabetical order from right to left. The seating arrangement was meant to convey collegiality and equality even though there were some power differentials across the group and within the respective founding families. Of the eighteen elders, an internally selected person served as a hybrid mayor-governor of Jubilee and its five areas. That person, called the Chief Elder, served for a six-year term. In the fifth year of their term, the Chief Elder would indicate if he intended to stay on or step aside. This announcement would then allow another to assume the mantle of leadership. Every five years, there was an election where votes were cast across the five areas, which consistently reaffirmed the prior arrangement among the elders.

For the last ten years, James Richardson served as the Chief Elder. James Richardson descended from Jackson Richardson, the second person to acquire forty acres under Sherman's order. A longtime friend of Ruby's grandfather Calvin, Jackson served with her grandfather as the under-minister for Mustardseed Baptist from its inception. Save for Chief Elder James Richardson, who sat center, the flanking began with the Almost family, represented by grandmother Etta and grandson Edward Almost. The Brown family was next, represented by father Baker and son Walter Brown. Next to the Browns were the Calhouns, represented by Ruby's parents Ronald and Lucy Douglass-Calhoun. Beside the

Calhouns sat Chief Richardson at the center. To the chief elder's right, the Edwards family was represented by two brothers Jonathan and Jacob Edwards. Then came the Jacksons, represented by grandmother Mary Jackson and granddaughter Mable Jackson-Douglass. Then beside the Jacksons was the Morris family, represented by husband and wife Louis Morris and Susan Brown-Morris. Following the Morrises was the second Richardson, James's son Michael Richardson. Rounding out the council at the end of the half circle sat the Williamses, represented by mother and son Lucretia Almost-Williams and Daniel Williams.

The Chief Elder stood and called the meeting into session. "We will now begin the final business of today's convening of the council. First, we have a progress report from Mr. Reginald Calhoun. As the council is aware, Reginald has served as the cultural coordinator and event planner for the annual Jubilee Festival for the past ten years. I understand that he will apprise the council of the progress made and present a short proposal for our consideration. Subsequently, we will turn our attention to the last item on our agenda, the council's determination and evaluation of Ms. Ruby Calhoun's recent work and performance. The council shall specifically inform Ruby of a series of decisions. First will be the council's assessment regarding her most recent performance at the 60 Minutes interview. Then the council shall issue our recommendations regarding any new or changing roles for Ms. Calhoun following the signing of the Voting Rights Act of 1965. All in favor, raise your right hand and say yea."

"Yea." All seventeen raised their hands and confirmed the Chief Elder's order of discussion.

"Before we begin, I must report something to both of you, Reginald and Ruby. We received word from our contacts in Washington, DC, just in the last hour. We have been informed that President Johnson has confirmed that he shall sign the historic bill in nine days, on Friday, the sixth of August." The Chief Elder took his seat.

Neither Ruby nor Reggie knew that the signing had been assured and confirmed. They looked at each other, hands intertwined underneath the table, and Reggie winked at Ruby as if to say, *Rubes! You did it! You did it!* Ruby's heart began beating so fast she thought it might jump onto the table just to shout at everyone, *You're welcome!* But Ruby thought it unwise to say anything aloud, given the coldness of the council. She released Reggie's hand and placed it over her heart to calm it.

As Chief Elder Richardson took his seat, he directed Reggie to begin. "Reginald, the council is ready for your report and proposal. You may begin, Mr. Calhoun."

Reggie stood and cleared his throat. He began his report on the festival. Even though he was only speaking when presenting, Reggie had a melodic tone that made everyone sway their head in rhythm. "Thank you, Chief Elder Richardson and council elders, for your time today. This year's festival promises to be the very best in the history of Jubilee. We are in store for the jubilee of all jubilees in Jubilee! The one and only Mr. James Brown has already begun rehearsals with his band, the J.B.'s. Mr. Brown has indicated that the sound equipment we have installed is excellent. I heard the rehearsal for his newest, hottest jam released just last month, 'Papa's Got a Brand New Bag,' and when I tell you, the groove was out of this world! OOOOO-weeee! Mr. Brown asked that I personally tell the council that he looks forward to, and I quote, 'Celebrating Jubilee's brand new bag!'" Reggie spun around in a circle as he recounted James Brown's words.

Several council members clapped with joy upon hearing the news. This energy shift made Ruby feel more relaxed. The council was already nodding and swaying their heads to Reggie's rhythm. Ruby was relieved to follow Reggie, assuming that his energy and approach might lessen the stings that surely awaited her.

Reggie continued. "After a little back and forth, I can also confirm that the show will open with Stevie Wonder."

The council smiled with approval and excitement.

"And that's not all, folks." Reggie grew more animated in his delivery. "Mr. Gordy also promised we would witness a battle as a part of the Motown showcase—the Four Tops versus the Temptations! That's right, you heard it here first! Mr. Berry Gordy said that 'Detroit loves Jubilee! And nothing says independence like the Motown sound'!"

Reggie was on fire. All of the women council members jumped out of their seats, forgetting their stoic posturing altogether. Even those who remained seated were ecstatic. Reggie and Ruby's mother, Lucy, who was out of her chair as soon as he said "the Four Tops," couldn't contain her joy and began singing and praising Reggie.

"Sugar pie honey bunch! Go on with your bad self, Reggie. That's my son! Okay!"

Reggie smiled from ear to ear and waited for all of the noise to subside. Finally, when he felt the room was quiet and relaxed, he laid on his final surprise.

"Oh, I am sorry. I realized I said the Four Tops versus the Temptations. That was incorrect."

"Oh no. Huh?!?" several of the elders voiced their upset and confusion aloud.

"Are they coming or not, Mr. Calhoun? This sacred room is not for untruths and spectacles!" Chief Elder Richardson demanded.

Reggie played coy at first and appeared like he misspoke and as though he was going to take back the announcement. "My apologies, Chief Elder Richardson. I misspoke," Reggie falsely confessed.

"AWWWWW!" Several council members sucked their teeth, and Lucy started to look angry and embarrassed.

"I meant to say . . ." Reggie spoke with a low register and then higher as he restated the information with a surprising end. "I just forgot to mention a key ingredient. It will indeed be the Four Tops versus the Temptations . . . VERSUS the Supremes! That's right! Diana Ross will be all the way live!"

Reggie's chest was all the way forward, and his grin-turned-smile was enrapturing. Everyone was on their feet. Reggie received a standing ovation from everyone in the room.

Ruby was so proud of Reggie. She had wondered why he had insisted on coming to Detroit the past year with her and Geneva because he never attended the forums. Ruby just thought maybe he was trying to get signed at Motown; it had never occurred to her that he was working on the festival and this bounty of surprises. Ruby felt so fortunate to have been born alongside her clever and talented brother.

For several minutes, the group, including Ruby and Geneva, stood and applauded and shouted and praised Reggie for all he had accomplished. Then all the elders turned to Ronald and Lucy and clapped for them, praising them for blessing Jubilee with these powerful twins. Finally, Chief Elder Richardson couldn't contain himself. When he heard Diana Ross was coming to town, the Chief Elder instructed everyone to regain their composure to continue with the business at hand.

"Mr. Calhoun, you have truly impressed the council! This festival will surely be one for the ages. Now, are you sure everything is in order? We don't want anything to go wrong here."

"Sir, everything is copasetic! They are all rehearsing as we speak. Mr. Gordy will have all three groups here the night before and has informed me that he wants to personally meet, I quote, 'the parents of that divinely gifted Ruby.' Unbeknownst to Ruby and Ms. Geneva, he and one of his trusted advisors have kept up with all the Jubilee happenings. Mr. Gordy has also attended Ruby's last two forums in Detroit. So impressed by her, he has even listened to some of her recorded speeches as well. So we all have Ruby to thank!" Reggie looked over at Ruby and winked and clapped for her. He knew that Ruby had no idea of any of this, and it was his intention to build a wall around his sister—a wall of joy and truth.

Though Reggie's applause for Ruby was only accompanied by Geneva's claps, it was all Ruby needed. She felt a smile well up from deep in her belly.

"I see. We look forward to hosting and celebrating with Mr. Gordy, Motown, and Mr. James Brown." Chief Elder Richardson looked at Reggie with eyes suggesting that he sit down and conclude his remarks. Chief Elder Richardson was sharp-witted and sensed that Reggie was also laying it on thicker than necessary to try and soften whatever the council had in store for Ruby.

"Yes, but also there is the matter of my proposal, Chief Elder." Reggie followed up on the statement to remind him that he had been promised the time to report and propose.

"You are right. Please continue." Chief Elder Richardson grimaced and waved his hand.

"Every year, Jubilee shells out thousands of dollars for the supporting musicians for the festival. We could save a lot of money if we were willing to convert the old cotton mill near my home into a music conservatory with lodging. I have already been able to build up a community of artists around my home, and we have thought ourselves as Jubilee's Bohemia—"

"More like Sodom and Gomorrah," Elder Louis Morris stated matter-of-factly and loudly enough to interrupt Reggie's flow.

His wife and fellow elder, Susan Brown-Morris, affirmed her husband's statement. "Mmmm hmmm."

Reggie tried to ignore their comments and continue, though their use of the Bible to mischaracterize the community he had built really got under his skin.

"In Jubilee, we should be welcoming all Black people from all walks of life. This place was built on Black talent. We will need talent from every corner if we are to have a prosperous place. This will especially be critical after independence." Reggie's voice pivoted into an imitation of his father's ministerial bravado.

"So what are you proposing, Mr. Calhoun?" the Chief Elder inquired impatiently.

"I am proposing that we build a music and art conservatory in the old cotton mill by my house. We can train our own elite group of in-house talent who would be a part of our community. This alone would be saving us thousands of dollars in costs. As it stands, we now pay a large sum for the musicians and artists. We pay for bus and train tickets and lodging every year for the annual festival, not to mention all the other functions we have during the year. Why pay a drummer when we could have one on scholarship? Several residents have offered to be instructors and mentors at the conservatory. . . ."

"So you've already recruited people for this endeavor? And before you have spoken with the council nonetheless?" Chief Elder Richardson interrupted Reggie, highlighting what he saw as an intentional disregard for custom and procedure.

"Recruit, no. Inquire, yes. I would not waste the time of this esteemed group without doing my due diligence. For just the supporting musicians and artists at this year's festival, we are spending several thousand dollars alone. When I spoke with both Mr. Brown and Mr. Gordy, they asked if we had in-house players I could vouch for, and I had to tell them no. We do not. You see the problem there? We cannot always rely on folks coming from out of town. Just because some folks are afraid of people who are different living here is not a good reason either." Reggie cut his eyes at the Morrises as he finished.

"Well, Rome was not built overnight. Therefore, Mr. Calhoun, we are not prepared to give any answers today. I can tell you right now, many in our community are traditional and conservative. They will not abide with the . . . let's call them 'tendencies' that some in the artistic community participate in."

"Oh, I see. Folks can play your favorite songs and cook your festival food and paint that glorious painting you keep above the mantle of your fireplace. Still, they are not welcome to be educated or live here? The only tendency I am seeing is self-hatred." Reggie's joyous tone had turned sour and defiant. "Besides, only a fool would believe that the 'community' is not already in Jubilee." He looked at the Morrises and the rest of the elders and ended his cold stare with Michael Richardson.

"That's enough of that, Mr. Calhoun. Let's stay in the place of gratitude and not travel down this dark path," Chief Elder Richardson interrupted, noticing his son Michael's reaction to Reggie's remarks and stare.

"With all due respect, I am not finished, sir. The bylaws state that any meaningful proposal shall receive a temporary yea or nay vote for further consideration by the council," Reggie shot back.

"And who exactly said this proposal was meaningful?" The Chief

Elder put his hand to his ear as though he were listening for support for Reggie's proposal.

There was not a sound. Reggie looked to his parents for support. Both Ronald and Lucy shook their heads in disappointment with Reggie. They looked away toward the Chief Elder, a signal that they were unsupportive and embarrassed. Ruby grabbed Reggie's hand to offer her support. She could feel Reggie furiously trembling.

"I see. Fear is the only 'tendency' that jeopardizes Jubilee. Mark my words, you all will rue the day you disregarded me and my vision. I am willing to bet that in thirty years, the world's spotlight will be on Atlanta and not on Jubilee. Atlanta will be on the world's stage, and we will haplessly witness it over here in Jubilee, driving in to take part rather than the other way around. Mark my words!" Reggie pointed his finger at each of the council members.

"That is absolutely enough! You sit down and be quiet right this minute!" Reggie's father stood and reprimanded him, beating the Chief Elder to the act.

"What Elder Calhoun said! That is certainly enough, Reginald," Chief Elder Richardson added his admonishment as several of the other elders nodded in agreement with his sentiments.

Reggie pulled his seat back so that it dragged loudly on the floor. He then sat down, placed his hands on the large table, and pulled his seat forward with another long screeching drag. Several of the elders sucked their teeth as Reggie dragged his seat forward, which, combined with the screeching of the chair, gave an echoing cacophony of disharmonious sound.

After a few beats, the room's acoustics released the unpleasant sounds and gave way to a new quiet. Then, Chief Elder Richardson stood again and pointed at Ruby, instructing her to rise before the council. Once Ruby was standing, the Chief Elder took his seat and brought the group back to order.

"We now commence with informing Ms. Ruby Calhoun of the council estimation of her work. The council will now share its recommendations for her future work." As Chief Elder Richardson spoke, he looked to his left and right, queuing up the day's final discussion before adjourning.

Although Ruby had entered the room anxious and worried, the news of the signing of the bill, Geneva's affirmation, and Reggie's indomitable performance gave her a new sense of peace and courage. As Ruby stood before them, she said to herself that come what may, she had succeeded. Ruby was confident that she had more than completed the many tasks that had been set before her.

"As you know, Ruby," the Chief Elder continued, "the council has been quite pleased with your work and the successful nature of your missions. For the last ten years, you have been on time, careful, and inspiring."

Ruby nodded her head.

"This is why we are all, and when I say *all*, I mean all eighteen of us, so thoroughly disappointed in your *60 Minutes* appearance. It was a time to put everything you have learned and done into action. And while you have many champions amongst the elders—I count myself as one of them—your self-righteousness could have cost us everything. I hope you understand that. Yes?"

Ruby looked puzzled and fixed her face a bit before answering. "No. I do not understand."

"Are you quite sure? Because I am told that Elders Ronald and Lucy had a thorough discussion with you about the discontent of the council. It disappoints me . . . it disappoints us that you still seem resistant to understanding our dismay."

"It is never my intention to disappoint or cause any harm to Jubilee. I believe my selfless and tireless work for the last ten years reflects that. What confuses me is why everyone seems to be letting the white people over at CBS off the hook. Has anyone heard of EDITING?" Ruby scanned the room, looking for nods and raised hands. Some elders did nod, though none raised their hand. Ruby continued, "I cannot control, nor will I accept responsibility for things beyond my control. And let's talk about disappointment. I am disappointed that a place founded upon the fact that white people harm Black people seems to have decided that I would do anything to jeopardize Jubilee! Me! Ruby, a Black woman, descended from the formerly enslaved hands that built this place. I have only given up my dreams and ten years of my life, traveling since age twenty-one!" Ruby scoffed.

"What's done is done. This is not a debate. You are entitled to your opinion, and we are entitled to ours. It is our estimation that your missions, as previously set forth, are now complete. Despite the unsettling interview, the council is grateful to you. Ms. Calhoun, we would like to thank you for your many years of service."

After the Chief Elder raised his right index finger, members rose one by one. Each expressed gratitude to Ruby. Some chose to just say a simple "Thank you." Others, including her parents, the Williamses, and Michael Richardson, spoke a little longer, enumerating some of her accolades accrued along the way. Then, unexpectedly, Geneva raised her hand. After being acknowledged by the Chief Elder, she offered remarks that moved Ruby, Reggie, and others to tears.

"Thank you, Chief Elder, for the opportunity to address Ms. Ruby Calhoun in this forum and sacred space. As you all know, I have traveled all over with Ruby. And what I can tell you is that she is a force of nature. Ruby is a light—kind and intelligent, bright and gifted. She has sat in front of a room full of rabid racists and offered words so loving they were moved to become allies in Jubilee's quest. She has been before rooms of jaded Black folk who chose to flee the South to seek a better life. And even then, she shared from her well of compassion and affirmed their experiences. She did so while also reinforcing the importance of the lives of those the great migrants left behind. Ruby has taken every note and piece of advice I have given her with grace and poise, even when I could tell she disagreed or did not understand."

Geneva then turned to look directly into Ruby's eyes. "Ruby, it gives me great pleasure to present you with two commendations. One from my alma mater Howard University's School of Law. The second from the president of the United States, Lyndon B. Johnson. It reads, 'It gives me great pleasure to commend Ms. Ruby Lee Calhoun for her tenacity, courage, and leadership. Ms. Calhoun is a true example of the greatest of Americans. On behalf of this great nation, thank you for your service. The twenty-eighth day of July in the nineteen hundred and sixty-fifth year of our Lord.'"

As Geneva finished the final words, her voice quivered, and when she finished, she too was in tears. She handed the two commendations to Ruby, and the two of them hugged. So moved by the events, Reggie joined the hug, wrapping his long arms around them both.

Ruby was so surprised by everything, having expected the equivalent of a good old-fashioned whooping. But instead, everyone had thanked her. And even though she had determined to move forward without the need for affirmation, she felt it helped close out such a long chapter of her life.

"Thank you, Ms. Crenshaw. And congratulations, Ruby!" said the Chief Elder. "Everyone in this room felt so relieved and happy to move forward upon the news from Ms. Crenshaw. When Ms. Crenshaw arrived just a few hours ago and reported that the president would be signing the bill, we were so pleased. We had no idea that she also possessed these"—his eyes looked to Geneva—"prestigious commendations. Now that we have that sorted, we can move to the matter of the future."

Ruby wiped the tears from her face and regained her composure. Ruby looked up to the Chief Elder with a gesture confirming that she was present and following the discussion.

"After much discussion, following your wedding to elder and my son Mr. Michael Richardson, you will begin two years of international missions. He will accompany you on these missions in place of Ms. Crenshaw. Ms. Crenshaw will be here in Jubilee overseeing the legal implementations of Jubilee's independence per the Voting Rights Act of 1965. Once this bill is signed, effective at 12:01 a.m. on Saturday, the seventh of August, Jubilee will be an independent territory of the United States. Some things will still have to be worked out regarding voting in elections, budgets, and developing Jubilee's own constitution. That said, we are on our way, which means we will need to act as a state, as a nation. You will serve as our liaison to the many countries of the world. Think of it as our international ambassador. You shall be the first Black woman to have such a large role, and we believe that you can do it. That said, you will not do any press or media without approval from the council. And when such media and press are approved, Michael shall handle all media and press requests and interviews. Michael, who will also serve as the council's eyes and ears, will begin his appointment as Jubilee's Secretary of State and your direct supervisor."

"I can tell that this is supposed to sound like a step up. But this sounds like a step all the way down. So I will be married off, and my husband will be my boss as I go around in uncomfortable dresses and pantyhose and drink tea and biscuits? This is not what I want! Has anyone ever stopped to think about what I want? Don't I deserve the opportunity to choose my own path after all I have done for my community?" Ruby was visibly irritated and upset.

"Last I checked, there are many white men who'd kill for an ambassadorship, especially one with the ability to travel the world. Perhaps you need some time to think it over. I imagine this must be a lot at once," the Chief Elder spoke with a gentler though authoritative tone. "Ruby, we have always thought of your happiness and believe that you and Michael will have a wonderful life. No one said you had to immediately have children. You two could have a few years where you get to see the world without the expectations and responsibilities of children. From the council's perspective, that is a wonderful gift of happiness in and of itself."

Ruby's shoulders sank, and she lowered her head. Then, after a look of deep consternation and several minutes of silent pause, Ruby cowered before the heavy demands of the council.

"I see. My gratitude to the council for this opportunity. I gladly accept." Ruby raised her head and looked directly at her parents as she spoke those words.

"We are pleased to hear and delighted that you have accepted the position. In the meantime, the council has also requested you begin a speaking fast for the next nine days. That means that you will not speak publicly or do any media or press during this period. We do not need nor can we afford any further distractions. Besides, you have wedding planning to busy yourself with anyway."

Ruby felt sick. Nausea rumbled in her belly. She swallowed her pride once more and spoke as shortly and briefly as she could. "I understand." She nodded her head affirmatively as she made eye contact with each of the elders beginning from the left to the right of the half circle.

Reggie was shocked and saddened by the whole thing. He knew that Ruby did not want anything they outlined. Reggie also understood that she probably felt like she had no choice. Reggie knew it was not in Ruby's nature to be disagreeable. He also knew that Ruby's challenging the council on multiple fronts was very hard for her.

Most of all, Reggie could tell Ruby was exhausted. That Ruby had run out of fight was made even more clear to him when she bowed her head, paused, and then agreed. Reggie's insights were spot on, as Ruby would confirm for him during their slow walk home. As they passed the statue of the founders in the center of Jubilee Square Park, Ruby explained that she felt the whole thing was a lost cause. Ruby explained to Reggie that she felt it was no longer worth it to try anything different. When Ruby's parents hadn't come to her aid, she was exhausted by the battle with the council. She also shared with Reggie her personal revelation that there was more for her than Jubilee. Ruby also knew that neither the Council of Elders nor her parents would understand. She no longer wanted to be browbeaten into anything else. No more missions. No more campaigns. Definitely not an ambassadorship and indeed not a marriage to Michael Richardson, whom she absolutely had no interest in. Ruby figured it was easier to agree, take the commendations, and figure out something with Reggie later.

Ruby knew that both she and Reggie were dissatisfied. However, Ruby knew that nothing could be done to have the council or their parents, for that matter, change their ways. The council was unable to imagine anything other than what they thought was right and good. The meeting all but confirmed that. What they would be or would do instead, they did not know at the time, but they both knew it definitely would not be what the council desired. And so Ruby and Reggie decided on that walk home through Jubilee Square Park to find another way by any means necessary.

1 AUGUST 1965

Sunday service began somber, as the congregants were not sure what awaited Jubilee. The news of the president's confirmed signing of the Voting Rights Act of 1965 had not been shared with the residents. Therefore, it had been determined that Sunday service would be the best time and place to convey the news. Ahead of the service, the church was outfitted with multiple outdoor speakers. The speakers were placed outside the building and throughout Jubilee City. The service was also recorded and aired over public radio so that all residents in the five areas could hear the news simultaneously.

There was a palpable ambivalence amongst the congregants. The last time they had convened was before the *60 Minutes* interview with which many had expressed their displeasure. Geneva, Ruby, and Reggie were all in their usual locations. Reggie sang a glorious version of Reverend Cleophus Robinson's "How Sweet It Is to Be Loved by God." Reggie's voice rolled and soared, and the choir kept pace right with him. As Reggie reached the end of the song, Ruby stood and clapped. She felt the message of the song all through her body and knew then why Reggie had told her he would sing something special for her on what was to be their last Sunday at Mustardseed Baptist Church. And as Ruby looked around the church, it was clear that the song's message was what everyone needed that Sunday. With all the tension, confusion, and worry about the future of Jubilee, Reggie's voice offered a necessary and needed ease, comfort, and knowing that soothed their souls.

As Reggie and the choir returned to their seats, Reverend Calhoun took to the pulpit. On this day, he described his message as a classic and simple New Testament truth.

"Church, on today, I want to announce that God is good!"

"All the time!" members responded emphatically.

"And all the time, God is good. And hasn't he been so good to us, hasn't he been so good to Jubilee? And when I think about God, his Son Jesus, and the Holy Spirit, and how they have been so good, so able, I cannot help but give them all the praise! Amen."

"Amen," the church responded.

"On today, our message is gonna come from a simple and always meaningful place. When my father, Calvin John Calhoun, the founder of Mustardseed Baptist, first taught me the Bible, he started not at the front of the book, nor did he start at the back. So, saints, we will go exactly to where he led me—to the foundation of our church.

"Please turn to Philippians, chapter four, verse thirteen . . ."

Before the pages turned, many of the most devout in the church already knew the scripture. So not only did they not need to turn the page, but the devout began to recite verbatim and in unison the words with the reverend.

"'I can do all things through Christ who strengthens me.' Again, 'I can do ALL things through Christ who strengthens me.' Now turn to your neighbor and say, 'Neighbor, you can do all things through Christ who strengthens you and me.'"

On cue, the congregants turned to one another and restated the scripture. The devout men who stood as the scripture was read restated it aloud rather than sat and turned to their neighbor.

"Alright, Reverend, now that is a word!" one of the congregants shouted as they finished speaking with their neighbor.

"You see, when you have Christ on your side, there ain't nothing you cannot do. There is not a mountain that cannot be moved, there ain't a job you cannot get, there ain't a bill that you cannot pay, there ain't a disease that cannot be cured. There is nothing that can stand in your way. You can do ALL things. And ALL means ALL, as my father taught me as a child learning at his feet."

"Amen."

"And you see, when you grow up with the notion that you can do ALL things with Christ, you are unstoppable. You can say to the United States government, Jubilee shall be independent. And you know what the president will say . . . Do you know what the president has said? Effective 12:01 a.m. on Saturday, the seventh of August, Jubilee shall be independent! All things!"

Initially, it took a few seconds before people realized that he had just announced that they had been assured independence. Folks were so caught in the rhythm of the reverend's words and the familiarity with the scripture that it took a moment before people began shouting as the realization came over the congregants, pew by pew. Some ran up and down the aisle. Others fell to the floor and cried and thanked Jesus over and again. One woman ran straight out the door hollering "Hallelujah" and ran back in and up the aisle. By the end, she was standing at the altar speaking in tongues. A few people near Ruby began to rub her shoulders. Then, with soulful repetition, they said, "Thank you, Ruby. Thank you, Ruby. Thank you, Ruby! God bless you, Ruby. God bless you, Ruby. God bless you, Ruby!"

When Ruby believed no one would notice, she briefly broke her speaking fast, turning her head slightly. "Thank you! God bless you too."

The church never quieted down, though the reverend attempted to wait for some modicum of silence. Finally, when the reverend realized that quiet was no longer possible, he gave in to the noise and intentionally sought to amplify it.

"Saints, let's make a joyful noise unto the Lord. We can do ALL things through Christ who strengthens us. Jubilee is free! Choir, now we don't always do this, but today I think it's only right. Reggie, play us some good old-fashioned Pentecostal shouting music!" The reverend directed his son, the choir, and the congregants all at once.

Reggie followed, directing the band and choir, and they began playing and singing as instructed. No sooner than the first few chords struck did the reverend pace back and forth across the stage. After a few back and forths, the reverend and Lucy walked down the aisle. They then swiftly exited the church, walking and joining the praise of those listening outside in the overflow. As they praised and walked outside, so too did the rest of the congregation. And before anyone knew it, they were all in Jubilee Square Park, jumping with joy and praise and pride. The unplanned service in the park lasted for nearly an hour before everyone ended with hugs and gratitude and headed in every direction back to their homes and vehicles. Meanwhile, no one had noticed that Ruby never left the church. Instead, Ruby found the unexpected emptiness of the church peaceful.

She walked around it as though it would be her last time. Memories played in her mind of being a small child and then a teenager, reciting Psalm 23 the first time she spoke before the congregation. As she walked through the pews, she rubbed her hands against the red fabric lining the seats. Ruby noticed the sweat stains on some of the rows from all the emotions worked up over the years. She looked forward at the stained glass, its vibrant oranges, reds, and blues portraying Jesus's baptism by John the Baptist. The next set illustrated Jesus's crucifixion and then the third day resurrection. A smiling cry came forth from her heart as Ruby walked up to the pulpit. There at the pulpit, Ruby turned her father's Bible to her favorite scripture, Psalm 23. Ruby then began softly and slowly reciting it, strolling as she exited the church.

The LORD is my shepherd. I shall not want. He maketh me to lie down in green pastures; he leadeth me beside the still waters. He restoreth my soul: he leadeth me in the paths of righteousness for his name's sake. Yea, though I walk through the valley of the shadow of death, I will fear no evil: for thou art with me; thy rod and thy staff they comfort me. Thou preparest a table before me in the presence of mine enemies: thou anointest my head with oil; my cup runneth over. Surely goodness and mercy shall follow me all the days of my life; and I will dwell in the house of the LORD forever.

While reciting repeatedly, Ruby had walked from the pulpit, out the church doors, down the stairs, and all the way home. As she walked and continued reciting Psalm 23, she could hear the congregants' praises and shouts and joy echoing in the distance. All had seemed to join the jubilee chorus of Jubilee in the center of Jubilee Square Park.

When Ruby rounded the corner of her block, she took off her heels, walking barefoot as she began speaking the final lines of the scripture with quiet confidence. Finally, she reached inside her purse, grabbed her keys, and opened her front door. Crossing the threshold, Ruby pulled several of the bobby pins from her perfectly coifed hair and threw her shoes inside.

"Amen," Ruby confidently concluded the prayer as she shut the door.

6 AUGUST 1965

The residents of Jubilee had been in celebration all day. Vibrations of joy and delight only increased once it came across the wire that President Johnson had officially signed the Voting Rights Act of 1965 bill into law. Finally, Jubilee's independence was official. Geneva was in Washington, DC, in the Oval Office for the ceremonial signing ritual. Geneva sent the wire of the historic news as soon as she was able. Attending the signing alongside Dr. Martin Luther King Jr. and critical proponents of the legislation was among one of the greatest highlights of Geneva's illustrious legal career.

The evening prior, Geneva had informed Ruby that she had prepared and left a special package for her to open on the evening of the signing. "It's a surprise, and I wish I'd be here when you open it, but there is no way I can make it back to Jubilee from DC in time. So just promise me you will not open it until after the wire comes to Jubilee announcing that the bill is signed." Geneva made Ruby pinky swear.

Ruby would follow Geneva's directions and not open the package until such time that the news broke and the sun had set. Although Ruby didn't know if she would be able to resist opening it, she did convey to Geneva she would respect her wishes. Ruby was curious about its contents and had stared at the sizeable, thick manilla envelope all day. Yet, as curious as Ruby was about what was inside, she also had packing to do and her own letters to write.

There were so many items to attend to and so many details to cover that at some point, she lost focus on Geneva's mysterious package altogether. Instead, Ruby gathered her most personal items and placed them in the trunk she inherited from her grandmother. Without thinking, Ruby grabbed Geneva's package and placed it into her messenger bag with her passport and other identification. She locked the trunk and placed the key in her purse. Ruby then placed her purse into the messenger bag. She zipped the messenger bag closed and hung it from her shoulder. Reggie had told her to place the trunk on the enclosed back porch, and someone would fetch it for her. Neither Ruby nor Reggie wanted to draw any unnecessary attention to their actions and behaviors that day for fear that their plans to leave Jubilee would be upended.

In the days following the council's orders, Ruby was on a speaking fast, or what she felt was an involuntary vow of silence. Ruby hadn't spoken to anyone other than Reggie and hadn't left the house. Then, Sunday night, while everyone was still praising and celebrating President Johnson's news about signing the bill into law, Reggie snuck away from the park. When he arrived at Ruby's house, he had sweated through his entire outfit and was dripping all over. Despite the clear evidence that he had been an avid participant in the spectacle at the center of Jubilee Square Park, Ruby knew Reggie was pretending. Ruby knew that it was all a show, all a part of the plan they conjured in the walk home after the council meeting.

"Rubes! They bought it, lock, stock, and barrel. You shoulda seen how they fell for my act! Phase one of 'Operation Get Out of Dodge' is complete. I need to take a bath before we get started on phase two and prepare for phase three." Reggie was already inside the bathroom when he finished speaking. He closed the door and stepped into the bath that Ruby had prepared for him anticipating his arrival.

"Rubes! This bath feels amazing! Man, I needed it. My body is so sore from all of the dancing and singing and jumping and all. Who knew how pretending can wear you out! I feel like I just finished opening night at a Broadway musical." Reggie chuckled to himself.

Ruby prepared some tea as she waited for Reggie to finish his bath and freshen up. Then, to ensure she and Reggie had a clear mind, she steeped a simple brew of fresh bay leaves from her garden, two sticks of cinnamon bark, and two stars of anise. While Ruby plucked a few fresh leaves from her bay leaf bush, she realized how much she would miss the little garden she made for herself. As Ruby clipped the last bay leaf, it occurred to her that she would probably miss the garden more than she would miss so many of the people she'd known her entire life. The irony of missing a garden more than her community made Ruby sentimental and pretty sure that she was making the right choice for herself. The revelation was yet another confirmation that she was on the right path. There was nothing more for her in Jubilee, and she couldn't let any emotional ties hold her back from pursuing her happily ever after.

As the tea brewed, she reread PJ's letter. Ruby replayed with small delight how she'd gotten it back from her mother earlier in the week at the family breakfast after her parents had laid into her pretty intensely. Ruby loved her parents tremendously. But as Ruby reread the letter, something else dawned on her. Ruby recognized that somewhere along the way, she allowed the love she had for her parents, for Jubilee, for her missions to outweigh the love she possessed for herself. Ruby couldn't be too mad with her parents; they were only acting in the ways Ruby had permitted for all the years where she put everyone else's needs before her own. When she finished rereading the letter, Ruby held it close to her heart for the last time. She hoped that her response had reached PJ back in Atlanta; there was an important role PJ had to play in her and Reggie's escape.

Useless thoughts of the mail being lost or diverted started to fill her head and caused a stir of anxiety to rise. To ease her worry, Ruby closed

her eyes. As her eyes closed, she tried to envision PJ's face as the letter arrived and the look of surprise and happiness the message would undoubtedly cause. After a few beats and breaths, Ruby grabbed a white candle
from her kitchen cabinet. She placed the candlestick on the silver holder
and lit it. She watched the fire grow until blue rounded under the orange
of the flame. Once the fire flickered with strength, Ruby took a pair of
metal tongs from her kitchen drawer and used it to pick up PJ's letter at
the folded ends. Ruby placed the letter over the flame and watched as it
began to cluster and change shape and color as the candle's light burned
it. So engrossed was she in her burning ritual that she hadn't noticed
that Reggie had finished his bath and was dressed and standing there
observing her in the kitchen.

By the time Ruby's eyes caught Reggie's, he was already moving his
mouth to speak.

"Just when I thought I knew everything about you, I learned something new. I have to admit, I didn't take you as a pyro." Reggie laughed,
hoping to ease the anxiety he could see mounting at Ruby's shoulders
when she saw that he was observing her.

"Finishing a personal ritual is all. Almost done. Have some tea. I
made some. It's sitting over there." She pointed to the stove where the
two cups were resting as the brew steeped. "You mind grabbing them and
taking them into the front room?"

"Sure. No problem." Reggie walked over to the stove, grabbed a tray
from the kitchen cabinet, and placed the two cups of tea on top. As he
strolled into the front room, Reggie couldn't help himself. He had to say
something.

"Rubes, that letter wouldn't happen to be the one that had Mama all
bent outta shape, would it? Even with the burnt edges, I can still see the
'PJ B. A. R.' at the bottom from here."

"Huh?" Ruby played coy. She was annoyed that Reggie still remembered the letter.

Sensing that Ruby was playing secretive, he figured now was the best
time to reveal what he had already put together.

"Now the 'Bar' last name part still has me guessing, but I think I pretty much figured out what's going on. I figured it out at the family table that morning."

"Figured out what exactly, Reggie?" Ruby doubled down on the coy routine.

"Look, I know and have met a lot of people, Rubes! You may have been born ninety-nine seconds before me, but that don't mean I can't catch up. And it definitely doesn't mean I was born yesterday." Reggie sought to disarm Ruby. He really wanted Ruby to be open with him and be at ease.

"If we are really going to pull this plan off and leave Jubilee, we have to be honest with each other."

Ruby nodded, indicating she understood and agreed.

"Now, we both know . . . " Reggie concluded as he took his first sip of the tea. "This is some good tea, Rubes! But I digress . . . What was I saying? Oh, that's right." Reggie snapped his fingers. "We both know that you have no interest in being in some arranged marriage, let alone with Michael Richardson!"

"That is definitely true. If Mama and Daddy were paying attention and were not so worried about consolidating some kind of power arrangement, they would see that Michael doesn't even like—"

Reggie interrupted Ruby so that by the time she said her last words, they were saying them together. "Doesn't even like women!" Ruby and Reggie both looked at each other after they said it aloud. They'd both thought the same thing about Michael for years for different reasons. Even still, neither had said it aloud in front of the other.

"And to add to that, I am pretty sure that PJ stands for Patricia Jo, so we know that you and Michael are most certainly not a match." Reggie spoke fast to make his words continuous with their previous statement and slip in his sleuthing of Ruby's secret.

Because Reggie had been so quick, Ruby could only react naturally, as she had no time to think or pretend or deflect. She just looked at him and hugged him. As he embraced her, Ruby began to cry. At first, her tears were soft and gentle. And then, after a few moments, they began flooding her eyes until it seemed they had finally given way for her to shed the mask that had been holding her back all her life. Reggie made her feel safe. Ruby knew that Reggie was a kind and open-minded person who loved people from all walks of life. Even though he was not gay, Reggie had spent many years traveling and supporting his many Black creative and colorful friends. Reggie had been there to support folks during their breakups, the breakdowns, the hiding. He had even hosted his fair share of small indoor parties in Jubilee where those who felt different could feel free and safe.

"I take it that I hit the nail square on the head there, Rubes?"

Ruby looked up at Reggie with her tear-stained face. "You sho did!" She pinched his shoulder.

"Okay, now that we have that cleared up, there is something I have been unable to figure out."

"Now, what's that, Sherlock Calhoun?!?" Ruby smiled and relief poured off her face and teeth as her grin twisted into a look of "What is it now, Mr. Nosy-Pants?"

"Patricia Jo, I am sure, is the PJ who wrote the letter and certainly lives in Atlanta. I met her back in Detroit at one of Ruth Ellis's well-known speakeasy functions for family and allies. . . ."

Ruby interrupted, previously unaware of two things Reggie said. First, she didn't know that Reggie had met PJ, nor was she aware of a Ruth Ellis speakeasy for family. "Wait, you met her at a family function? I recall meeting Ruth Ellis at a Detroit forum, but we aren't related to her. So we have family in Detroit, Reggie?!?" Ruby asked, puzzled by these unknown details.

"C'mon, 'family' is just a little code word for folks who are different and like and keep the romance and company of people of the same sex. Rubes, it's 1965! Get with the lingo."

"Hmmph," Ruby interjected as Reggie continued to explain.

"I would have said 'homosexual,' but that's not how Black folks like to be referred to, and the term even makes me cringe." Reggie shook off the word. As he did so, Reggie thought of Black folks' awkward reaction to the word "homosexual." After a brief pause, Reggie continued. "Such a white thing to call yourself. Anyways, yes, we met in Detroit. Let's just say that Berry Gordy isn't your only fan. Patricia Jo told me that she came to see you in Atlanta and that you had invited her up to check you out on your next forum if she could, which happened to be in Detroit. She wound up at Ruth Ellis's weekend speakeasy. It's the place to be for family in Detroit. And Patricia Jo—I mean, PJ—was looking for a place to just be and decompress."

"Looks like I ain't able to keep much from you, huh!" Ruby was surprised. She was stunned that all of this had gone on without her knowledge. Even more, Ruby couldn't believe that Reggie had been keeping this to himself for at least a year.

"Which leads me to the bigger question. I recall PJ saying her last name was something on the order of McCall or McCombs or something like that. Not Bar?"

"Ahhhhh." Ruby laughed heartily, realizing Reggie was trying to crack their code. "It's McCombs for sure. Bar isn't the last name. It's an acronym. B period, A period, R period. Stands for Burn After Reading! It's 1965, sir! Get with the lingo," Ruby playfully repeated Reggie's advice and imitated the tone and texture of his voice.

After a short laugh, Ruby finished explaining and answering Reggie's question. "Burn after reading, which was exactly what I totally forgot to do. That's how our nosy, intrusive mama found the letter as she was going through all my things. I was so tired the night I read the letter from preparing for the interview that I forgot to burn it after reading it. We've exchanged letters for over a year, but there had been a few weeks since our last communication. So when I got the letter and read it, it just made me feel so good, so loved, so in love. Then the following day I forgot about it. By the time I remembered, the letter had come up missing. And when I tell you I looked all through the doggone house!" Ruby sucked her teeth. She recalled unsuccessful attempts to find the letter only to discover her mother had planned to drop it on her at the breakfast table in front of the family.

"Burn after reading! How ingeniously secretive! I have been racking my brain since breakfast with Mama and Daddy. I knew it had to be Patricia Jo, but I didn't want to bring it up until I could figure out the last name and had all the puzzle pieces worked out. But when I saw you with the letter again, and this time you . . . it was being burned. I thought if I didn't say it now, we might never talk about it, and I would never fully solve the mystery of Ruby's pen pal!"

"I will give you this, Reggie. You are consistent, consistently all in my business. Haha!"

Ruby and Reggie laughed and hugged and laughed. Ruby felt as though a huge weight had been lifted off of her shoulders.

"As long as you know I love you, and I will always support you, that is all that matters to me! My life is your life. Your life is my life," Reggie offered affirmation.

"My life is your life. Your life is my life," Ruby reaffirmed.

"Okay, now that we have that sorted comes the matter of the rest of the plan. Phase one is done: *pretend like it's all good*. We have both played the part of the obedient Calhoun children, going along with the elders to get along. Next, we need to figure out how we exactly get out of here. How do we slip away? And now, I am wondering, do you think Patricia can help?" Reggie queried.

"I am sure she will. I wrote telling her that I was leaving to be with her and start our life in Atlanta together. I told her that you would be with me, and we would need to stay at her place for a little while until we figured out our own living situation in Atlanta," Ruby answered.

"Do you think she got the letter?" Reggie was a little anxious.

"I am pretty sure she has, but no matter what, I know if we show up at her front porch, she will open the door and give us shelter." Again, the love Ruby felt for PJ was evident.

"Okay, Rubes, that sounds solid enough. Besides, if that doesn't work out, I do know some folks in Atlanta we can stay with, even if for a few days . . ."

"PJ is solid. It will work out," Ruby interrupted with confident assurance.

"Okay, PJ's place it is," Reggie responded with relief and also to move on and discuss the remaining elements of their plans.

"Now that's settled," Reggie continued, "there is also the matter of getting out of town. Our car being gone would be a dead giveaway, especially if folks see us driving off. Any person with eyes will think it's weird that we are driving off amidst Jubilee's greatest jubilee. So after careful thought, I determined that the train was best. That way, we won't have to drive through Westmoreland and Borderton where more folks could spot us and our direction of travel."

"The train! Yes, that's it. Great idea, baby brother! And there's that one just after midnight that would be perfect." Ruby clenched her fist as she could feel the plan coming together. "Were you able to get the tickets for the last train to Atlanta?"

"I sure did. Leaving the Jubilee station at 12:35 a.m. and arriving in Atlanta at 4:05 a.m.," Reggie sang-answered Ruby.

"You didn't buy them, did you? We don't need anybody tipped off." The anxiety was evident in Ruby's voice.

"No sweat, Rubes. The same person who will pick up your trunk and my bags works the train that night and lives in Atlanta. He's coming in to sing some backup for James Brown's set. He will lead them on the train and hand us the tickets at the station. And because he is from out of town already, no one will pay him any attention. Phase two is solid. I was more concerned about phase three, but now with PJ in the pocket, we are all set. Rubes, we are almost there." Reggie was excited. "You smell that?" Reggie took a long pull of air in through his nose. Ruby followed suit. "Smells like freedom, Rubes." Reggie slapped his knees, taking pride in their collective cleverness.

"Freedom, huh . . . We are almost there." Ruby closed her eyes and visualized she and Reggie arriving at PJ's steps and her new life beginning. Then, of course, there was the matter of when their parents discovered they were gone, but she would handle them accordingly when the time arrived.

"One step at a time is always the surest way forward," Ruby said aloud as she opened her eyes.

"One step at a time indeed." Reggie put his right hand up, and Ruby slapped him a high five.

"Okay, what else is there?" Ruby wanted to make sure their plans were near flawless if not at least thorough.

"Don't forget to write Mama and Daddy," Reggie remembered and reminded Ruby. "We don't want them calling the authorities and having them looking for us like we are missing. So I will be writing them too. I also thought that it might be good for you to write Michael Richardson as well. Everyone will likely ask him where you are. And we also don't want that fool faking concern and involving any authorities as well."

"Makes sense. I will make sure I do that. Now, should I leave the letters here in the house or drop them at Mama and Daddy's and Michael's?"

"Naw, leave them sitting right on the table." Reggie pointed to the silver tea tray. "I like the image of it being left for them on a silver platter! Ha!" Reggie was gleeful as the plan came together. It seemed more and more foolproof, metaphoric even. "And I will do the same, though I don't have any of the fancy trays you do."

Ruby got up from the couch, walked into the kitchen, and grabbed the second silver tray that had come in the set. She handed it to Reggie.

"Here you go! There were two in the set. And it seems to me that if we do it the same way, it will be clear to everyone that we are in this together and that we left together."

"Great point! I have to admit—I am so glad that this is happening. I have wanted to leave for the last few years, but I always felt like I couldn't leave without you. I didn't want to leave you behind. And you know how the council is about those who leave!"

"DEFECTORS!" they both said together, imitating the voice of Chief Elder Richardson.

Reggie kept going. "And so I stayed. I had a bag packed in '64 when it looked like independence was coming. But when it didn't, I figured I would at least wait for the day when Jubilee was independent. So when that day came, I said that I would independently walk myself right on up outta here! I had a letter written to you and everything," Reggie confessed.

"Really? So you were just gonna leave your twin behind? So I see how my baby brother gets down." Ruby pinched Reggie again. "Haha! I'm just kidding! If you didn't know before, now you know that I deeply understand the call to leave Jubilee."

"Ruby, can I tell you something—this crazy idea that has been rolling around in my head?" Reggie's tone sounded like Ruby's when she confessed her relationship with PJ.

"Of course you can, baby brother." Ruby rubbed his shoulders.

Then, taking a few moments to himself before divulging, Reggie took a large swallow of tea and began sharing. "I call it Marquette Social Club," Reggie confessed.

"You call *what* Marquette Social Club?" Ruby queried, puzzled.

"So remember when I told you about the Ruth Ellis speakeasy in Detroit?"

"I do." Ruby nodded and listened intently.

"Ever since I went to a few of Ruth Ellis's gatherings, I have imagined something bigger. Something even more than what they have going on there. What if there was a social space that welcomed Black people from all walks of life. A place where Black gay people, the ladies, and the fellas can feel free to enjoy a drink and a dance. For the artistically gifted and for open-minded folks like me too? A place to commune, as they say, 'with the spirit in the dark'?"

Ruby smiled and bobbed her head approvingly as Reggie shared more of his idea.

"There is a sense of freedom that just comes over you when you're at Ruth Ellis's place. I want that for more people and something bigger than just a house. A place. A real place. And I just know that Atlanta is the place to make that dream a reality. I was trying to get the council to understand it the other day. And I wasn't even presenting the whole idea, just the notion that we could develop a creative commune or conservatory.

But as you can see, they are a close-minded, old-fashioned group of people who are more concerned with how everything looks than the reality of what it is. I am not mad at them though. And strangely enough, I kind of get it. I just wished and hoped that Jubilee could be that place, and then I wouldn't need to search."

"Reggie, that is a beautiful dream. Just seeing how your face glowed as you spoke it aloud to me really warms my heart." Ruby hugged Reggie tightly. "Thank you for sharing that with me, baby brother." Ruby winked. "Looks like we both had some confessing to do. And even more, looks like we both will be chasing our dreams in Atlanta. Scratch that! Not chasing dreams. Realizing our dreams. Manifesting together!"

"Here's to the Marquette Social Club!" Ruby glowed with endorsement as she and Reggie clinked their teacups and headed to the porch to watch the moon and be still together.

As Ruby watched the Supremes finish their set, she recalled that night of confessing and planning and the stillness of the moon to quell her lingering anxiety. All her letters were written and sitting on the silver tray in the front room of her home. And although she knew that everyone was preoccupied with celebrating, she couldn't help but think, *What if someone finds the letters before they are meant to be found? What if the train is late or the guy forgets my trunk? What if my parents already suspect?* All the 'what ifs' bounced up and down in her mind. She wished she could say something, but between her speaking fast and Reggie being onstage, Ruby had to accept, believe, and keep the faith.

Reggie was onstage serving in his usual capacity as the master of ceremonies for the annual Jubilee Festival. From the time the wire came down and the news of the signing broke, the city had been in full celebration mode. An impromptu Mardi Gras had broken out, and folks were throwing beads and candy, handing out cupcakes, balloons, and hats. Everyone had been presented with specially made t-shirts for the event. The t-shirts were black with "Jubilee Is Free" in red and green. Folks had driven into Jubilee City from Borderton, Westmoreland, Eastland,

and Oceanair for the festivities. Celebratory energy was emanating from every person; all were excited that they had pulled off this extraordinary feat of independence.

The concert officially kicked off at sunset with everyone wearing their specially made "Jubilee Is Free" t-shirts. Ruby, not one for wearing t-shirts, never felt at ease with it on. She and the t-shirt had been in a tug-of-war for most of the day. When Ruby danced or waved her hand with the music, the t-shirt would rise, and she would tug at it and stretch it back down. As she clapped for the Supremes, Ruby pulled at the ends of her t-shirt, annoyed that it refused to cooperate.

All three of the Motown groups had put on a rousing show. Everyone was singing and clapping and dancing. When the Four Tops sang their hit "I Can't Help Myself (Sugar Pie Honey Bunch)," Ruby saw her parents doing their romantic two-step over in the special box for the Council of Elders. The way they danced and looked so free made her heart smile; it also assured and reminded her that her parents were none the wiser when it came to her and Reggie's plans. From the looks of it, they were absolutely clueless, and so too was all the rest of the Council of Elders.

Chief Elder Richardson had been waving his hand with eyes mesmerized by the beautiful women of the Supremes for the entirety of their set. His wife, Mrs. Ruth Brown-Richardson, nearly fell to the ground after he brushed her aside when he caught eyes with Diana Ross. Chief Elder Richardson wasn't alone in his fandom. As each Motown act performed, several pockets of loyal fans revealed themselves. They screamed the group members' and Stevie Wonder's names and performed the entire routine as they did. Some folks even wore the same signature fashions for which each musical act was known. By the time the Supremes took the stage, teenagers wearing their hair in the group's signature bouffant had rushed forward to the front of the stage. Several had pushed past Ruby and had ruffled her shirt and made her nearly lose track of the messenger bag she had been holding tightly.

Before the Supremes began, Diana Ross stopped the introduction music. To everyone's surprise, she wanted to speak directly to the people of Jubilee before performing. Diana Ross stretched her arms out to their full wingspan. Then she pulled the microphone to her mouth. "Congratulations, Jubilee! Motown loves you! The Supremes are proud to be here to celebrate this history. Ain't that right, ladies?" she looked to her groupmates Mary Wilson and Florence Ballard. Both Mary and Florence nodded their heads in agreement, smiled, and raised their microphones, exclaiming, "That's right! The Supremes love Jubilee!"

Their voices rang with elegance and excitement, and everyone shouted how much they loved them and Motown in response. Lost in the excitement, Ruby hadn't noticed that her shirt had rolled up again from dancing until the Supremes left the stage. As they exited, Ruby pulled her shirt down. Ruby was feeling even more anxious because shortly after James Brown's set, she and Reggie would be leaving Jubilee and probably never coming back.

Suddenly, the Supremes came back to the stage along with Stevie Wonder, the Four Tops, and the Temptations. Stevie Wonder borrowed Reggie's microphone, speaking to the crowd. "Jubilee, Motown has one more surprise for you!" After he spoke, all of the performers turned and pointed to the back of the stage. Within seconds, Berry Gordy was at the front of the stage.

"I couldn't leave without expressing my congratulations to all of you," Berry Gordy's voice beamed with levity as he spoke from the microphone Stevie Wonder handed him. "I want to say a very special congratulations to Ms. Ruby Lee Calhoun! Where's Ruby? Somebody get a light on that brilliant young woman, please!"

The lights flailed around until they spotted Ruby. She was standing midway in the crowd next to Tom Chewey, the lead cameraman from the *60 Minutes* crew. Tom pointed his large oak staff in Ruby's direction to make her aware of Berry Gordy's call and request for her. When the light came over her, Ruby froze. Ruby had been so preoccupied with securing her messenger bag and fixing her shirt she hadn't been listening or paying attention to the rapidly unfolding events.

Tom tapped Ruby and said with a kind smile, "I think that spotlight's for you."

When she looked up, Berry Gordy's eyes met hers. Berry Gordy continued. "Ruby, you are amazing. Those speeches you gave in Detroit really impacted me. I mean tremendously." Everyone began clapping as Gordy continued. "I mean, really and truly impacted me! Changed my thinking in so many ways. More than I have time to say tonight. That said, I couldn't leave Jubilee without personally and publicly thanking you. In honor of your incredible work, and on behalf of Motown Records, I am proud to present this check for five thousand dollars to create the Ruby Lee Calhoun scholarship to support students in Jubilee. We hope this helps those who want to go on to college—here or anywhere else!"

The crowd went wild. Ruby was stunned. She couldn't believe what was happening. Then, Berry Gordy began signaling for her to come up on the stage. Ruby walked forward, and as she did, the crowd parted and made way for her.

Soon enough, Ruby was onstage receiving the adoration of all the Motown acts and then a massive hug from Berry Gordy himself. Ruby had an out-of-body experience. Berry Gordy presented Ruby with the check and shook her hand. He reached for the microphone again and said, "Thank you, Jubilee, for setting the example of what can be possible for Black people in this country. That is also our mission at Motown—to show America and the world that Black people are people of excellence. Congratulations again, and have a wonderful jubilee, Jubilee!"

As quickly as he had taken the stage, Berry Gordy and the Motown acts were all swiftly whisked off. Their security detail escorted them onto their signature blue-and-white buses, and they began their long drive back to Detroit.

Ruby was still at the center of the stage when Reggie tapped her and whispered, "Okay, superstar, don't forget we got places to go and people to see."

With Reggie's reminder, Ruby snapped back into action and promptly exited off the side of the stage. She walked through the crowd, where everyone was rubbing her shoulders and congratulating and praising her. She walked through until she reached Chief Elder Richardson and Mrs. Richardson, who were in a special box at the right of the stage, and she handed Chief Elder Richardson the check.

At that moment, Chief Elder Richardson was both grateful and envious of Ruby. He held her hand as she gave him the check, and after getting over his own sense of feeling upstaged, he spoke with an unusual tone of kind familiarity. "Great work, Ruby. The ancestors are surely smiling upon you on this day. This scholarship shall do wonders!"

As she thanked Chief Elder with her eyes, Ruby turned to walk back and noticed Michael, who was in the box with her parents and the rest of the elders, motion in her direction. Michael looked as though he might even follow her back to where she had been standing.

Ruby calmed her mind with the visual of her and PJ seeing each other in a matter of hours and got back in rhythm. She began to walk briskly back, looking out for Tom Chewey to relocate her spot amongst the crowd. But as Reggie continued to remind her, no one needed to suspect anything. Neither of them wanted anyone trying to talk them into staying, shaming them, or trying to stop them. They had to get on the train and see what the world had in store for them. Maybe they might return. Maybe they wouldn't. In any case, even as Ruby watched all the joy and festivities, she knew she couldn't let fear or sentimentality derail their plans.

As she returned to her original spot, she felt Michael Richardson tap her shoulder. When she turned to her left, he was standing next to her, smiling. Michael following her was concerning. She and Reggie hadn't discussed what she should do if Michael decided to attach himself to her during the festival, nor had they anticipated the whole Motown spectacle, though the more Ruby thought about it, the more she began to think that maybe Reggie had a clue about what Berry Gordy had planned. Given that Reggie had organized and coordinated the festival down to the finest of details, Ruby believed he had to have suspected something. Or perhaps it was all unexpected.

In any case, at the time they were planning, none of these events seemed like factors to consider, and so they didn't. And now, with Michael literally breathing on her neck, she was running out of ways to soothe her anxieties. Of course she knew Michael would surely be in attendance. Still, she figured he wouldn't be paying her much attention, as was his usual disposition toward her. Michael was the type who slid off somewhere with someone. That person was usually another young man when he thought the town or his parents or both had their attention elsewhere. This time, however, and for whatever reason, Michael was all up on Ruby. Ruby knew she would have to quickly figure out how to ditch him and not raise any suspicions. For any onlooker, it just appeared that the husband-and-wife-to-be were going to have a groovy time to the funky sounds of South Carolina's own Mr. James Brown and his world-famous band, the J.B.'s.

"Hey, isn't that Edward Almost over there? Wonder why he's standing by himself?" Ruby knew what she was doing. She knew that if she brought Edward to Michael's attention, he would indeed find a way to leave her sight. Edward and Michael were usually thick as thieves.

At first, Michael didn't look back. Ruby could tell Michael didn't seem the least bit concerned. Even odder to Ruby was that Michael seemed as though he already knew Edward's whereabouts. And then, a small blessing happened just as James Brown began gliding across the stage, gyrating to "Papa's Got a Brand New Bag," his opening number for the evening. Michael had been dancing behind Ruby, and it was making her entirely uncomfortable. Ruby played along and sighed to herself, thinking of how to get out of this unexpected entanglement with Michael. Finally, she turned back to shoot her look of disappointment at Edward for not being as enticing to Michael's attention as he usually was. But when Ruby looked back, Edward was no longer alone nor solemn looking anymore. Between the time she mentioned it to Michael and now, Edward had been approached and joined by Daniel Williams. Edward and Daniel opted out of the elder's box and were standing side by side at the back of the crowd.

While they were out of the sightline of the elder's box, from Ruby's vantage point at the middle right, she could see them both clear as day. As James Brown really started grooving, Ruby could see Edward and Daniel talking into each other's ears and dancing. Of course, they weren't dancing with each other per se but more dancing next to each other. But they were close enough that every few movements, they would brush along each other's sides. In a short time, Edward shifted from lonely to the life of the party. In fact, he seemed happier than Ruby ever recalled him looking in all the years she had known him, even more so than when he and Michael would run around town and hang out. Ruby knew that this was her chance to distract Michael and relieve herself of his gaze and presence.

"Come on, Ruby! I know you can get down better than this. From over in the box, I saw you doing more dancing during the Motown set. Everybody loves James Brown!" Michael's tone was demanding and not alluring at all.

"What you say?" Ruby pretended she didn't hear Michael, though his words did break her stare back at Edward and Daniel.

Michael stepped in front of Ruby, grabbed her hands, and looked into her eyes. "We are supposed to be married in a matter of weeks, and people expect us to at least look like we enjoy one another's company, Ruby! So come on now. Have some fun!" Michael sounded kinder this time as he tried to sway Ruby's hips a little into motion.

"You are so right." Ruby looked at Michael with sweetened eyes. "It's just that I was so caught up in trying to learn the step that Edward and Daniel were doing back there. I mean, they know how to really get down!" Ruby began imitating their steps. Before Ruby even finished her sentence, Michael's eyes were set upon the back of the crowd. Ruby pretended as though she couldn't tell Michael was no longer paying her any attention. Ruby could see the look of surprise and a tinge of jealousy filling up Michael's face, and she knew he would be leaving soon.

"Huh, what . . . what you say again?" Michael was already in motion to leave, his head leaning in Edward and Daniel's direction.

"Doesn't matter. You're right, so let's get on the good foot, Michael!" Ruby had a mischievous grin on her face. Michael didn't notice, so caught up in what Edward and Daniel were up to as he was.

"Yeah . . . yeah . . . the good foot. That's right, Ruby! So you go ahead, and I will be back . . . But, uh, I think I need to use the bathroom." Michael sounded panicked. Michael was not even looking at Ruby anymore nor in the direction of the bathrooms. Instead, Michael's feet pivoted toward a path to the back of the crowd.

"You *think* you have to go to the bathroom? Or you *have* to go to the bathroom?" Ruby tried to sound disappointed and confused.

"Sorry, Ruby. Yeah, I need to go to the bathroom. Good to dance with you. See you in a few days for the discussion with the wedding planner. You look beautiful as always, even in a t-shirt."

With that, Michael was off. Ruby watched as Michael moved with definitive purpose. First, Michael walked toward the edge of the right side to stay out of view of the elder's box. Then, after he got to the edge, Ruby saw Michael move swiftly in Edward and Daniel's direction.

Ruby was sure not to stare or keep her head turned back for too long. She didn't want to have the elders thinking anything of the brief exchange between her and Michael.

When Michael hadn't returned by the end of James Brown's set, Ruby let out a deep release of relief. James Brown's set was fantastic. Ruby was astonished at how much stamina and energy he maintained for the entire hour he performed. He dazzled the audience. When a few of his men came from backstage and put his signature cape-robe over his shoulders, James Brown hunched over like he would pass out. The two men held him up as he waved to the audience. Just as he neared the stage's exit, James Brown threw the robe off, pushed the two rather large men aside, and glided from one side of the stage to the other. When he reached the middle, Reggie threw him the microphone. James Brown grabbed the microphone, spun in three complete circles, fell to his knees, and spoke.

"Now, I couldn't just leave Jubilee, South Carolina, without getting down on my knees and congratulating this wonderful place on the historic achievement! I know what it's like living here in South Carolina, and what has happened here is nothing short of a miracle." He then stood, the men returned with the cape-robe, and James Brown saluted the audience. He then turned to the J.B.'s like a military colonel. "Now, J.B.'s, hit me one time for Jubilee!" They played a loud rhythmic boom. "Hit me again for Jubilee, two times!" *Bam. Boom.* The J.B.'s played the rhythmic boom twice. "Hit me again for Jubilee, twenty times!" *Bam. Boom. Bang. Dun. Bam. Boom. Bang. Dun. Bam. Bang. Boom. Dun. Bam. Boom. Bang. Dun. Bam. Boom. Bang. Dun.* After the twenty hits, James Brown turned and shouted an electrifying "OWWWWW!" and saluted the audience again, followed by each band member who saluted at once.

It wasn't until James Brown had congratulated the crowd on Jubilee's independence that Ruby looked back again. Ruby turned, curious to see if Michael, Edward, and Daniel were all together or still there. All three were nowhere in sight. Even Tom Chewey and his oak staff were gone as well. Ruby figured everyone could tell the night was coming to an end and wanted to beat the crowd out of the park.

"Thank you, and good night, Jubilee!" James Brown adjusted his robe and walked off accompanied by the two heavy-set men. Each band member peeled off one by one, following him onto the bus waiting for him backstage.

Reggie grabbed the microphone. "Jubilee, let's hear it for South Carolina's own, the hardest working man in show business, the one, the only, Mr. James Brown! And the world-famous J.B.'s!"

The audience roared. By the time they had finished clapping, the bus was rolling down the road and off into the distance.

As the cloud of dust flew up from the back of the bus, Reggie informed everyone, "It is now midnight, and in just sixty seconds, Jubilee's independence will be official." Some in the crowd began exiting the park, while many others stayed behind. When it was getting closer to 12:01 a.m., Reggie looked at his watch and started counting down.

"Ten, nine, eight, seven, six, five, four, three, two, one! Happy Independence Day, Jubilee!"

As Reggie finished the countdown, fireworks shot up into the sky. Reds, yellows, oranges, and greens filled the sky. People hugged and kissed. One man got down on his knee and proposed to a woman, who clearly said yes as they embraced with the ring on her finger. The elders all celebrated in their box. As the last firework fizzled out, the elders headed out and in the direction of their homes. Ruby's parents waved good night from afar to both her and Reggie as they walked out of the box and into the park toward the family home.

"Now you don't have to go home, but you do have to get on outta here." Reggie laughed-instructed-informed the audience that the performances were concluded.

As the audience began leaving the park, Reggie looked out into the audience to find Ruby. He saw her standing off to the side. When Reggie's eyes caught Ruby's, he looked at Ruby and then looked at his watch. That was Ruby's signal that it was time for her to head to the train station. She needed to look like she was going home, which was a few minutes in the opposite direction of the station.

Ruby looked at her watch, and it was 12:05 a.m. She knew it would take a little less than ten minutes to complete the walking journey to her home and then the train. Ruby adjusted her t-shirt for what felt like the fiftieth time and gave Reggie the look that signaled she would meet him at the station. Though she looked to be sauntering and had been on her feet for several hours, the image of boarding that 12:35 a.m. train made her feel reinvigorated.

As both she and Reggie had anticipated, her indirect path to the train station had gone unnoticed. Other than a few out-of-towners, the pathway to the station and the platform were pretty empty. The council building was empty and quiet. In the distance, Ruby could hear the continuing celebrations and the cheers of the drunk and overly merry folks who would be partying into the wee hours of the morning. Ruby looked at her watch and saw it was 12:20 a.m. on the dot. She'd made it. The feeling of relief and belief started to well up inside her, and she remembered Geneva's package was in her bag. Ruby fumbled around to pull it out. The bag dropped to the ground with a large thud. Ruby kneeled down to pick up her purse, keys, and the package that had spilled out.

A hand came down from above her head to lift her up. Just as Ruby rose from the ground and stood, she noticed a tall, long oak staff. She realized it was Tom Chewey from the *60 Minutes* crew who must have been heading to Atlanta on the same train.

"Thank you, Tom," Ruby politely responded.

Tom looked at her and nodded. "So, Ruby, you are world famous now. How does it feel?" he asked with an unassuming grin.

"I wouldn't say famous. Just Ruby. Thank you again for helping me up."

Tom smiled, then turned his head, looking down the rails as though he were trying to spot and see the lights of the train in the distance.

Ruby was more concerned with getting to Geneva's package. She looked around first to see if anyone else had arrived or if Reggie was there yet. Then, Ruby checked her watch and saw that it was still 12:25 a.m. Very soon, the train would be arriving, and she and PJ would finally be together. Ruby felt ineffable joy.

When Ruby opened the package, she was amazed. The package contained a short letter wrapped around what looked to be at least a thousand dollars. Ruby read the letter while simultaneously slipping the wad of cash into her messenger bag and rezipping it quickly. The note was short but illuminating.

> To our gem of the ocean, Ruby. May your journey be the blessing to you that you have been to everyone you have encountered. I too once loved a woman and understand the calling of the heart should never be ignored. But unfortunately, I wasn't brave enough to see it through. I have always regretted it. I hope this money helps as you start anew.
>
> Love and solidarity always, Geneva

So many different thoughts raced through Ruby's mind. Her eyes welled up with tears of love and shock. She had no clue Geneva suspected anything. But then again, nothing ever really got past Geneva. And Ruby certainly had no idea about anything related to Geneva's personal or love life. Geneva always seemed a solitary figure consumed with her work. Yet the more Ruby thought, the more she realized that she and Geneva were similar, and perhaps Geneva had sensed that over their ten years together.

The letter then transformed from a mere gift of sentiment and support to a letter of permission for Ruby to be brave and courageous and not let work consume her entire life.

As Ruby contemplated all the layers of meaning in Geneva's words and gestures, she felt a nudge at her back. When she looked over and left her whirling thoughts, there was Reggie. He was standing beside her and reporting that the train was less than ten minutes away. He was sweating and a little out of breath, but he was next to her and on time. They embraced each other.

"Looks like we made it, Rubes!" Reggie put his right hand up in the air.

"We sho did!" Ruby slapped him five.

Reggie looked at his watch again. "Twelve thirty a.m. Just think, Rubes—five minutes from now, we will be boarded and on our way!" The two high-fived again.

Just as Ruby was wiping the sweat from Reggie's hand off her palm, she felt a slight rumble beneath her feet. It was quiet, so she thought that it was perhaps the train's vibration that was five minutes in the distance. Then came another rumble. And then another rumble. It felt as though the entire platform was shaking. Then Ruby heard the few other folks awaiting the train make subtle noises of confusion as they too felt the tremors.

"You feel that, Reggie?" Ruby asked with concern in her voice.

"Oh, probably the rumbling train coming." Reggie was unphased and focused more on boarding the train. "Oh, there's our guy!" Reggie pointed to the double doors that opened onto the platform. A young Black man came running through the double doors onto the platform, pulling what looked like her trunk and a host of other bags.

"Well, that's all. Three minutes before the train." Reggie slapped the guy five and looked down the rail line as the lights beamed from a distance.

Ruby tried to forget the tremors, but then another came, and then another. And then a huge one rumbled so hard that the bags and trunk fell over and off the pulley. Ruby grabbed Reggie, feeling her feet losing balance.

And then came another rumble. Then Ruby heard the oak staff make a loud rumbling pound on the ground.

Tom turned to her, Reggie, and Reggie's friend. "That vibration is the sound of my people. The Cherokee people." Tom spoke confidently as he removed his glasses and stood completely upright.

"I don't understand," Ruby and Reggie remarked, puzzled and in unison.

"Ms. Ruby, my full name is Tsula Thomas Chewey. My ancestors once called this land home before being forcibly moved west. We are standing across Jubilee, and we are here to reclaim the land that was stolen from us."

3

THE PARABLE OF NEW
JERUSALEM, UGANDA

"One, two, three, four, five, six, seven, eight . . . fifteen, sixteen, seventeen, eighteen . . . twenty-eight, twenty-nine, thirty . . . fifty-four, fifty-five, fifty-six, fifty-seven, fifty-eight, fifty-nine, sixty."

Mary counted aloud the first sixty seconds of her morning. Her eyes had opened after the sun rose, but she was not groggy. Mary felt alert and alive for the first time in a long while. Before placing her feet on the wooden floor of the bedroom, Mary wanted to take a full minute to let the newness and the healing she felt after sleeping in the room for the night take hold. For most of her life, Mary had been up and running well before sunrise, racing around to make it on time for her work. This relatively late morning where her eyes popped open with the sun already overhead gave her the feeling of triumphant satisfaction. Sitting up, Mary looked around at the wallpaper along the walls. As her feet hit the floor, she felt the cool sensation of the polished wood press against her toes. Mary rose from her bed covered in her favorite orange-and-green muumuu.

Within a matter of minutes, Mary had remade the bed, fluffed the pillows, and slid her hand across the top sheet until the last wrinkle had been removed. When she was finished, the room looked like a pristine hotel room awaiting a new guest. Because making the bed in such a precise fashion had not only come naturally to Mary but also had been her job, she wasn't really aware of her behavior. The whole thing had happened so instinctually and automatically. Once the bed was made and the curtains were fully opened, the sun gleamed on her face. And as though awaking from a daze or trance, Mary snapped back and turned around. As she looked at the pristinely organized room, the polished floors, and the decorative wallpaper, she grinned and then laughed aloud.

"Mary, this is your home and not your job anymore." She followed her laughter with a self-reminding command.

As though the affirmation had implied unstated directives, Mary walked over to the bed that she had just rendered into a perfect and inviting form. She pulled the cover at the middle as though she was shaping it into a tent. The middle of the sheet rising made the pillows fall over to the floor. Once the pillows were on the floor, she pulled and then snatched the cover off and threw it to the side. Looking around at the decorative wallpaper, Mary looked for the corner she knew that always curled at the end and never stuck.

"I've always hated you." Mary plucked at the wallpaper in search of a place to pull or tug at it.

After a few seconds, Mary found it and peeled back the wallpaper to the original wall of mahogany wood, revealing a red emergency button. She was surprised she'd never noticed it before.

"Now it makes sense why they covered up such beautiful wood with such ugly paper!" Mary grinned and laughed aloud again. She wanted to be sure that she enjoyed the short time she had alone in the house and used the quiet morning to free herself from the shackles of having been the home's primary housekeeper for the last twenty-five years.

Mary became the primary housekeeper of 2201 Herzl Road, having inherited the role, following her mother's retirement. That Mary was waking from the bed with sheets and pillows that she had washed and ironed for others for almost thirty years was a surreal feeling. The wallpaper, which featured antelope and deer in nature, she had always hated and didn't know why the family would have covered the walls with paper and glue. There were other parts of the house that she looked forward to reconfiguring and refashioning, but that would have to wait.

Realizing that she had already spent at least fifteen minutes making and unmaking beds, counting and staring, and ripping and pulling at the wallpaper, Mary headed to the kitchen to get into action.

There were a number of tasks that Mary needed to complete by the time her family arrived. There was breakfast to be made. The rooms needed to be ready for her children, husband, and her mother as well. Mary knew that they would arrive at the top of the hour, exactly on time, on the porch with their belongings, excitement, and empty stomachs.

Mary began cracking eggs and cooking a variety of meats to provide a big breakfast buffet that would amaze and impress her children, mother, and husband. As the food cooked, Mary scanned the other rooms of the house to ensure that everything was as it should be. She also went through each area determining who would go where and why in case there was any disagreement or arguments about their new permanent lodging. The wallpaper, which she abhorred, was all around the house, and it nearly distracted her each time she went into a new room. Mary was just about to begin peeling off the paper in one of the rooms when she began to smell that the breakfast sausages were on the verge of transitioning from crisp and delicious to burnt and inedible.

Mary ran into the kitchen and cut off the cooking fires and pulled plates from the cabinets. Bowls and utensils were placed on the large table in the dining room. The food was laid out on the kitchen table so that her family would be able to help themselves and bring their plates to the dining room. Just as Mary was laying napkins down on the dining room table, she remembered the disarray of the bedroom.

Realizing that her husband might think something strange or even terrible happened in the room if he found it as she had left it, Mary raced to the bedroom.

Even faster than she had when she awoke, Mary quickly grabbed the pillows and dusted and fluffed them back up. She took the bedspread and sheets and placed them gently on the mattress. Soon enough, the bed was crisp and wrinkle-free. The corners were flattened and patterned, and the sheets and bedspread were tightly tucked underneath the mattress. Mary grabbed the torn wallpaper from the floor, balling it up in her hand to throw away. Heading down the hallway and back toward the kitchen, Mary could hear the familiar sounds of her four children's voices ringing with curiosity and excitement. Although Mary was expecting them, their arrival felt earlier than expected.

Mary looked at the clock in the kitchen. The clock showed 8:50 a.m., confirming that they had arrived ten minutes ahead of schedule. Mary quickly threw the tortured wallpaper into the kitchen receptacle and washed her hands. She thought about trying to quickly change her clothes, as there was an outfit that she had hanging in the bureau especially for the occasion. But now there was no time, so Mary figured she'd just make a special dinner and change into her outfit that evening.

Mary dried her hands and headed to the front door. Entering the hallway, Mary could see that her four children were already on the porch with little bundles of clothes and other items gathered together. Her husband, Daniel, was behind the children with several bags in each hand full of items that Mary had instructed him to bring. Mary's mother, however, seemed to be nowhere in sight. Mary unlocked and opened the front door and went out to the porch to greet everyone and direct them into the home.

All four children were bouncing with excitement and ran inside right past Mary. Daniel, who was holding so many bags he looked as though he might tilt over, managed to give Mary a huge kiss on her lips and then on her forehead. Mary felt so proud as she heard her children running inside. The unexpected affection from Daniel made Mary feel so warm and victorious, she almost forgot that she still hadn't seen her mother.

"Maama is standing on the side of the house. She is afraid of the neighbors recognizing her," Daniel informed Mary, releasing exasperation in his voice that loosened as he let the items he was carrying fall to the floor. Mary stepped out further onto the porch and peered around to the side of the house; there her mother was, eyes closed, hands clasped in prayer.

"Maama! Maama! What are you doing? Please come inside."

Her mother, who looked to be finishing a prayer, waited for a few moments before opening her eyes and responding.

"Didn't I raise you to never interrupt a person while they are speaking with Jesus?" Mary's mother's mild voice rang with admonishment.

"Maama, unless you are saying 'thank you,' I don't know what you would need to be praying on the side, hidden like that for." Mary's retort of confusion and question met her mother as she approached the porch.

"Oh, that is you, Ms. Mary! Good morning to you! Wasn't sure who that was . . . Is that Ms. Martha? Oh my! I haven't seen you since I was a teenager at Bible study camp. How kind of the family to invite you all over after their return!" Isaac, the head of Herzlton's security, startled both women, who hadn't realized that someone had been paying attention to their interaction.

"Good morning, Mr. Isaac. We are the family," Mary responded with a noticeable smirk, and she and her mother, upon seeing the head of security, scurried quickly into the house. As she entered the house, Martha responded with a quick wave.

Mary closed and locked the door before Isaac could respond any further. Mary stood in the hallway for a few seconds trying to determine if she had taken the right actions, especially now that Isaac had witnessed her and her family entering the home with bundles and baggage and other items. And while Mary knew she was not up to anything suspicious or wrong, the timing of Isaac's approach just didn't fit with how she had planned to bring the change in the home's ownership to their attention. Nonetheless, Isaac was aware something was up and had already likely informed the neighbors that Mary's entire family was next door.

"I just don't trust it," Martha said, the voice rolling into Mary's ears and breaking her train of deep thought.

"Ehhh?" Mary turned around, where her mother's look of concern awaited her.

"I just don't trust this whole thing." Martha was more emphatic the second time.

"There is not anything to not trust. I have the deed and all the papers. This is our home. Everything is in order." Mary spoke with intoxicating confidence. And although Mary was a bit bruised by her mother's doubts, she did not let it show. As long as they had all their paperwork and proof of ownership, Mary felt there was nothing to be concerned about other than the nosey neighbors and any hiccups that occurred in their being accepted into the community.

"The food smells good, baby, and I am so hungry I could eat an entire elephant." Daniel came up and stood between his wife and mother-in-law, hoping that his presence would shake the emerging stalemate between the two. Daniel held Mary at her waist and pulled her into his chest. He hugged her and whispered into her ear, "Thank you."

"Come on, everyone. Let's eat this wonderful breakfast your mother has prepared," Daniel yelled out to the children, who had each been in the careful yet chaotic process of claiming a space or room or both. As the children ran into the kitchen, Mary went behind them to ensure that they didn't make a mess of the kitchen and overfill their plates with portions they would never be able to finish.

"Maama, let's eat and be grateful for what God has provided our family." Daniel's smile and words coaxed Martha, and the two grabbed plates and entered into the kitchen. As the clock struck nine, laughter and chewing were the only sounds filling the house.

9:00 A.M.–10:00 A.M.

The shuttle was completely empty. Miriam found it odd that no one else was aboard the bus yet. After waiting for more than an hour inside the airport, Miriam realized that in her choice to take an earlier flight, she hadn't paid much attention to the departure and arrival time of the next flight from Tel Aviv. Because Miriam had been so frustrated with her family and longed to see Isaac, she took the first flight she could, happily traveling separately from her family and others in the community. The two weeks she had spent in Israel felt like months. For most of her life, her family and community members would spend many a Friday evening following the ceremonial Shabbat prayers and customs, fantasizing about what Jerusalem would look and feel like when they visited.

When Miriam was a child, she didn't think much of the conversation amongst the adults. She instead just wondered, *What if the ancient structures and locations from the Talmud are real and intact?* Of course, Miriam was aware that there had been many transitions and migrations over the centuries—walls torn down, burned down, destroyed, rebuilt, torn away, and rebuilt again. Miriam was more taken with the power that the idea of Jerusalem had over her family and the many members of the community. Miriam couldn't remember a time when she was actually not within earshot of her community. Initially, when Miriam appeared to be the first to arrive at Entebbe Airport, she was delighted. The solitude the travel and arrival had afforded gave Miriam time to be on her own for the first time in twenty-five years of living. Waiting an hour inside the airport had been long enough, so once Miriam couldn't take the monotony of the airport, she headed to the regularly scheduled shuttle to and from Herzlton, the Jewish settlement nestled between Kampala and Entebbe.

For the first ten minutes on the bus, Miriam was unbothered, and her aloneness had not yet felt unusual. After ten minutes became twenty, Miriam went back inside to inquire about the status of the usual flight, given that there was only traditionally one flight every few days that could even go between Israel and Uganda, provided there may be a few changeovers in between. As she awaited the supervisor's status update about the flight, Miriam recollected how she had gotten to Israel and what she'd been taught about her community and its origins. Beginning at the top of the year, the community had been celebrating the seventy-fifth anniversary of the founding of Herzlton. Miriam, like all the children in the community, learned in school about the origins of the settlement and the quest for a homeland that captured much of her imagination and understanding of Jewish history. Somewhere around the age of six, all children were taught the story of the settlement. The name Herzlton was in honor of Theodore Herzl who'd convincingly proposed before the Zionist Congress a plan to have a Jewish settlement in Uganda rather than wait upon such to be made available in Palestine. In 1903, Herzl's plan received a majority vote but also was poised to splinter the group. Many were against Herzl's plan and viewed the settlement in Uganda as mere consolation and distraction from the goal of Jewish resettlement of Jerusalem. But there were some who were in areas of Europe where they sensed that their long-term safety may not be a guarantee, and a settlement elsewhere might prove beneficial. Those who were against Herzl's proposal believed that he had only sent a team of scouts to assess possible locations. And while that was true, there was more to it.

By 1904, one hundred families, known as the Founders, had developed a secret agreement with the British government that also had support from the king to establish a Jewish settlement in or near Lake Victoria. Those one hundred families hailed from Austria, Britain, France, Germany, Poland, and Russia and staggered their arrivals to avoid detection by the Zionist Congress. By the time Theodore Herzl made his formal presentation again in 1904, nearly all one hundred families had already settled in the contracted area. Like other children born in Herzlton, Uganda was the only home that Miriam knew. She was not familiar with Europe other than it being shown on a map and the horrifying and terrifying stories of the Holocaust survivors who joined the community in the years before her birth.

At some point between remembering grammar school and these early lessons and memories, the supervisor had returned to the desk and was trying to get Miriam's attention.

"Ma'am ... Nyabo. Ma'am ... Nyabo." The supervisor's voice rotated through tones of confusion, frustration, and professionalism. It was not until the supervisor appeared to have given up and began to turn around and walk back to the office behind the desk that Miriam snapped out of her nostalgia.

"Yes, yes. You were saying?" Miriam spoke with a jittery rapidness and also a tone that sought to stop the supervisor in his tracks as though she had been listening to him the entire time.

"Ma'am, it appears that Flight 404 has been delayed." The supervisor's voice was matter-of-fact.

"Delayed! Are you sure?" Miriam was dubious and assumed that the supervisor was not a good listener and hadn't jotted down or remembered the correct flight information.

"Yes, ma'am. Chartered Flight 404's arrival time has been rescheduled," he responded with a kind tone that didn't suggest the frustration brewing underneath.

"That's impossible! There must be some sort of explanation." Miriam was visibly annoyed and increasingly agitated.

The supervisor didn't respond immediately. Instead, he turned around and headed to the office.

"Hello, sir! Where are you going?" Miriam's voice was now becoming loud enough for others in the facility to have a front seat to her ongoing exchange with the supervisor.

He took his time and scanned over notes that were coming through a printer in the office. "Ma'am, it says here, 'Flight 404 rescheduled.'" The supervisor walked out of the office with a great deal of purpose. The supervisor turned the readout so that it faced Miriam as he pointed to the information and deciphered the codes for her.

Miriam's face scrunched in such a way that it made her look like the determined impatience and worry of a latchkey kid who had lost sight of their house key long after school had let out for the day.

"Ma'am, this letter here . . . R . . . tells the reason for the change. The code used underneath the R indicates that no one was boarded because the chartered flight was rescheduled. Ma'am, the plane is still in Tel Aviv."

"I don't understand."

"The plane is still there."

"This doesn't make any sense."

"Perhaps there was a weather pattern that caused the delay. Our pilots do take great pride in safety first. In either case, why don't you leave a contact number? I will call to inform you of the flight status."

The supervisor's words and tone proved persuasive, as Miriam wrote down her home number. She finished writing and looked up to the supervisor with eyes asking after some sensible logic to quell her racing mind.

"Ma'am, this will be checked and is a priority." The supervisor was increasingly compelling in his ability to assuage Miriam's angst. He continued, "Unusual activities regarding any flight to and from Entebbe must immediately be reported to security and state officials. The authorities will sort out this matter and ensure that everyone is safe. As I said, the weather could easily be the explanation."

At this point, the supervisor walked around the desk partition and escorted a calmer Miriam back outside. Miriam thanked the supervisor and reboarded the shuttle bus.

10:00 A.M.–1:00 P.M.

Mary passed her mother a freshly washed, wet plate. Drying the plate, Martha remained quiet. Her continued silence was growing louder and louder to Mary's sensitive ears and heart. She had always been able to sense her mother's unease or discomfort even as a small child. Her ability to tap into her mother's inner emotions had grown acutely after her father's sudden death. When Mary was five years old, her father died in his sleep in bed next to her mother. Mary awoke and saw her mother in the kitchen alone. Being the daddy's girl she was, she raced to the bedroom to wake her father up and shower him with morning hugs and kisses on his cheek. As she entered the room, she felt a small chill crawl up her tiny back. Had Mary been older, she may have taken that chill as a sign to proceed with caution, but she was so young and innocent, she had no real clue of what she would find. All Mary wanted was to bring her father a happy surprise of her adoration in the morning and see his warm glow as his eyes opened. Although he had initially felt a little warm, as Mary tried to wake him up and her panic set in, her father's body grew quieter, more still, and colder.

Mary lifted his eyelid and was horrified when all that sat behind his eyelid was the white of his eye, the pupil residing elsewhere. Unable to understand what she was witnessing, Mary thought she may have jumped on her father too hard or injured him in the process of hugging him, and now he was blind. Too young to understand that his pupil had rolled to the back or top of his head, Mary figured that if she told her mother that she may have blinded her father, her mom would know what to do. Mary didn't scream or yell, run or jog; she walked with as much poise and calmness as her five-year-old body could muster.

"Maama, I think Baba may be sick." Mary's innocent voice flew into Martha's ears with the precision of a small axe on its last chop of a great tree.

The wet dish that was in Martha's hand fell to the floor as she immediately ran into the bedroom. A doctor confirmed later that day that Mary's father had succumbed to a heart attack while he was asleep. And although her mother had been religious before her father's death, Martha became extremely so after his death, dedicating herself to leading the largest Bible study camp in the region.

All Mary knew was that her mother had a deep inner turmoil that she wouldn't or couldn't express outside of the quiet solitude of prayer. As a result, Mary blamed herself. No one had ever taken the time to tell Mary that her actions had not affected her father. That he was already dead when Mary entered the room, which she figured out on her own after many years of self-blame and hidden episodes of sadness.

After Mary's father's death, Martha never dated or married again and thus never had any additional children. Mary always noticed her parents' age gap; her mother was twenty-one, and her father was fifty-one when they were married just before Mary was born.

"Don't you think Baba is so happy for us?" Mary handed another wet plate to her mother, hoping to break the silence. The sensation of the wet plate in her hands and her mother holding the plate as she dried it had drudged up memories of finding her father. While Mary had not thought of this ordeal in forty years or even had a full discussion with Martha about it, the vibration of the moment felt familiar, like a reminder that her father's spirit was guiding and protecting her and her family.

Martha, however, remained silent. This time, the silence made Mary feel unsupported and defensive. She could no longer take Martha's quiet punishment and odd prayers on the side of the house.

"Maama, what's wrong? I feel like you are trying to make it so that I am not allowed to be happy about this house and what it means for my family!" Mary didn't mince her words, and though her voice was raised, it neither rose to disrespect nor loud enough for the children and her husband to hear from other parts of the spacious home.

There was a pause even still after Mary's outburst. Martha dried the plate and then dried her hands. She turned to Mary, who was near tears awaiting Martha's response.

"You must not read anything from my being punished by God. That is my cross to bear. When you are happy, my sweet daughter, I find happiness in your happiness." Martha held Mary's wet hands, pressing into them the warmth from her heart for her daughter.

"I don't understand. Why are you being punished? God loves you!" As soon as the words left her lips, Mary knew they were unsuccessful.

She had tried for many years to get her mother to release herself from the overwhelming sense of blame and responsibility for her husband's death.

"I can feel Baba is here right now, don't you?" Mary was desperate to get her mother to open up and share her feelings.

"I felt his presence with me until I entered this house again. When we walked up to the home, it was like I could feel him leaving me again. And of course, why would he want to be in this house? And so that's what I am praying about. Asking God to forgive me for coming back here to live. I asked Jesus to bring my beloved husband's spirit of protection back upon me."

Martha said more than she meant to say. As soon as she began to divulge the substance of her prayer, she regretted it. It was unlike Martha to share the subject or requests embedded in her prayers with anyone; not even her pastor was privy to their contents. But on this occasion, maybe it had been the four decades of silence on the topic between Martha and her precious daughter that made her speak it aloud and confess.

Mary's face moved between confused concern and a desire to minister to her mother's broken heart. Martha, noticing her daughter's search for what to say and how to say it, just grabbed Mary, wet hands and all, and hugged her. Martha hugged her until she felt their heartbeats meet and then join in rhythm. At first, Mary was surprised and unsure, and over the near minute of their embrace, she found ease and comfort resting her head on her mother's sturdy and broad shoulders.

"I find happiness in your happiness. That is all you need to know. The rest is for me to handle." Martha's words were tender and calmed the pressing anxiety that had been bubbling up within Mary as they washed the dishes.

Mary had other questions, but their importance decreased as her heartbeat moved into a new rhythm. Mary decided she would ask on another occasion, and that breaking through Martha's silence and resistance was a big enough triumph to mark the moment this new home represented for her family. As Mary and her mother washed and dried the last dish, Daniel returned to the kitchen.

"What are you two beautiful ladies doing in here?" Daniel asked rhetorically, smiling from ear to ear. He and the children were all on a high, filled with the joy and possibility they found as they explored their new residence with piqued curiosity.

"The children love this place. They didn't even argue about who slept where and why. Looks like this house is already working its magic!" Daniel grinned and laughed a little, thinking his words would resonate at the intersection of a joke and truth.

As though they were intentionally coordinated, both Mary and Martha turned to Daniel and smiled back. Mary's laughter was more genuine and tinged with relief, while Martha's was an artifact of politeness built upon the hope that her daughter's querying and mentioning of her deceased husband might subside or end altogether. Mary, who had been running around the house cooking and cleaning since the night before, felt her legs growing weary. Daniel sensed Mary's fatigue and encouraged her to rest or, at the very least, join the children in the family room.

"We now have rooms to choose from. Baby, I will take care of the lunch. I saw it prepared inside the REFRIGERATOR . . . I just have to say some of these words out loud. ROOMS! REFRIGERATOR! This house is a miracle!" Daniel was so carried away by the amenities and the dramatic shift from their one bedroom with an outhouse arrangement that he couldn't help himself in noting the overall and drastic improvement in the family's quality of living.

"Yes, lunch is already prepared and only needs to be taken out of the cooling shelf and placed into the oven," Mary spoke quickly to remind Daniel to pick up where his train of thought had derailed.

"Yes. Yes. I will take care of lunch, and you two rest some, or at least enjoy our new home."

Daniel shooed Mary and Martha out of the kitchen and down the hallway. Mary found the whole thing pretty sweet, while Martha's reluctance became visible even to Daniel. In response to sensing his mother-in-law's lack of enthusiasm, Daniel gave Mary the "Is everything alright with Maama?" look. Mary nodded and shrugged to indicate she thought so but was also unsure and had picked up on the same vibe as Daniel.

Mary and Martha walk into the family room as Daniel whistled a joyful melody in the kitchen while preparing lunch for his family. The children, who had been bouncing with excitement since the night before, were fast asleep in the family room. An inviting voice of a narrated cigarette commercial rolled off of the floor-model television playing in the background as Mary watched her children sleeping with a tremendous sense of peace and accomplishment. Mary wanted to ask her mother how she felt watching the children sleeping so quietly and also how this modern home might change their lives for the better. But Mary chose to keep the thought to herself, remembering how her mother responded in the kitchen when they were washing dishes.

"The children were so excited all night. You should have seen how Daniel and I worked overtime to get them into bed and quiet." Martha's unexpected reflections eased Mary's mind.

Hearing Martha make these unprompted remarks gave Mary an indication that her mother, while slow to embrace the home, was on her way to fully being able to do so.

"Maama, thank you for everything that you have done for me, for my family. This home—"

Martha interrupted Mary as she transitioned back into the uncomfortable topic of the new house. "Let's make an agreement right here, right now." Martha's whispered voice was stern.

"Agreement about?" Mary half pretended not to know what Martha meant.

"We all agreed that we would live here. But can it not be a constant topic of conversation between me and you? It makes me uncomfortable." Martha sighed as she spoke, releasing an unknown sensation of relief that had been rumbling in her chest ever since she arrived at the house.

"Maama, I am not trying to make you uncomfortable. I apologize for making you feel that way." Mary was near tears and felt very upset that her excitement and need to discuss the house was triggering discomfort for her mother.

"You have done nothing wrong, my sweet daughter. You are doing the right thing for your family, and you have no responsibility for the sins of my past." Martha was kneeling before Mary, hoping to quell her daughter's rising upset and sadness.

"It is not a sin to have been a housekeeper. So what you worked for the white people and took Herzlton money for doing so! There is no sin in taking care of your family!" Mary's voice rose, and two of her children nearly awoke at the sound of her raised tone.

Before speaking, Martha observed the children and ensured they were still asleep. After being certain that they were not awake, Martha turned back to Mary, who was increasingly confused and upset.

"I feel shame for having worked in this community for fifty years, especially because this land was just taken from families by the government. But there are details that maybe someday I will share. For now, know that I continue to ask for God's forgiveness for my past actions." Tears rolled down Martha's usually stoic face.

Upon seeing her mother's tears, Mary was no longer able to hold back her own. As Mary cried, she wiped her mother's tears and helped her back up to her feet.

"Maama, please sit here and rest. I will accept your agreement, but I cannot promise that I understand everything." Mary was now kneeling before her mother, and tears blended of confusion and joy welled up at the corners of her eyes as she continued. "After all the cooking, cleaning, and childcare we have provided in this house to this family for seventy-five years . . ." Mary was unable to finish, as she could feel that the statement required her full chest and unleashing of her emotions, which would most certainly wake her children. Mary kissed her mother on the crown of her head and left the room as quietly as she could.

When she exited the room, she heard Daniel's joyful whistling. And as though it were the call of an enticing siren, Mary followed the whistling in the air until she was led back to its source in the kitchen. Daniel was well into his one-man show when Mary walked into the kitchen. She hadn't seen Daniel this excited in a very long time. The sight of her joyous husband eased Mary's increasing upset with Martha. And even though she was smiling when Daniel realized Mary was standing behind him, her tear-stained face betrayed her smile.

"Baby, what is wrong? Everything is so right. What could be wrong, baby?" Daniel pulled Mary into him and wrapped her in a strong, protective hug. He could feel Mary's upset entangled with her heartbeat as they embraced. Daniel let Mary go and pulled a chair out from the kitchen table. He poured her a cup of tea using the hot water he had been boiling on the stove. After pouring the hot water over the teabag, he sat next to Mary at the kitchen table.

"Now, tell me what has dampened your joy, my love?" Daniel's eyes were open and sincere as though he was looking directly into Mary's heart and shining a light on the exact coordinates of her upset.

"It's just that Maama . . . that Maama . . . It's just that . . ." Mary was also becoming anxious.

"Take a breath, my love. Take a sip, and I will wait. Then tell me." Daniel rubbed Mary's hands, hoping to offer her some ease and comfort.

Mary took a deep breath and exhaled. She put the teacup to her lips and blew another breath over the tea. She took a few small sips. As the warm tea traveled through her body, Mary felt some ease and began where she stopped.

"It's just that Maama isn't as happy as I thought she'd be. When the Hoffmans turned the house over to me, I couldn't wait to tell her. We had come from housekeepers to keepers of the deed of the house. I just thought that by the time she walked inside or arrived at the front door, she would finally show her excitement and leave the fear behind." Mary felt immediately better just getting her disappointment and frustration out. Until she spoke those words, she hadn't realized how her mother's disposition for the two weeks leading up to the family moving in had registered with her in such a deep and clear way.

"Give her time. She would not have come if she was too bothered or didn't have some level of excitement about it." Daniel offered his insight with hopes of aiding in Mary's comfort and perspective.

"We've agreed not to talk about it, but I don't know if I will be able to keep that agreement. And then she is speaking in these strange, mysterious ways, talking about sins of her past and other things about God punishing her. I don't get it."

"You know the old folks who are super religious are also superstitious too. Maybe it's her superstition getting the best of her. Remember, she is a part of the generation that remembers when the white Jewish families first arrived. She remembers the families who'd been displaced by the community and their fight with the government over their rightful claims to the land. I know when I was growing up and my parents were still alive, I first told them about how I planned to make you my wife. You know what they told me? 'Be careful.'"

"Be careful?!?" Mary had never heard this story before and was shocked to hear that Daniel's parents would advise him to be careful about her. Daniel's parents had always been so loving and supportive, and she was surprised to hear of this caution.

"Not of you per se," Daniel tried to assure Mary while coming back to finish his story with increasing regret for having decided to share the story. "Be careful about your job. They didn't think that working in Herzlton was unsafe for US. They know of the curses that were put upon Herzlton by the tribes whose ancestral land this is. They believed in the power of hexes and revenge. We can look seventy-five years later and see that things have worked out to be relatively peaceable between Herzlton and the Ugandan people. It has been seventy-five years of a razor's edge peace, especially to people like my parents and other descendants of the original tribes of this land." Daniel could tell by the look on Mary's face that his point and intention were not clear.

"I am trying to say that the older generation has a different relationship to this place. And if I am completely honest, I think their hexes worked. I mean, look at where we are living and these electronics and amenities. You know what I have been whistling all this time?"

Mary paused for a second and thought. Until Daniel had asked, Mary hadn't thought much about what Daniel had been whistling. Rather, Mary had been most attuned to Daniel's joyfulness, which she'd hoped would be more infectious, especially to Martha.

"Now that you ask, I have noticed, and at first I thought it was familiar. Like something I've heard before, but it sounds faster than what I remember."

"It is the harmony to my tribe's song. It is probably familiar because it was sung at our wedding and some other times over the years. And you are right—it is much slower. But for some reason, when we walked up and you answered the door, it all hit me. This is our HOME! An awareness came over me about the moment of accomplishment this was. I guess that's why this story about my parents came back to me just now." Daniel was processing new thoughts and responding to Mary at the same time. "When you answered and opened the door, I understood that this was what the old magic accomplished. Returning here as an owner felt like this indescribable feeling of being restored." Daniel was standing and beaming with pride, his hand outstretched to Mary.

"I had not thought about all of this like that. How beautiful and true!" Mary was now standing. The couple began to dance around the kitchen floor to the rhythm of Daniel's whistling. Mary's once tired legs and feet felt rejuvenated and youthful. The couple moved with harmonic swiftness and agility. As they made a final twirl, Daniel dipped Mary and pulled her up, and they shared a passionate kiss.

"Mmm-hmm. Now that's what I call happiness!" Daniel proclaimed after the couple's long and impassioned embrace. For a few moments, the couple just stared into each other's eyes. It was as if they had been transported to the beginning of their romance; before they had children; before Daniel lost his job as a dispatch operator after the government downsized communication companies across the country; before the financial struggles; before life complicated the love and marriage they shared.

Daniel took Mary by the hand and walked her up to the window box. "Look at the front yard and the green grass. That's where our children will play and imagine their futures." Daniel's finger moved around as though he were following the future positions and actions of their four children. "And then one day, it will be just you and me. And we will see our grandchildren play in this same front yard as we watch from the porch."

Daniel's exuberance and sheer belief in the positive virtues of the home's prosperity for the family made Mary forget all about her concerns about Martha.

"Yes. I see it too. I love you." Mary kissed Daniel on his cheek, impressed and swept up in his energetic forecast of their future.

"This is the fresh start we all needed. Being cooped up in that small one-bedroom shack was hurting all of us. And then with you being gone five days out of the week, the last fifteen years have been hard, to say the least. But look at us now!" Daniel started sliding around the floor in his own happy dance.

"I think we should also tell the children what is going on. They have some idea, especially since they had to bring all of their clothes and toys, but I want to make sure they know what is really going on." Mary moved back to a chair at the kitchen table and gave Daniel a look that instructed him to sit back down. Daniel did one last striding glide and flopped into the chair.

"I agree. They should know that God has blessed us with this home. They should know they now have no excuse for not becoming all that God has meant for them to become in this life. Just imagine if you or I had been able to start early in life with the foundation of a beautiful home with all the amenities and a great school nearby!" Daniel agreed with Mary, adding his own mandates to what would be discussed with the children.

The timer rang to indicate that the food was ready. Daniel gathered the children into the dining area for lunch while Mary went into the bedroom to retrieve the deed for the house. It was important to Mary that her children see an actual deed, see what ownership looked like, and know that this was their home. She wasn't sure what questions they would ask or what her answers would be. As Mary pulled the deed from beneath her pillow, she committed to being open and honest if her children asked questions.

Everyone was seated and awaiting Mary's arrival. The children, while wide awake, all had some form of sleep in their eyes or creases on their faces from the positions and materials they slept on. Their looks of recent waking and innocence made Mary see her children as even more adorable than usual.

"Everyone, let's hold hands and bow our heads. Jjaja will lead us in blessing the food as usual," Mary instructed the family.

"Heavenly Father, we come before you and your mighty throne giving thanks for your Son, our Lord and Savior Jesus Christ. We thank you for sending him to this earthly plane so that we may be worthy enough to make our way into Heaven to behold your mighty throne. We thank you for blessing and keeping this family."

Daniel and Mary looked at one another, appreciating that Martha had referred to the home as a blessing.

"We thank you for covering us in the blood of Jesus. We ask that you bless the food prepared before us. We ask that you bless the hands of those who have prepared the food before us. In the glorious and powerful name of Jesus Christ, this we ask with gratitude for all things you have done and will do. Amen!"

"Amen!" The family completed the prayer in rousing unison.

The family was quiet and peaceful as the fresh-baked bread, rice, and baked chicken were eaten. Although they had all had a large breakfast, lunch had arrived right on time; for they were all hungrier than each of them thought. The children were the first to finish. And just as Mary was taking her final spoonful of the soup, her oldest began the questions.

"Maama, so this big house is all ours? We picked out rooms, and I just want to make sure we are not going to have to leave like we had to with the other places we lived."

"Edward, I understand that it has been hard on everyone having to move four times in this last year. I promise you—this is our home for good." Mary reached for the deed underneath her chair. Before Mary could answer, her mother interrupted.

"Edward, remember that we must always have gratitude. Even though there were four different places we had to live in the last year, remember friends and others who were not as fortunate and currently may have no place to live at all." Martha's voice was matter-of-fact but infused with a grandmotherly warmth.

"Thank you, Maama." Mary nodded and acknowledged her mother's reminder. "I know it has been a hard year for us, especially after your father's job was eliminated by the government. But today is a new day for all of us. You see this in my hand?" Mary unfolded the deed and held it upright, showing it off in a rotation across the large dining table. "This is called a deed. It is a legal document that means that the person whose name appears on it and has it in their possession owns the property." Mary's tone was that of a schoolteacher.

"A deed? A deed." Edward asked and answered himself out loud.

"Yes, son. This means that we are the owners." Daniel reinforced Mary's lesson, pointing to the place where her name was printed and signed on the paperwork.

The other three children immediately began to shimmy and shake and dance.

"Yay! YES! This is the best day ever!" The three younger kids were out of their seats and gyrating, smiling, and cheering.

Edward, nearly a teenager, wasn't as easily excitable. The look of confused curiosity on his face reminded Mary of her own when she asked questions of her mother. Seeing that expression reflected in her son triggered Mary's commitment to forthrightness.

"Baby, is everything okay? You don't seem happy by the news like your brother and sisters."

"I am happy, Maama. It's just that . . . It's just . . ." Edward became shy and stuttered as though he feared the reaction to his truest thoughts.

Relating to Edward's disposition, Mary reached over the wide table and grabbed Edward's hand. "Go on and say what's on your mind and heart. We want to know." Mary was gentle and encouraging.

"Okay, you three. Have a seat and get quiet so that we can all pay attention and listen," Daniel deftly commanded the younger children who immediately stopped and sat back at the table.

"It's just that isn't this place for white people only? How did we get here? And why would white people let us have all of their furniture and fancy electronics? It just feels too . . ."

"Too good to be true?" Mary finished Edward's statement, which gave him comfort.

"Hmmph." Martha's reaction was audible to everyone, who looked at her for a second before Mary responded.

"Here's the thing. Jjaja and I worked in this house for a total of seventy-five years. Jjaja for fifty of those years and me for twenty-five years. Jjaja raised the Hoffman children and then I raised their grandchildren. The family decided that they wanted to move to a faraway place that they feel is their homeland like how Uganda is our homeland. You know the place Jerusalem from the Bible?"

"Yes, Maama." Edward's confusion had moved to a fascination with the biblical overlap.

"Good. Well, that's where the family went to live. These folks are not just white; they are also Jewish. And that means they are descendants of the Hebrews who once called Jerusalem home. When I was around your age, the same white people who helped these families get the land that makes up Herzlton here in Uganda, well, they told them they could have the land in and around Jerusalem again. The place is called Israel." Mary was careful about her words and could tell her son was absorbing everything she said like a sponge.

"So Jerusalem is not just in the Bible. It is still around today?" Edward asked.

"Edward, don't be foolish now. Everything in the Bible is real!" Martha admonished Edward for his disbelief of the infallible nature of the scriptures and stories of the Bible.

"Maama, please." Mary cut her eyes at her mother for disrupting the flow of her explanation and continued. "Last year in America, Egypt agreed to acknowledge and no longer be at war with the Jewish people and their nation of Israel. Herzlton families had never been to Jerusalem or anywhere else after they left their homes in Europe to come to Uganda and establish and build the community. And because of the conflicts with other countries, many of the families were afraid to travel there. But after the agreement, many started visiting, and some decided to move there permanently. You understand?" Mary felt as though she was beginning to go beyond her capacity for historical explanation and did not want to confuse or misrepresent the facts.

"So the white people who lived here wanted to go back home and gave you this home because they didn't need it anymore." Edward stated his takeaway aloud with the hopes that his version was also recognizable to his younger siblings who'd ask him a million times about the conversation later if the discussion wasn't simplified.

"Basically, yes. Son, yes." Daniel added the words that accompanied Mary's affirmative nodding.

Anticipating that more questions would come, Mary held her breath and prepared to answer or provide clarification.

"I hope it works out for them because I am not giving up my room or that television or the radio or this space. Besides, Uganda is our Jerusalem, so we shouldn't be the ones moving around all the time anyway. I say, thank you and goodbye!" Edward was now dancing around himself, and his siblings all joined in.

"Thank you and goodbye! Thank you and goodbye!" The children danced around with all of their fancy and agile moves. Daniel loved it and found it entertaining while also ringing true of his own tribe's relationship with Herzlton. Daniel soon joined in.

Soon enough, everyone, except for Martha, was dancing and repeating "Thank you and goodbye!" Mary was dancing and singing with the relief that she'd survived what she thought may have been a continued inquisition.

As everyone danced, Martha began clearing the table and made a point not to disrupt the family's joyful dancing. After placing the last dish into the sink, Martha looked out the window and saw the big bus had arrived from the airport. She called out to Mary upon seeing the bus stop and door open.

"Mary, come here please!" Martha raised her voice but kept her tone casual so as not to alarm Daniel and the children.

"Maama, what is it?" Mary asked, winded from dancing and celebrating in the dining room.

"Look! Do you see it? The bus is back?" Martha's concern was clear in her voice.

"Yes. That is fine. Maybe not everyone planned to stay in Israel or maybe they came back to retrieve some things and will leave again," Mary responded with a confidence that belied her own bewilderment at the sight of the shuttle.

The bus door opened, and one white woman came off of it. Mary and Martha watched for a few more minutes to see if other people emerged from the bus. Martha let out a deep sigh of relief when the driver handed the woman her luggage and drove off.

"See. That's just Ms. Miriam from next door. The family probably sent her back to gather a few items. I told you they were all leaving." Mary pretended to be sure, even though she nearly let out a similar sigh of relief when her mother did.

"Everything will be fine." Mary rubbed her mother's back, hoping to help her release the intense anxiety that rose from Martha's shoulders.

1:00 P.M.–3:00 P.M.

The bus was hot. As it rolled around the bend into Herzlton, Miriam's thoughts raced. During the ride, she had replayed her decision to go ahead of the charter flight on a commercial airline.

Miriam figured that once she arrived, she would be the first on the shuttle and use the long ride to even out tensions with her family. Instead, Miriam found herself sweaty, bothered, and alone on the long and empty bus ride. The shuttle bus, which was usually full of the sounds of chatter among the returning families, was filled only with the sounds of bumpy roads, the bus driver's attempt at small talk, and the static-filled radio broadcast.

Over the course of the long ride, Miriam went in and out of sleep. The hours it took gave her a chance to use sleep to mitigate her anxiety and the sheer and unusual discomfort of the temperature of the bus. Noticing that Miriam was asleep as the destination approached, the driver called her name several times until she awoke.

"Ms. Miriam . . . Ms. Miriam . . . Nyabo," the driver politely but loudly beckoned Miriam from her sleep.

"Uh, yes. Yes." Miriam awoke, gathering her wits and taking note of the approaching entry into Herzlton.

"Ma'am, we will be in Herzlton at one p.m. sharp." The driver's voice echoed from the front of the bus with a hint of delight underneath his reverberating tone.

Miriam gathered her purse and reached inside for a handkerchief to wipe the sweat from her brow. After returning the wet cloth back to her purse, Miriam reached inside and retrieved her sunglasses. Sensing that her eyes were puffy and her face was undone, Miriam thought the sunglasses would help to hide her face well enough when she stepped off the bus. When the bus pulled up in front of her house, Miriam felt a coolness come upon her. Isaac waving and flagging the bus from the porch was especially exciting for Miriam. Miriam had longed to see Isaac, having been in Israel for the last two weeks. And the sight of his smiling chocolate face made her almost forget the dismay she had carried back to Uganda.

No sooner had Miriam's feet hit the sidewalk than Isaac was standing beside her.

"Welcome home, Ms. Miriam," Isaac greeted her as he went to the side of the bus with the driver to collect her bags from the storage area.

Miriam grinned and reached inside her purse, pulling out an envelope. She handed the envelope to the driver and turned to walk toward her house.

"Ma'am . . . Ma'am . . . ," the bus driver spoke with an urgent though respectful tone.

"Yes, sir." Miriam didn't look back, replying to the driver as she walked toward her house.

"This is less than my usual fee." The driver spoke up, concerned about the funds lacking in the envelope.

"The flight should be coming in later, and they will pay your full rate upon their return. We will need two trips from the airport this time." Miriam was now a few yards away from the driver, who looked confused and on the verge of anger.

Unbeknownst to Miriam, Isaac reached into his pocket and gave the driver an additional envelope. The driver quickly scanned the money, nodding approval to Isaac.

"Forgive Ms. Miriam. She was not aware that she would be responsible for the whole fee," Isaac calmly whispered.

"You have a nice day now, Ms. Miriam." The driver broke from his quiet exchange with Isaac, hoping that his near upset hadn't registered or created cause for Miriam to complain and have him replaced.

"You as well. Don't forget that the others will be needing the bus service when they arrive as well. Best to check with the supervisor at the airport about the time of the charter's arrival."

Miriam scanned the street and didn't see many neighbors. Most everywhere she looked there were numerous Herzlton Black support staff leisurely walking and working—finishing landscaping here, washing windows there, sweeping, and so on. Were it not so hot, Miriam may have thought the absence of her neighbors outside strange. But between the long travel to Uganda and the long bus ride home, Miriam wanted to take a nice bath and decompress. When Miriam turned around to continue up the walkway to her front door, she noticed a familiar face in the window box next door.

"Is that you, Ms. Mary?" Miriam placed her right hand above her head like a visor to block the sun.

Mary waved from the window box.

"Oh my! Is that Ms. Martha?!? I don't think I have seen you since I was a little girl! Come on out now." Miriam, joined by Isaac, gestured for Mary and Martha to come out of the house and say hello.

Mary and Martha stood on the porch, waving empty hellos. Due to her intense sweating, Miriam was unable to discern Martha's and Mary's disingenuous smiles.

"Ms. Martha, you are a sight for sore eyes. I'm sure Ms. Mary tells you how often I ask about you and how you are doing." Miriam waved and smiled as she spoke.

Neither Mary nor Martha spoke any words. They continued their smile-and-wave routine, hoping that Miriam would eventually go inside.

"It's pretty hot out today, Ms. Miriam. Maybe it might be good to get inside and unpack?" Isaac interrupted Miriam's growing gaze on Mary and Martha.

"Do you think Ms. Martha knows what happened to my father?" Miriam whispered to Isaac through her waving and smiling at Mary and Martha.

"I am not sure. Let's get inside and get these bags unpacked." Isaac's voice shifted from that of an attending assistant to more of a peer.

"Good seeing you both." Miriam turned and headed back into the house as she offered her final wave to Mary and Martha.

"Welcome home, Ms. Miriam." Mary's fake smiled nearly cracked as she gave Isaac a look of gratitude for whatever it was that he said that helped to distract and move Miriam along and into the house.

Miriam had been in the bath for a while before her mind began to race into memory recall. The soothing olive oil made her skin and emotions less prickly than when she arrived. She was very excited to see Isaac but hadn't spoken more than a few sentences to him since she came inside the house. Miriam quickly proceeded into the bathroom and began running her bath.

Miriam closed her eyes for much of the time in the bath in an effort to empty her mind of any negative thoughts and also of any anxieties she felt. It was her anxiety and anger that had gotten her into the situation she was currently in now. Several days into the Israel trip, she longed to be home in Herzlton, smelling the fragrant freshwater aroma of Lake Victoria. Miriam sensed something strange was going on. Miriam's first sign was that many of the people from her family and the community had personal items awaiting their arrival. Her mother had the beautiful vase that adorned their family room shipped and waiting for her in Jerusalem. When Miriam asked her mother why she'd shipped the vase, she waved her off and didn't answer. But that was not unusual for Miriam and her mother, who rarely ever, if at all, got along with one another. The youngest of four children, Miriam was her father's indisputable favorite, and everyone in the family knew it.

Miriam's next sign that something was awry arrived in the form of a conversation with Rachel, her childhood best friend. Over lunch, Miriam and Rachel commiserated about how much their families were getting on their nerves. After a few bites of their food, their conversation transitioned to future marriage and family plans. Those topics were not unusual on their own, as Miriam and Rachel spoke often about their dreams of a husband and raising a family. Different this time, however, was that Rachel revealed that she would be married in a week while the family was in Israel.

"You are getting married next week?" Miriam was shocked and her response so loud that it garnered the attention of the full restaurant.

"Please, Miriam. You are causing a scene!" Rachel admonished Miriam, whose face shifted from surprise to betrayal.

"How could you keep something like this from me? And to whom, by the way? You aren't dating anyone." Miriam tried to recover from her bruised ego, shifting the attention back to Rachel's violation of their sisterhood-like friendship.

"It was a surprise to me too, for the most part. I am embarrassed by it, and so I just couldn't bring myself to tell you." Rachel confessed.

"Embarrassed? I don't understand." Miriam was intrigued.

"My family arranged for me to get married during this trip to a man I have never met." Rachel's voice trembled.

"Arranged? What's this all about?" Miriam had more questions even as Rachel seemed to be offering answers.

"I am not sure how this all started. It is my understanding that practically all of the founding families planned over the last year to secure a place in Israel, especially once President Amin began fighting with Tanzania and enlisting mercenaries to assist him. That's what this trip is really about. I thought you knew at least that much, given your father's plan to be buried in Israel earlier this year."

"Pardon me if I am not following or seeing the connection between my dead father and your arranged marriage." Miriam took exception to Rachel's mentioning of her beloved father who'd died at the top of the year.

"Since that agreement between Egypt and Israel, almost all of the founding families met and determined whether or not they will stay in Herzlton. Many believe that there is no need for Herzlton anymore, especially when the original Jerusalem has been secured and returned to the Jewish people." Rachel's voice was no longer trembling with embarrassment but rather that of the tone she used with her pupils at Herzlton Academy.

"Wait! So am I the only person who doesn't know about any of this? People are planning to stay here and not go back?!?" Miriam's growing impatience was matched by her feelings of betrayal and outsiderness upon hearing this new information.

"I thought you knew. In fact, I thought everyone knew. It was your father who really started the idea of leaving Herzlton. Given how close you two were, I figured he had told you or at least planned to tell you before he died."

"He didn't! He didn't!" Miriam's tone bordered on rage.

"I am sorry, Miriam. If I had known you hadn't been told, I would have told you. I wonder why your family has been keeping it from you. Is there something going on? Some issue that you and your family are having that might explain why you were being kept in the dark?" Rachel's sincerity and compassion were clear to Miriam.

Miriam, however, had no intentions of revealing anything at this lunch, especially about the existing family turmoil. "I am not sure. Maybe everyone just thought that I would want to be near where my father was buried instead of back in Africa." Miriam spoke with a straight face, hoping to avoid further inquiry from Rachel.

"Samuel Meyerson," Rachel responded without any hesitation.

"Who? What?" Miriam was confused.

"That's his name. The name of the man I will be marrying next week." Rachel spoke matter-of-factly.

Miriam couldn't hide the surprise on her face, nor could she hide feeling blindsided.

"So that's it. I guess I should thank you for at least telling me. But then I don't think you planned to." Miriam's betrayal rose to open aggression toward Rachel.

"Look, Miriam. I understand how you feel. No one discussed anything with me either. I only learned of whatever I know because of my parents' plan to marry me to Samuel, which they set up when we were all last here for your father's shiva last summer. With the ongoing turmoil in Uganda and the involvement of the Israeli government to free the hostages at Entebbe Airport in January, many think it is time to abandon Herzlton. The founders all have their own plans, and the children are expected to follow and be obedient." Rachel was trying to empathize by revealing her own sense of betrayal and lack of agency in the plans.

"We are the same age, so has my mother married me off to some man here in Israel too?" Miriam was both snarky and concerned.

"I would imagine that you would know that. All the last children of the founders received notice during the summer in Israel from our future husbands or wives. You haven't received any letters?" Rachel was suspicious.

"I haven't gotten any letters, let alone a letter of marriage, marriage request, or marriage arrangement. In fact, I just thought we were back in

Israel to visit some new family that had recently arrived from America." Miriam reserved her anger for her mother, whom she planned to confront immediately.

"Unfortunately, Miriam, that's all I know. I can tell you that I am pretty sure that your sisters are likely planning to stay and not return to Herzlton." Rachel offered this last tidbit with the hopes of salvaging whatever remained of her longest friendship.

Miriam wondered what skeletons in her own closet were known that would cause her alienation from the community's plans to leave Uganda. Rather than share more with Rachel, Miriam just nodded her head. Miriam smiled to offer some relief to her friend with whom she now knew she was sharing the last lunch of their twenty-five-year friendship.

"Miriam, I love you like a sister. I cannot imagine going through with this marriage without you being by my side. That is why I needed to have lunch with you today. When I told my mother that I wanted you at the wedding, she told me that she was not sure if that would be appropriate. I was confused and made it a point to just come clean with you about this arrangement that I hadn't shared, even though we have always told each other everything." Rachel began crying uncontrollably.

Miriam pushed her chair back and walked around the table to console her. Miriam left money on the table and lifted Rachel from the chair, then they walked hand in hand out of the restaurant.

The memory of the lunch made Miriam feel nauseous as she opened her eyes and moved the bubbles from the middle of the bathtub underneath her chin. Recalling her lunch with Rachel brought about more anxiety and sadness, as the rest of her trip in Israel had all been downhill from there. The argument with her mother echoed and rang in the back of her mind as the bubbles began melting underneath her chin. Hoping to wash it all away, Miriam pulled air into her lungs and lowered herself into the bathwater until her face was fully covered. The water, which splashed as she lowered herself, rose to the brim of the tub, some of the water spilling over the side in a puddle that slowly moved in a stream underneath the bathroom door.

After a few seconds under the water, Miriam closed her eyes again and began searching her memories for her father's face. A tall and steady force, Miriam's father had always been the one who understood her and offered her patience. In a family of four children, being the last born always made Miriam feel like she was also always the last to find out things. Miriam also felt an intense competition over her father's affection and attention with her mother. For most of her life, Miriam was unaware as to why her mother chose her of her three other sisters to be the one in such stiff competition. It wasn't until the summer of her father's death and burial that answers regarding her rivalry with her mother surfaced. As everyone gathered and shared reflections and fond memories of her father, Miriam became overwhelmed by the sheer grief of losing her father, feeling a great sorrow rising up inside of her. Unaware that the sorrow had already manifested into tears rolling down her face, Miriam was initially confused by all of the hugs and back rubs that came racing in her direction. And while she hadn't timed her outburst, Miriam's mother spoke as her emotions poured out in front of everyone. In response to Miriam's actions making her the center of attention, her mother spoke words she immediately regretted but couldn't take back.

"Miriam, everyone has lost him. Not just you! You have always been such a self-involved child. I'd hoped that his loss might bring us closer and help me understand why he had been so insistent on having another child, especially knowing I was done with having children."

Everyone gasped after Miriam's mother spoke these words. Miriam jumped up and looked at her mother with eyes sharpened like daggers. But rather than saying any words, Miriam pulled air from deep inside her gut and screamed. She screamed so loudly that everyone, including her mother, covered their ears. The two didn't speak much, even after they arrived back in Herzlton a few weeks later. In fact, the second trip to Israel had been the first time Miriam and her mother had spoken in any meaningful way since.

Miriam began counting down from one hundred as she floated just beneath the surface of the bathwater, hoping that the descending numbers would quiet her mind. But as Miriam counted, an inkling of intuition churned. As she counted down, Miriam decided to lean into her intuition and allow events to replay, figuring there was some purpose to it all.

A pristine image of her father came to the forefront of her mind. Miriam saw his white beard and brown eyes; she saw his smile and the creases at the ends of his nostrils.

As Miriam sat upright, more water spilled over the tub and crept underneath the bathroom door. Her father's presence made Miriam feel at ease for the first time since he had died. Miriam felt an inner peace with her decision to leave ahead of everyone and skip the charter flight in favor of a commercial flight that had two different layovers, believing that it was the house that had brought him to her.

A sudden knocking at the door made Miriam jump, causing more water to splatter to the floor, the puddle now becoming a pool that was seeping out underneath the door.

"Everything okay in there?" Isaac's deep voice pulsed through the door.

Miriam didn't immediately speak back, gathering herself and her thoughts.

"Everything okay in there?!?" Isaac's voice grew louder as he began to twist and turn the bathroom doorknob.

"Yes. Yes. I am fine." Miriam's voice was scratchy but confident.

"What was that? I couldn't hear you," Isaac spoke back while still twisting the knob.

Miriam jumped from the bath and grabbed the towel hanging over the sink. She slid toward the door, unlocking it and nearly falling in the pool of water on the floor.

"Everything is okay." Miriam cracked the door open and peeked out.

Isaac stood back to provide a respectful distance from the door and turned his gaze away so as not to appear to be staring at Miriam.

"You've been in there over an hour, and there is water all on the floor." Isaac pointed at the water-soaked floor.

"Place a towel down so that the water doesn't damage the floor. I don't need my mother barking at me about another thing!" Miriam shut the door and pulled the drain plug from the tub. As the water made its loud gurgling sound down the drain, Miriam looked at her body in the vanity while drying her hair. Miriam was nearly lost again in thought when her stomach began to ache and twist and turn, and she found herself kneeling before the toilet vomiting.

Isaac was asleep on the sofa by the time Miriam had refreshed and composed herself. Watching Isaac sleep, Miriam observed his face with the intensity of a scientist. Miriam watched as Isaac's eyelids fluttered and his cheeks filled and released air. Isaac's smooth skin seemed to shine even when he was asleep, which greatly amazed Miriam. Soon enough, Miriam was standing before him, watching Isaac's fluttering eyelids with loving amazement. She then sat beside Isaac for a few minutes, following the rhythm of his breathing pattern.

Next to Isaac, Miriam felt safe. She had been so uneasy for so many weeks, and the feeling itself was intoxicating and soothing. Miriam laid her head against Isaac's shoulder and neck. When he awoke, Isaac smiled and kissed Miriam on her forehead.

"I missed you." Isaac's ever more soothing baritone voice vibrated over Miriam's body.

"I missed you too." Miriam looked up at Isaac with romantic vulnerability.

"How was the trip? Did you get to see your father's headstone?" Isaac asked with a kind inquisitiveness.

"The trip was terrible. I did see the headstone, but that was the beginning and end of the highlight of the trip for me," Miriam confessed.

"Oh no! What could have gone so terribly wrong?" Isaac turned to Miriam.

"I don't think everyone is going to come back home. Rachel told me most of the families planned to stay in Israel." Miriam looked for the surprise and shock on Isaac's face as she revealed what was for her a bombshell revelation.

"Ahh. I see." Isaac was unmoved by the information.

"Why aren't you surprised? I certainly was!" Miriam was suspicious.

"I am not surprised by the information. I am surprised that you are surprised," Isaac remarked.

"Why wouldn't I be surprised that the community planned to abandon the place where I was born and raised? Wouldn't you be surprised if your cousin Idi and your family suddenly revealed to you they would be leaving Uganda for pyramids in Egypt?" Miriam was offended.

"That would be a surprise mostly because Uganda is our home. This is the land of my people. Leaving feels like exiting the womb without being fully formed." Isaac's tone was serious and stern.

Miriam rubbed her arms and then her stomach as she processed Isaac's womb metaphor. "What does that mean, Isaac? I don't follow."

"It means, it is not surprising that white people would want to abandon Africa. That is what white people have been doing throughout Africa for quite some time. And to be clear, Africans abandoning Africa is a very different case than what you are describing." Isaac spoke confidently.

"But I was born in Uganda. And so was Rachel. And so were my siblings and all of the young people in Herzlton." Miriam was indignant.

"So are you saying you are Ugandan? Are you saying you are African?" Isaac was not amused by Miriam's conflation of her birthplace with his.

"I am saying that this is home. Israel is a home of sorts, but it is not where I was born. I was born here. Raised here. And I don't think I want to leave just yet, if at all." Miriam's tone shifted to one of graciousness, noticing that her words had offended Isaac's not-easily-offended sensibilities.

"You had to know that at some point this may come to pass. The community was formed and started by Zionists. Why would they continue in a New Jerusalem now that the Americans have helped negotiate peace and acknowledgment for Israel?" Isaac inquired.

"Because seventy-five years is a long time. I understood my father wanting to be buried there, but leaving all that we have built behind to be in a place that is destined to be in a continuous battle is not appealing to me." Miriam hoped sharing her true feelings might ease the mounting tension.

"And you don't think that Herzlton is not a site of continuous battle? Well, I am sorry to be the bearer of bad news, but from the beginning, this place has been very contentious. There have been stories, moves, and rumors for decades of the Ugandan government and military taking Herzlton back. If it weren't for the money that the community pays the government, this place you call home would have been gone." Isaac noticed Miriam's astonishment.

"Really?!?" Miriam's eyes widened until they appeared stuck open.

"Yes. Really! The land that was given was also land that was taken. And when land is given and taken, those who originally possessed it will always long for its return. Their history and their culture and their blood are in the land. Herzlton is really a name for a corrupt deal made with white people to make money. That's what many of US think when we hear Herzlton." Isaac could tell that Miriam had never thought of her community and the land that was Herzlton in this manner.

"So everyone really is leaving?" Miriam recognized the sobering reality.

"I am not sure. But I do know many of the families have been selling off furniture for months. Others even signed over the deeds to their helpers. Some others have created a leasing agreement with their helpers. Your friend Rachel's family . . ."

"Yes, what about Rachel's family?"

"That house is completely empty. You didn't recognize any of the furniture in Israel was the same as what was in the house?" Isaac queried.

Miriam hadn't thought much about the surroundings of Rachel's home in Israel, preoccupied as she was with the arranged marriage and wedding that occurred a few days after their revelatory lunch.

"Now that you mention it, I do remember the fine china dishes used for the wedding were the ones that the family kept on display in the cabinet in their dining room here." Miriam felt pieces of a puzzle that had once confused her coming together.

"I have been assuming that you were clear about staying, and so no one really included you in the schemes of leaving." Isaac admitted.

"Really? You knew then!" Miriam, feeling relieved of the long-standing confusion, was now invested in getting to the bottom of this plot whereby she was an outsider.

"Yes. When your mother and the rest of your family said 'Goodbye' to me, I felt the finality in their voices. I saw in their eyes they would not be returning. In the weeks since the community left for Israel, the newspapers have been speculating that Herzlton was sold to the military, and that all the Jewish people who left Uganda were planning to stay in Israel now that the peace agreement with Egypt was fully implemented."

"Hmmph, I do not plan to leave anytime soon." Miriam's sense of entitlement matched her crossed-arm defiance.

3:00 P.M.–4:00 P.M.

"Entebbe International Airport, Charter Division. This is Aaron. How may I assist you?" Aaron answered the phone at the first ring.

"This is Captain Jones of the charter flight from Israel to Entebbe. We are awaiting and requesting permission to land in Entebbe." The captain was noticeably frustrated.

"I am sorry, but I do not have the authority to provide that permission. I will need to call the appropriate government office." Aaron was nervous, and his anxiety made his voice raise. He thought he was whispering. However, he was loud, and anyone in the terminal could easily hear him. Hearing his voice echo, Aaron looked around the relatively empty terminal and noticed he and a new security guard were alone in the terminal. Aaron took a breath to release his nerves and return to a professional tone.

"That is unacceptable. We have been delayed already and were supposed to have landed this morning. We have twenty-six people on board all with Ugandan citizenship and passports! We cannot stay in a holding pattern for too long! Do you understand?!?" The captain's forceful impatience sent chills down Aaron's spine.

"I understand, Ssebo. I had a woman arrive earlier who made an inquiry about the flight. Our system showed that it had been rescheduled. Per our policy, I placed a call to the government office that oversees air travel and international relations. I was told that they would be back in touch within the hour." Aaron offered extra assurance.

"Within the hour! We are supposed to land at sixteen hundred! What is going on over there? We have never had this problem! Your people are the ones who gave the green light to depart a few hours ago, and now we don't have permission to land? Get to the bottom of this! Now! My copilot will be looking for the dispatched signal permitting us to land within the hour." The phone made a few clicking sounds before going dead.

Aaron paced from side to side, trying to figure out what to do. He was terribly afraid of what would happen if the flight landed without being cleared. Aaron knew that no matter how and why the plane landed, as the terminal and division supervisor, he would be held accountable. Sure that such an ordeal would rise to a high penalty and land him in jail, Aaron began to think about his wife and children waiting for him at home. He channeled their faces for encouragement and strength. As Aaron thought fondly of his family, the new security guard was excitedly walking in his direction.

To avoid the security guard's involvement, Aaron composed himself quickly, smiled, and waved to give the appearance that all was well. The security guard waved back, returning to his station and detail. Aaron scrolled the phone directory for the contact number that he called earlier. He wrestled back and forth in his mind, contemplating whether or not he should call again. Just as he was about to lift the phone, it began ringing. Aaron's heart jumped at the sudden ringing of the phone. He let it ring a few times to allow his heartbeat to slow and to catch his breath so that when he answered he sounded as professional as possible.

"Entebbe International Airport, Charter Division. This is Aaron. How may I assist you?" Aaron's tone had an undercurrent of hope as he awaited the sound of the voice on the other end, presuming that it would be a government official. When Aaron heard the voice on the other end, however, he became even more flustered.

"Yes. This is Miriam Hoffman. I inquired about the status of the charter from Israel this morning." Miriam was on the other end with an innocent enough inquiry, although her timing only applied more pressure on Aaron.

"Yes, ma'am. I was planning to call you a little later once I had the necessary confirmations."

"And do you?"

"Not necessarily, ma'am."

"Not necessarily?" Miriam parroted Aaron's response as a sign of her rising annoyance.

"I can confirm the charter flight from Israel bound for Entebbe is up in the air."

"Okay. And what is the arrival time?"

"I cannot as yet confirm that. I can confirm that the flight . . ."

"You can confirm that the flight has left and is in the air but not when it will land? Israel is not that far away!" Miriam's impatience was clear.

"Nyabo, ma'am, please give me a little more time. I have spoken with the captain of the flight, and I am awaiting the call from the authorities with the code that will permit the flight to land. This is standard protocol. No flights are allowed to land without an authorized code. I understand this is terribly frustrating, but I also do not want to miss the call by tying up this phone line." Aaron dug deep and pulled from the well of his most professional confidence.

"I see. Yes. Well, I will leave you to it. I definitely don't want the phone line tied up. You will call as soon as you have the confirmation? Yes?" Miriam was more understanding and cooperative.

"Yes, ma'am. I certainly will. You can expect to hear from me within the hour." Aaron spoke with an assurance he really didn't have.

"Thank you." Miriam hung up.

As Aaron hung up the phone, his anxiety reached new heights. Sweat droplets fell from his forehead and rolled down his nose onto the counter. Aaron looked back at the phone directory to locate the number again, this time determined to call and get some answers. He couldn't allow himself to be the punching bag for these people calling about a flight over which he had no power.

To avoid having to search through the directory again, Aaron wrote the number down on a small piece of paper just in case he would need to call repeatedly until an answer arrived. Just as Aaron finished writing the last digit of the phone number on the small piece of paper, the phone rang again.

"Entebbe International Airport, Charter Division. This is Aaron. How may I assist you?" Upon hearing the voice on the other end, Aaron was immediately shaken upright, his posture shifting to one of great deference and surprise.

"Is this the Charter Division supervisor?" The woman's voice responded back. "I have President Amin on the line. I am patching him through now."

"Yes, Nyabo." Aaron was dutiful while also extremely afraid.

"Thank you, Grace. Aaron?"

"Yes, Mr. President. I am here." Aaron was both scared and impressed.

"You will receive a code shortly that will authorize the charter to land. It is important that upon landing, the passengers are delayed."

"Delayed?" Aaron asked, sounding both fearful and befuddled.

"Yes. They mustn't board the Herzlton bus until after six this evening. This is a matter of national security and in service of your country! Is that something that you can accomplish?"

"Yes, Ssebo . . . Yes, Mr. President. I will make sure that we slow down their exit from the plane and receiving their bags from stowage. That will certainly take up a significant amount of time."

"Grace, are you there still?"

"Yes, Mr. President. Ssebo, I am still on the line."

"Get that code over to Aaron. Good day, Aaron, and thank you for your service!"

"Thank you, Mr. President!" Aaron wasn't sure what he'd agreed to nor the intention behind delaying the plane and passengers. Aaron was just happy to know that the plane would be landing soon and that he would soon be getting Miriam off his back, off his phone.

"Aaron are you there?" Grace asked with a robotic tone.

"Yes, ma'am. I am here."

"Give Air Traffic Control the code 808DNAL. They will report that to the pilots on the flight, and that will permit them to land." Grace's robotic tone felt like speaking with a machine and not a person.

"Yes, ma'am. Code 808DNAL. Anything else I should . . ."

The phone clicked off abruptly as Aaron asked his question.

"Hello . . . Hello?" Aaron asked puzzled, pulling the phone away from his ear and examining it with his eyes.

Aaron hung up the phone and wrote down 808DNAL on the small piece of paper underneath the number he'd previously written down.

The phone rang again.

"Entebbe International Airport, Charter Division. This is Aaron. How may I assist you?"

"Air Traffic Control here. Calling for the landing code for charter flight 242 from Tel Aviv to Entebbe."

"Yes. It's 808DNAL. Code number 808DNAL." Aaron could hear the typing and other voices in the background sounding as though they were guiding and communicating with other flights in the air.

"Code 808DNAL has been inputted and is now being relayed to the captain and copilot. Estimated time of arrival is at seventeen hundred zero seven."

"Okay. I have the time of arrival as one–seven–zero–seven."

"Correct." The operator hung up.

4:00 P.M.–5:00 P.M.

Clearly agitated, Miriam paced back and forth.

"Aren't you hungry? You should have something to eat. I placed some leftover pot roast in the oven for you to eat. Eat something." Isaac tried his best to calm and redirect Miriam's energies. But Miriam paced back and forth as though she couldn't and didn't want to hear Isaac's advice. Miriam had been this way since getting off the phone with the supervisor at the airport, and as time continued to pass with no new information or confirmation, she was growing more and more worried.

"The supervisor said that the flight was up in the air. That means it will land soon. I am sure that everything will be okay." Isaac kept speaking in an attempt to latch onto the train of thought he saw passing through Miriam's mind.

"This is all strange. I suspect the government is involved. I know you will think I am a conspiracy theorist for saying that, but that's what I feel deep in my bones. Until the last few years, the government has been very accommodating and even encouraged a relationship between Herzlton and Israel. It was the community that didn't feel it wise to leave. Now when we do leave, the plane is suddenly rescheduled with no arrival time. People have leased and sold a strange, hidden agenda. What is going on, Isaac?" Miriam stopped mid-pace and looked directly and demandingly at Isaac.

Isaac was half listening to Miriam as she meandered and hadn't recognized that she was indeed questioning him directly. "I know as much as you do, Miriam."

Isaac's response was unconvincing. "Hmmph. We already know that's not true. You knew about the fact that many in the community were planning to never come back. I didn't. You are also the head of security for Herzlton. My father specifically chose you because of your perceptive intelligence and also because you are the president's first cousin. And this has his name written all over it. Ever since he has gotten into bed with that Gaddafi, there has been a target on my community's back." Miriam, who tended to keep her political beliefs to herself, was now revealing just how deeply she believed that the Ugandan government was untrustworthy after so many years of supporting the community and their cause.

"Whoa . . . Whoa! Let's not get carried away here. This community has been here for seventy-five years, and that would not be possible if there was no support from the government."

"Yeah, I can only imagine how much the government loves receiving those checks every month. Just before he died, my father confessed to me that the community was pulling twenty-five thousand dollars from the vault every year in payment to the government!" Miriam was self-righteous and sarcastic.

"What exactly is the point of this? Getting yourself into a rage or continuing to be upset is not going to make the plane land or arrive faster. And also, didn't you say that you went ahead and left before everyone? If you cared so much, why aren't you on the plane with the 'community'?" Isaac was feeling verbally assaulted by Miriam and decided it was time that he gave Miriam as good as she was dishing out.

"I left because . . . because . . . because . . ."

"Because why? Because what?"

"Because . . . because of you." Miriam felt herself becoming light-headed and collapsed to the floor.

Isaac, who had been upset by her continued shouting and insinuations, had his back turned to Miriam and hadn't realized she had fallen to the ground. Isaac turned and was terrified by the sight of Miriam unconscious on the floor. Isaac lifted Miriam, carrying her from the family room to her bedroom down the hallway. Although Isaac had unpacked Miriam's bags and placed the items back into the closet, the white envelope with her name on it he'd found inside her luggage earlier was atop the pillow. Isaac laid Miriam down, brushing the letter aside. After placing Miriam on the bed, Isaac rushed into the kitchen. Isaac grabbed a drying towel and ran hot water over it, warming the towel with the hot sink water. Isaac returned to Miriam's bedroom and placed the towel on her head.

"I told you, you needed to eat something and calm down," Isaac spoke his frustration aloud. Isaac checked Miriam's pulse, which seemed to be beating with normal regularity. Isaac stood over Miriam, hoping that her eyes would open and that she would awake. But after several minutes of watching as Miriam lay with her eyes closed and little movement, Isaac took a seat along the wall to observe her. Isaac was full of regrets as he tried to chase the increasing worries about Miriam from his mind. Isaac plucked his temple, self-induced punishment for his lack of recognition of Miriam's agitation as a sign that he should have heeded.

Eventually, Miriam's chest began to rise and fall with air and a calmness that assured Isaac that she would recover just fine. Now, sure that Miriam would recover from her fainting spell, Isaac racked his mind to think of what he could do to get answers about the flight and also figure out who, if anyone, was returning. While Isaac was fully aware that Miriam's family had no intentions of returning, he wasn't exactly sure of the current status of the rest of the community—only a few of the families stayed behind when everyone left for Israel. Considering all his options, Isaac knew it was time he made a few calls and checked in with the Herzlton security team. Isaac stood up and looked over Miriam once more before exiting the bedroom.

5:00 P.M.–5:30 P.M.

Martha prayed nonstop in her room after lunch. She battled feelings of unease after seeing the shuttle and Miriam arriving in Herzlton. At the time, Martha did her best to keep quiet as she and Mary washed the dishes. She even pretended to be happy while she played with her grandchildren, watching some children's programs on the television. When Daniel asked if everything was okay and if she was feeling better, Martha even lied to avoid his inquiry. Rather than tell him the truth that she was worried something bad was on the way, Martha smiled and said that she was just feeling "blessed." Meanwhile, Martha modulated between severe fear and nervousness.

Almost three decades after her retirement, Martha couldn't believe how Herzlton was unchanged. The cabinets, floors, windows, rooms—everything was as she last remembered it. Even the wallpaper that depicted stags in the forest was the same. The whole thing felt eerie. Martha knew she had to tell Mary what had been on her heart since the news about the deed transfer. Martha also regretted that she neglected to visit Mr. Hoffman before he died. As she kneeled by the bed she used to make, Martha felt tremendously guilty that she hadn't come the previous summer to see him off to Israel and was now living in the home.

Martha scanned the room and remembered the young children once had bunk beds in the room and how she would read them bedtime stories. She could see her younger self sitting in the rocking chair and reading the fables of her childhood until the children's eyes closed and their breathing went deep and grew loud into snores. The rocking chair was still in the same exact place, angled as though it had been waiting for her return. Martha felt haunted by the ghost of her former self in the room. Martha couldn't even remember much of the events of the day because the events of the past kept bullying their way forward.

Unable to beat the past back into submission in her subconscious, Martha pulled out her well-worn Bible. Unsure where to start or what scripture would assist her in easing her nerves and fear, Martha decided that wherever the book opened would be the place where her message lay. She placed the Bible onto the mattress, closed her eyes, and then opened the book. When Martha opened her eyes and saw that the Bible had opened to the book of Revelation, chapter twenty-one, all her fears were confirmed. Thinking to herself, *This is the end*, Martha pushed the Bible to the side and closed it. She stood before the rocking chair, which looked to be slightly swaying without anyone sitting in it.

Martha began reciting the Lord's Prayer.

"Our father who art in Heaven, hallowed be thy name. Thy kingdom come. Thy will be done. On Earth, as it is in Heaven. Give us this day our daily bread. And forgive us our trespasses as we forgive those who trespass against us. And lead us not into temptation, but deliver us from evil. For thine is the kingdom and the power and the glory. Forever. Amen."

As Martha recited the prayer, she felt a sense of relief. And so Martha recited it again and again. Martha recited the prayer over and over until she was chanting one long divine harmony, rolling and twisting and twirling her tongue as her head rocked back and forth.

"I see you! And you cannot have me or this family. I rebuke you!" Martha moved with the seriousness of an exorcist as she went to her purse and grabbed the holy water she kept with her at all times. She poured the water into her hands and began splashing and sprinkling it about the room. Martha flicked water from her hands onto the walls and then the bed. Last but not least, Martha saved the remainder for the seemingly possessed rocking chair. After rubbing her wet hands up and down the wooden arms and legs of the chair, she flicked water across the seat.

"Now be gone!" Martha commanded the presence she felt occupying the room. Opening the window, Martha moved her hands to guide the unwanted energy out the window. By the end of the process, Martha was both breathless and feeling accomplished.

Martha pulled the rocking chair to the open window and took a seat. She grabbed the Bible from the bed and opened it. She began reading the New Testament's beginning aloud, planning to return to the serendipitous Revelation passage afterward.

"The book of the genealogy of Jesus Christ, the Son of David, the Son of Abraham: Abraham begot Isaac, Isaac begot Jacob, and Jacob begot Judah and his brothers . . ."

An ongoing conversation from the neighbor's house managed to disrupt Martha's flow. Fully distracted, Martha looked up from her Bible and peered out the window. Martha noticed it was Isaac on the phone having a very intense conversation. The phone cord was stretching and contracting as Isaac paced back and forth, his face grimaced. Martha could make out most everything Isaac said, and even though she couldn't hear what was being said on the other side of the phone call, she discerned the telephone call's importance from Isaac's body language and tone.

"Cousin, what do you mean Kampala has been taken?!? You must help protect us!" Isaac stammered.

A sudden cough rumbled up through her chest and released itself without permission. Martha ducked before Isaac turned around to determine the source of the cough. Martha stayed on the floor and kept quiet. As she heard the window next door shut, Martha took a deep sigh of relief, hoping that her actions had gone unnoticed.

5:30 P.M.–6:00 P.M.

Miriam popped upright as if awakened from a coffin. Unaware and unsure of how she had gotten onto the bed and in her room, Miriam placed her fingers at her temples and tried to remember. The faint smell of olive oil on her wrists brought back memories of the bathtub, and after a few minutes, Miriam surmised that she must have passed out. She instantly felt embarrassed.

As the disorienting feeling wore off, Miriam stretched forward to relieve some of the pain in her neck that must have come as a result of collapsing to the floor. Miriam had hoped that the fainting spells would have stopped by now. As it was, Miriam had been hiding them for nearly two months by the time her mother witnessed one during a heated exchange in Israel. Miriam rolled her head around in a circular motion. She then placed her feet on the floor and attempted to stand. When she placed her weight on her feet to prepare to stand, her legs were wobbly. Attempting to push through her unsteady legs, Miriam pulled her strength into her spine to stand tall.

The effort proved unsuccessful, and her body responded to her attempts by throbbing with pain and returning the wooziness behind her eyes, swirling around in her head, and producing a brain fog. Her stomach churned and vibrated with a longing that required Miriam's hands to rub and soothe it.

Miriam took a few deep breaths and wiggled herself to the center of the queen-size bed. Once at the center, Miriam stretched her hands out and folded her legs in a semi-yogi-style pose. Miriam inhaled and exhaled several times until she felt the fogginess that had captured her brain relinquish its hold. When her right hand traveled toward the end of the mattress, she felt an envelope that she hadn't noticed was present and nearby. As soon as Miriam saw the looping vowels of her name in the cursive font, she knew exactly who had written the letter. Not sure when and why her mother had written her a letter, Miriam slid her right index finger underneath the open corner of the sealed envelope. The seal broke but not before extracting a little blood from a papercut.

A few drops of blood plopped onto the back of the envelope, raising two circular stains on the pristine white paper. Miriam sucked on the thin cut on her index finger as she pulled the letter out. Miriam immediately noticed the date: *April 10, 1979*. Miriam smirked, thinking about her mother's cunning having placed the letter in her luggage the night before her departure. Miriam thought that her decision to leave before the charter would have been a surprise, only to find that apparently her mother had already figured out and anticipated her plan. At first glance, Miriam didn't see any words that necessarily seemed important. But when her quick skim landed at the letter's closing that didn't say "love you" or "always" or any other generic shorthand for how a caring mother might end a note to her child, Miriam was shocked. The letter ended with the phrase: "Goodbye, Miriam."

Miriam went back to the beginning of the letter and began reading it. From the first sentence until the last one, Miriam felt outwitted, outmatched, and excommunicated all in one fell swoop. Miriam lifted herself from the bed and headed into the family room to reveal her brokenheartedness to Isaac.

As Miriam exited her bedroom, she could hear that Isaac was on the phone. His muffled voice sounded serious. Miriam could hear from the tenor of Isaac's voice that the conversation was not meant to be known to her. Once Miriam was a few feet away, a hot breeze swept through the open window and reached a door in the house that shut with abrupt and noticeable vigor.

"What money? Promise me you will keep us safe. Please don't let them come here . . . Hello? Hello!" Isaac pleaded.

"Who was that?" Miriam asked Isaac whose back was turned to her.

Isaac had been so engrossed in his phone conversation that Miriam's presence had gone unnoticed. "What was in that letter? I found it when I unpacked your luggage," Isaac sidestepped Miriam's inquiry. His approach was successful, as Miriam didn't ask again about the phone call. Instead, Miriam burst into tears, sobbing uncontrollably. Afraid that she might faint again, Isaac guided Miriam to a chair at the kitchen table. Once Miriam was seated at the table, she handed him the tear-stained letter.

"Read it. Just read it, Isaac." A dejected Miriam wiped her face with fresh tissues.

As Isaac read the letter, Miriam watched his face. She watched the lines in his forehead appear and disappear, rise up and fall down. She watched Isaac's eyes open wider and wider as he read the letter, his chest filling with air as he held his breath while reading. Miriam watched and peered, awaiting a sure sign that Isaac had fully read the letter, but his gaze was steady on the letter. As Isaac's chest released the air he had been holding, Miriam prepared to speak. Before she could do so, Isaac read the letter aloud:

Dear Daughter,

This letter shall mark our last communication. For twenty-five years, we have been at each other's throats. At first, I believed that our conflict resided in our mutual love of your father. Where the other children were loved by him, you were beloved. And I can acknowledge now that I resented him and you for it. I never told you (and I don't believe your father did either), but you were the child that he wanted, not me. Yes, I was the one who was pregnant. And yes, I know that as your mother it was ultimately my decision to bring you into the world. But in truth, it was your father that truly wanted you and brought your being to life. Our marriage was an ordeal, and many painful secrets and terrible indiscretions were buried with his body in the cemetery. I thought when he died that I would feel released from him, from the anger and resentment I held against my own daughter. But even months later, the feelings have not disappeared. Instead, they are in my bones and scorched across my broken heart. You must know that it is not that I don't love you. It is that your life was unable to repair the damage your father did to my heart many years before you were born. I never really wanted to leave England to start Herzlton nor did I really find it to be the New Jerusalem that everyone promised. Instead, I felt forsaken and sent away. I felt I had given up my whole life and the community that I had been born and raised in to chase men's dreams, men who cared more about being in control and having power than the true point of a homeland. I envy you. You have always loved living in Herzlton, and you seemed to get the whole idea of it in a way I was never able to. Your sisters understand and feel as I do. We each felt released from the purgatory of Herzlton even as you fussed and argued about returning. I thought when you arrived in Israel, your feelings would shift. I thought you would see that there is no replacement for a true home. That you would see that Herzlton was just an attempt to replace home. But you didn't. Instead, you fought back. You argued and you seemed determined to not only return to Herzlton but to live there for all of your days. This confused me. Were you choosing Herzlton because you knew how much I despised it? Did your father tell you the truth, and you wanted to explore what that meant? These are the questions I have asked myself. It occurred to me that maybe none of this was about your father or some high-minded vision or understanding of home. What if it was something else altogether? I know that you are pregnant. And I suspect that it is Isaac's. And I have decided the humiliation and embarrassment ends here and now, with you and with me. You are just like your father. We cannot allow our family to be corrupted any further. You will find the deed in the safe has been turned over to you as have any other family items we have left behind.

Goodbye, Miriam.

Isaac was exasperated and stunned. He searched Miriam's face for some sign that would confirm that the letter was untrue or false in some nature.

"I'm pregnant. And she is right. It's yours. I don't know how she knew. I am pregnant, and you are the father." Miriam's voice was firm and her posture assured.

6:00 P.M.–7:00 P.M.

Aaron was down to the last passport. He had stalled as long as he could, reading each name aloud to himself and reviewing it against the government watch list he was given ahead of the flight's arrival. The captain and copilot were becoming increasingly annoyed as Aaron pretended to be moving with urgency. The plane was significantly empty when Aaron climbed aboard. Besides the captain, copilot, and two flight attendants, there were just twenty-six people on the flight. Among the twenty-six passengers, there were only two men.

With so few people aboard and the flight landing at a quarter past five, Aaron knew that making the delay requested by the government would not be easy, especially if he wanted to escape any suspicion. Putting his customer service skills on full display, Aaron was extremely kind and pleasant. He walked to each row, greeted the passengers, and then asked for their passports. As he worked his way through the small group, he observed that all of those on the flight were all under the age of forty. This meant that they were either dual citizens or actually Ugandan citizens with a Ugandan passport.

The fact of the passengers' Ugandan citizenship made the prolonged and detailed check of the passports even more dubious, requiring Aaron to slide in a few passing jokes to keep impatience and doubts low. By the time Aaron got to the last passenger, both the captain and copilot gazed at him intensely, their faces screwed and patience worn thin.

"Last but certainly not least, Ms. Rachel Kochanski. It says here in the register that you left to get married in Israel?" Aaron asked studiously, looking back at Rachel for an answer.

Of all of the passengers, Rachel was the first who had any paperwork discrepancy. Aaron knew that this discrepancy was just what he needed to delay until the instructed time. When Aaron queried Rachel and then double-checked with a person over the walky-talky, there was a unified and audible sigh of frustration and disappointment from all on board. Rather than be directed at Aaron, discontent was aimed at Rachel, who cowered as she was asked the whereabouts of her husband and pertinent details regarding the marriage.

"Is your husband aboard?"

"No."

"Will he be joining you in Uganda at a later date?"

"No."

"You will please forgive me, but it is the protocol that I ask these questions. Are you quite sure he will not be coming to Uganda? Not even at a later date?"

"No. He will not."

"I see. I will need to report this over to dispatch so that the appropriate authorities are aware. What is your married name, ma'am?" Aaron queried as he saw his watch click past 6:10 p.m.

"Meyerson. Samuel Meyerson is his name. But as I stated, he will not be coming here. If you must know, we will not be married much longer." Rachel was embarrassed.

"Dispatch. I have a Ms.—sorry—Mrs. Rachel Meyerson on board. She reports that she was married in Israel as detailed in her departure documents but will not be joined by her husband, a Mr. Samuel Meyerson." Aaron tried to sound as official and dutiful as possible so as to keep up appearances, all the while not genuinely concerned.

"Dispatch here. Copy that. This has been recorded into the system," the voice on the other end reported back.

Aaron was proud of himself for thinking proactively when he

concluded the discussion with the dispatch. The whole thing looked and sounded very official, even though unbeknownst to those on board, the voice on the other end was just the security guard from the terminal. Just before the flight landed, Aaron received another call from Grace at the president's office. During that call, among other things, Aaron was informed that the new security guard was on special assignment and would be escorting the passengers back per the president's orders. Unlike Aaron, who was mostly afraid during the call, the security guard was suspiciously excited, elated even, by the task.

By 6:30 p.m., the quiet terminal was buzzing with the deplaned passengers' idle chatter and movements. As they waited for their baggage to arrive, several inquired with Aaron about the bus that would shuttle them from the airport to Herzlton.

"I phoned the driver at the time of landing. The bus will be here shortly." Aaron found he had repeated that response at least eight times to five different passengers. The first time Aaron answered, it didn't bother him that much that he had spent the last hour or so stretching the truth here, a small lie there. But after the fourth time repeating the statement about the bus, Aaron was growing more uncomfortable. On one hand, Aaron understood why the passengers and the flight crew were all visibly and audibly upset. On the other hand, however, Aaron wished he had followed his wife's advice and called out sick.

Aaron found the security guard's eagerness evidence that he was party to a much larger plot. Answering the persistent questions about the flight and then the shuttle bus made Aaron wonder how he had become some main player or coordinating figure in this government plan to delay this flight. Aaron held steady and just repeated the response, appearing unfazed. Aaron was immediately relieved when the shuttle bus pulled up. Aaron was glad to see the small group board the bus and head off to Herzlton. The security guard signaled two thumbs-up alongside a wide ear-to-ear smile as he jumped onto the bus.

Resolved to finish out the last hour of an eventful shift uneventfully, Aaron returned to the counter to complete the closeout paperwork.

Aaron approached the counter, and the phone rang. The sound echoed through the terminal and gave Aaron an instant headache.

"The president would like to thank you for your service. The bus driver has already informed us that he is on his way to Herzlton. Have a good evening and enjoy your wife and two children." Grace's robotic tone turned menacing.

The phone clicked as soon as Grace hung up the phone.

7:00 P.M.–9:00 P.M.

Mary watched with great adoration as her family ate the slow-cooked stew she had made. She could tell it was as delicious as she had planned because for the first time since everyone arrived, the house was absolutely quiet. The children's faces beamed with happiness, their eyes fully engaged with the stew and getting every morsel onto their spoon and into their mouths. The spoons clinked across the bowls, and Mary watched with great delight. Mary especially enjoyed watching Martha's satisfaction with the stew. One of Martha's favorite recipes, the blend of carrots, onions, and potatoes was combined with the beef and brown soup, resulting in a filling taste sensation.

"Baby, you aren't eating? You should enjoy this wonderful meal you have prepared for us," Daniel encouraged Mary after looking up briefly from his bowl and noticing her grinning rather than eating.

"I am . . . I mean, I will. I admit though that I am full of the joy I am feeling just watching the family I love so very much here in this place at this moment." Mary's happiness and fulfillment rolled through the air and conjured smiles from everyone at the table.

"This has been a long day—a long two weeks," Mary continued, "but this blessing was worth the wait!"

"Amen. Now you eat too." Martha cosigned Mary's perspective as she looked up from her stew which was nearly finished.

Mary began to eat her stew, which had cooled a bit but still remained rich in flavor even in milder temperature.

While Mary took a few bites and found herself scooping and eating through the stew with her own tunnel vision, Daniel began the family's dinner ritual of sharing their highlights for the day and what they would be praying for this evening.

"It looks like we let this delicious stew carry us before we shared our highlight of the day." Daniel looked around the table where everyone save for Mary was either finished or had nearly completed their dinner.

"I will start," Daniel began. "My highlight of the day was dancing in the kitchen with my wife." Daniel's smile filled his face as he continued. "I love you so very much, baby. It brought me so much joy to spin around with you through that kitchen, knowing how far we have come together and the blessing you are to me and our family."

Mary was deeply touched and dropped her spoon to run around the table and plant a kiss on Daniel's forehead. After kissing Daniel on his forehead, he pulled Mary onto his lap as the family shared their highlights.

"Okay, next let's hear from our baby girl, Charity. What was the highlight of your day?" Daniel wrapped his arms around Mary's waist as he asked their six-year-old daughter to share.

"The television! Oh, and Jjaja and Maama playing with my toys with me." Charity's sweet voice and her love of the television made everyone chuckle.

"I see. The television beat out your toys! I am impressed." Daniel, still laughing, looked to their middle child, Hope, as her cue to go next.

Hope, the shyest of the children, appeared reluctant.

"Go on, Hope. Tell everyone your highlight." Mary encouraged Hope, knowing that her encouragement usually helped ease her bashfulness.

"Ummm . . ." Hope looked down and paused as though she was afraid to share. Her eight-year-old mind appeared to bounce back and forth about whether or not to share her true highlight.

"Come on, baby. I know you have something. Let it out. We all want to know." Mary used her softest tone to coax Hope's answer and insight.

"Honestly, my highlight is that I won't be teased anymore by the other girls at school." Hope spoke her true feelings so rapidly and breathlessly that a big sigh emerged afterward. Mary and Daniel looked at one another with a shared feeling of shock. As they looked around, the children were nodding, and it was the adults who were the ones who were surprised.

"Baby, you were being teased? I didn't know that. I am so sorry. You know you can tell me these things. I am your mother and I will always protect you." Mary jumped up from Daniel's lap and walked over to Hope and kneeled beside her.

"We love you, Hope!" everyone at the table said together. Unplanned, the collective statement sounded staccato though nearly in unison.

Hope began to cry and rolled out of her chair and into Mary's waiting arms.

"Hope, look and listen to Jjaja. Don't worry your mind anymore. Those children are jealous of how smart and beautiful you are. When people don't know what to do with a bright light, they try and dim it and blow it out. But you shall not be blown out! We love you, Hope! And even more, Jesus loves you." Martha joined Mary's embrace and rubbed Hope's shoulders.

After a few moments, Hope had released the bottled-up feelings, and Mary stood up. Mary sat in Hope's chair and invited her daughter to join her by sitting in her lap. Hope immediately obliged. Hope moved with a newfound easiness.

"Okay, now that leaves the oldest of the bunch. Edward, what say you? What was our firstborn's highlight?" Daniel queried his son even as his eyes stayed upon Hope.

"Just now. Just now is my highlight. I know how afraid Hope has been to tell everyone. A few days ago, I saw a group of girls picking on her and I jumped in the middle. One of the girls went and fetched her brother who was around my age . . ."

"Really?!?" Mary, Daniel, and Martha gasped and reacted at the same moment.

"Yes, really! But don't worry. I made a lesson out of him. I made sure he learned that it was better to encourage his sister to leave mine alone than to come and try and defend her poor behavior." Edward's shoulders were broad with pride and strength, relishing being able to reveal how he rescued and protected Hope.

Hope jumped from Mary's lap, raced around the table, and hugged Edward so tightly that it made all the adults proud and deeply sympathetic.

"Jjaja, that means you're next." Daniel gazed over to Martha who was so taken with learning this recent example of her grandchildren's love and support of one another.

"My highlight is always the same: God is good! God is good . . ." Martha looked around the table, cueing everyone's expected response to her affirmation.

"All the time!" the family joined in response.

"That's right. God is good all the time!" Martha laughed with affirmative joy.

"And now you get the final highlight." Daniel looked at Mary who was sitting beside Martha.

"My highlight is every one of you. When I woke up this morning, I couldn't have imagined a better day! This has been one of the best days of my whole life!" Mary gleamed with pride.

After a bit more conversation and laughter, Edward led the children in clearing the dining room and washing the dishes. As the children washed the dishes, Daniel supervised and offered humor and levity to make the experience more enjoyable and keep the happy energy of the evening going. Meanwhile, Mary and Martha were at the dining room table engrossed in conversation. The discussion started with Martha calling Mary back into the dining room after Daniel and the children were completely out of earshot.

"Mary, stay here with me while they clean up. I want to talk with you." Martha's tone was calm, though Mary could tell that underneath it was something long in the making to be shared. Martha directed Mary to sit directly across the table from her as she closed the dining room's pocket doors.

"Okay, there we are. Funny how those doors haven't changed." Martha looked over to Mary and then took her seat. "Now that we have some privacy, I believe the time has come."

"The time has come? For what exactly?" Mary was curious but found her mother's tone ominous and a bit confusing given how Martha never ever gave Mary much information or answers to much anything, especially voluntarily.

"My precious daughter, the time has come for you to know the truth." Mary grabbed a tissue from the box on the table, holding it as though she was preparing for the downpour of tears from her otherwise stoic eyes.

"What's going on, Maama? What's it all about?" Mary reached her hand across the table to offer her mother comfort while also hoping to cajole a relatively quick pace for the discussion.

"As you know and can probably guess, I have had a good deal of difficulty coming to terms with living in this house."

"Yes." Mary nodded her head in agreement.

"The truth is that the issue really is not about having been the original housekeeper of this place for fifty years. At first, I thought that might have been a part of why I left the room when you came home two weeks ago with the news about the house being transferred to you. I thought to myself that night, *Has all my life come down to working and then dying in Herzlton?* The prospect really troubled me and brought back so many memories that I thought I'd forgotten." Martha wiped the edge of her eyes as tears began to well up.

"I understand the conflict of living in the house that you worked and cleaned and cooked in for years. After working in this place for twenty-five years, I admit that on the long ride home that evening, I heavily considered just selling the place. But then I thought about the quality of life and schools that my children would have just by virtue of living here. And by the time I finished the two-mile walk from the bus station home that evening, I knew this was meant to be, meant to happen. You know what I mean?" Mary looked to her mother for affirmation.

"I do know what you mean. It just hits differently for me because I was here when it all started. When the community was first being constructed, I remember the fights with the tribes and families that originally owned this land. I remember the curses and the bloodshed that came as this place became Herzlton. I remember being called a betrayer for working the job as a housekeeper. But the pay was better than anything I could find, and with my own parents being dead since I was a young child, I needed to take care of myself." Martha's tears rolled down her amber face like newly formed crystals excavated from a coal mine.

Mary rubbed her mother's hands and didn't interrupt, perceiving that this conversation was indeed the one she had been awaiting her whole entire life. While listening to her mother, Mary saw each of her younger selves taking a seat at the table, listening intently for answers to lifelong questions.

"This afternoon, I went into the room that is now my bedroom. Did you know that was once the room where all four children stayed until the rest of the house was complete?" Martha queried.

"I didn't know that. By the time I took over, it was a guest room," Mary replied.

"I spent so many nights in that room reading bedtime stories to the children. When they slept, I'd look out the window and stare at the house next door, wondering what the housekeeper there was thinking. Were we having the same experience at the same time?" Martha paused briefly and then continued. "Today when I went into the room, I could feel a presence, as though it had been waiting for me."

"Maama. Come on. Please don't tell me it was something about the Devil or Satan." Mary sounded like an impatient child.

"Child. You listen. Be quiet and listen. You have been wanting answers. Well, take 'em now. No telling if I will find the courage to do this another time!" Martha admonished Mary, who swallowed air and looked with apologetic eyes.

Martha continued. "As I said, I felt a presence. It was a familiar presence. Sitting in the rocking chair that I sat in for many, many years reading bedtime stories. I was afraid at first and grabbed for my Bible. I had never been in a situation of this nature before, so I didn't know the appropriate scripture. I closed my eyes and took a few breaths, placing the Bible on top of the bed. After a few seconds, I just flipped the Bible open so I could allow the Holy Spirit to guide me to the sign inside. And you know where it took me?"

"Where?" Mary was uninterested in guessing.

"The book of Revelation, chapter twenty-one. When I saw that, it scared me so deeply that I just closed the book. I searched in my mind for prayer and began reciting aloud the Lord's Prayer. I kept reciting it and chanting it until suddenly it was one long word that swirled and twisted from my tongue. The more I spoke the prayer, the more the rocking chair seemed possessed, swaying even though no one was seated. I walked over to the rocking chair and commanded the presence to be gone. After some time, I was able to guide it out the window."

"I am not following. Are you saying the house is possessed by some kind of demonic force?" Mary gestured as though she was going to get up and give up on the conversation with her mother, sensing the unfulfilled promise of long sought-after answers.

"Yes and no. As I sat in the rocking chair, I felt the familiar presence return. There was something else in the room, and I think my efforts shooed it away or at least moved it next door where the window was open and an odd phone conversation was underway . . ."

"Really a phone conversation?" Mary questioned and interrupted.

"Now you are the one off track, Mary. That is not important right now. Right now, what I am trying to say is that the Bible gave me the sign that the house and rocking chair had been awaiting my return. You see, once I finally got up and went back to the Bible, I conquered my fear and read. The church has always made me afraid of the book of Revelation, being as it is about the rapture, the Devil, and the great plague. But you know what chapter twenty-one covers? . . . I can tell by the confused look on your face that I may as well tell you. It details the regeneration of the promised land. It foretells of New Jerusalem. I get it now," Martha confessed, although she could tell that her words were still not fully clear to Mary.

"I guess that's where the nickname came from for Herzlton. But still, why are we here with the doors closed and secluded? That is something that everyone, at least Daniel, could also hear as well." Mary was bewildered with the prophecy talk and unconvinced that her mother was confessing anything meaningful.

"First, I can tell from your response that my attempts at getting you to take your daily Bible study were ineffective. Because if you had, you would know that the last book of the Bible is also the last book of the New Testament. And Jewish folks do not read that far. Many don't even go to the book of Malachi at the end of the Old Testament. What I am saying, my precious daughter, is that you are right. Coming here and living here was meant to be. The Bible offered me the only confirmation I would fully trust—a sign from the book itself. The Bible opening to exactly that place at that moment was not a coincidence. Instead, it was the rainbow sign like God gave Noah."

"Oh, I see. I understand. You received a sign that this was our home." Mary's voice rang with understanding even if it was limited.

"Yes. A sign indeed. And that sign also confirmed the familiar presence and that it was time to break the silence because he waited for me to return."

"Who is he? God? What is this presence? What are all of these riddles?" Mary was beyond confused.

"Your father! It was your father, who had waited on me to return. He waited in that chair because he knew I would notice. I felt his warmth and returned my attention to the Bible to accept the sign I asked for. He helped me see the sign, just as he helped you secure this house."

"But why would Baba wait for you here? He hated that you worked in Herzlton." Mary's questions and dismay came rapidly.

"Baba was not your real father. Baba is not your real father." Martha began to cry as she spoke.

"Baba is not my real father? What are you getting at? What are you trying to say?"

"Your father is the father of this household, Moshe Hoffman. You are the daughter of the father of this family, not the one you were raised in. Baba was a very kind and nice older man who was born with a defect that made it so he could never have children. When I became pregnant, he told me he would marry me and raise the child as his own." Martha fully released her shame.

"So you are saying that I am . . ." Mary was on the verge of tears herself but unable to cry because she was stunned.

"This house is your inheritance. You are the rightful heir to this house, for you are the daughter of the owner who also was one of the founders of Herzlton. When I was a young girl working here, I never thought that I would love anything about the people or the place. It was all white people, and they had displaced our people to create this place. But for some reason, we fell in love and were drawn to each other. I knew he was married to the lady of the house, but it didn't matter after a while. And then you came, and I refused to not have you. That caused a major issue for the family because the fear was that his wife would find out, and who knew what would happen to me, to us, then? But she never gave me a sign that she knew." Martha was no longer weeping. Instead, Mary's eyes had welled up greatly and the flood was covering her face. Martha reached her hands across the table and wiped Mary's face with the tissues.

"This home is your birthright. That's all. I refused to accept it because I had been hiding this terrible secret of my sin that blinded me from appreciating that your father did right by you. And even if his wife knew, they didn't treat you any different. In fact, when you shared the stories about working in the house for the family, I was always listening out for when they would treat you harshly. But that never happened." Martha stood up and walked over to the other end of the table and sat beside Mary, who wept into Martha's bosom as she continued to share.

"Your father's spirit waiting for me in that rocking chair was a long time coming. I was so sad that I decided not to come here before the family left so that he could die and be buried in Israel. I was angry with him all these years for living with the sin we had committed with what I perceived as ease. But he did love you. Hiding out in the secret of my own sin, I realize that the only person I had been punishing was you. You, my precious daughter, you deserved to know. You deserved to know how you came into being and also that you earned this home. This was not given to you; you were born with a claim to it. The family just honored it is all. And it was your poor mother who was so afraid that you would look at me with downcast eyes of disappointment and judgment. Please forgive me." Martha rubbed Mary's back as they both cried.

"Of course, Maama. I forgive you. I love you." Mary affirmed.

9:00 P.M.–10:02 P.M.

Scanning the window for signs of Isaac or the shuttle, Miriam grew more and more worried. She had been looking out the front room bay windows for a while before realizing that the shuttle that took the workers home also had not arrived. From the looks of the workers at each of the homes nearby, Miriam couldn't tell if they cared. No one was waiting at the sidewalk for pickup either.

The night was quiet, as nights usually were. The relative peace gave Miriam a lot of time to reflect and anticipate. She reflected on her mother's letter and decision to stay in Israel. She reflected on her combative relationship with her mother and her feelings of betrayal toward her siblings and the community members. She reflected on her father, whom she missed and adored.

Sitting on the porch, she recounted the many times her father would share stories about his life and the community as they sat on the porch in the evenings before she went to bed. Miriam missed his smiling encouragement and affection. It wasn't until she sat on the porch alone in the quiet that it occurred to Miriam that her father's choice to die and be buried in Israel meant all she had left of him in Herzlton was whatever had been left behind. This awareness made Miriam even sadder than she already was, and she rubbed her belly for comfort, promising her unborn child a better mother than the one she had. Miriam promised that her love for her child would be unconditional, and no matter what Isaac did or didn't do, she would always love, support, and protect her child.

Miriam's promises made her imagine her life moving forward. She wondered what life for her in Herzlton would be without her sisters, aunts and uncles, and even her mother. And while Miriam knew that Israel did not feel like the same kind of home space for her as it did for her family, she was unsure if Herzlton was home either. She just knew it was more home to her than anywhere else, mostly because it was the only home she'd known.

In recognition of her love and passion for Isaac, Miriam decided that she would stay in Uganda unless he left. Wherever Isaac went, she would follow, whether that be into Entebbe or staying in Herzlton. The affirmative feelings for Isaac led Miriam to recall when she and Isaac first met two years earlier. The community had interviewed different men to head up Herzlton's private security following the retirement of the head after thirty years of leadership and no heir apparent.

After a few weeks of interviews, Isaac appeared before the full community. Everyone, especially Miriam, was impressed with Isaac. The timbre of his voice was professional, sure, and confident. He spoke a series of languages and had done all his research on Herzlton. He knew when it was established, the founding families, and the overall arrangement between Herzlton and the Ugandan government. Isaac impressed everyone so much. When Isaac mentioned the fact that his first cousin was the president of Uganda, the job was his. The timing of Isaac's leadership of the security forces couldn't have been any better, and his connections to the government were essential. Whereas for years the Ugandan government had been favorable to Zionists and Herzlton, over the last two or so years, President Amin had become increasingly opposed.

There had been threats of taking the land back and a massive increase of an additional twenty-five thousand dollars added to the required annual tax payment to the Ugandan government. A year later, the peace agreement between Egypt and Israel brokered by the United States made it so that many of the European nations that had helped secure and pay the agreement with the Ugandan government were scaling back. By the end of 1978, several countries, including England, France, and Germany, removed Herzlton as a national budget item.

Beset with the sudden loss of revenue from Europe, the fate of Herzlton was hanging in the balance near the start of Isaac's tenure. The community did not hide the issue from Isaac. Instead, they made sure that he was aware that one of his primary duties was to protect it from a government or military takeover, mercenaries, and improve diplomatic relations between Herzlton and President Amin.

Within a few weeks of Isaac's start, the threats of a government take-over of Herzlton vanished. The Ugandan government provided a more manageable payment arrangement for the tax increase. Soon enough, ease returned to life in Herzlton, and everyone saw Isaac as the arbiter of that newfound peace. Recollecting Isaac's start in Herzlton, Miriam realized that it was within those two years that the plans to abandon Herzlton must have begun. European nations cutting Herzlton from their budgets was the beginning of the end. At the time, Miriam had been so swept up in Isaac that she barely noticed much of anything. Isaac was all that she could think about. Sixteen months into Isaac's tenure, Miriam discovered that the feeling was shared and mutual. Isaac too had a thing for Miriam, and both understood that it must be kept secret.

Unable to wait inside for Isaac any longer, Miriam grabbed a light blanket and took it to the small bench on the porch. She gathered a few of the candles underneath and lit them to add brightness to the dim porchlight. More time passed and the neighborhood grew quieter. With still no sign of Isaac, Miriam considered what she might say when Isaac returned. No longer afraid of his response, Miriam just wanted to see Isaac again. She regretted that she had been so slow to embrace him at her return. Rather than just hugging and holding him, she had chosen to delay her affection and wander off to the bathtub.

Miriam regretted that it was her mother who had forced her to tell Isaac. She had planned something more intimate and special than a handwritten letter of ex-communication and secret spilling. But as Miriam sat there waiting in the spring night quiet, she accepted that things happened as they had, and there could be no turning back now. Miriam was surprisingly relieved Isaac now knew that they had a child on the way. Miriam appreciated her mother's letter because it did the dirty work and revealed her harshness. Miriam felt lucky and smart for returning to Herzlton to be among the things and places she had known her whole life.

Miriam looked to the left and right of her house and thought about her siblings and father. She had for so long pictured that on the day that she shared her news of pregnancy, she would have run to her parents' home on the left and raced to her loving father's arms with the good news. Her father would have hugged her tightly and offered his words of support, and with that, Miriam would've raced to the house next to hers to tell her eldest sister. The two would have raced through the rest of the block to tell the family and so on. But as she sat there on the porch that evening, nothing was as she had imagined. When Isaac emerged at the end of the block, Miriam found she preferred things as they were unfolding over the fantasy. As Isaac neared, Miriam could see there was a troubled look on his face.

Miriam wanted to run out to him and hold his hand and tell him that she loved him. She resisted the urge and thought it best to allow Isaac to close the distance between them, given that so much had been shared unexpectedly. Isaac walked steadily. Suddenly, the loud noise of the shuttle rolling around the bend boomed through the quiet.

Miriam and Isaac both watched and listened as the bus's brakes squealed and made a slow roll toward the middle of the block. Miriam called out to Isaac, who was more keyed into the bus than to her on the porch.

"Isaac, please come inside so we can talk," Miriam called out. Isaac waived Miriam off. Miriam watched as Isaac looked increasingly alarmed by the shuttle's presence. By the time the bus stopped, Miriam understood from Isaac's additional hand gestures that he was concerned about the bus and who might be on board. His hand signals were meant to cue Miriam to head inside for protection.

Miriam recognized Issac's gestures as the signals that were a part of the emergency protocol. She too noticed that the sound and appearance of the shuttle were off. Herzlton shuttles were always the same color and size—white and blue. The driver was also always the same and visible from the window. This shuttle did not look like their privately owned vehicles. Instead, it was a repurposed school bus that had bars over blackout windows and a front window that made it difficult to make out the driver.

When the shuttle made its screeching halt, several people emerged from the homes on the block. Miriam noticed that all of them were the Black workers and support staff for the various Herzlton families. She also noticed that not only did the workers not appear to plan to board the bus; they were also watching on with fearful looks and postures.

"Go inside! Everyone go inside and lock yourselves in! Now!" Isaac's instructions echoed powerfully through the streets.

"I'm serious, everyone. This is not a drill!" Isaac reprimanded the onlookers, including Miriam, who was now walking off the porch and closer to the bus.

"What's going on?" Miriam heard a familiar voice ask. Miriam turned and saw that Mary too had come out of the house upon the curious appearance of this bus.

"You don't know that bus either?" Miriam asked Mary.

"I have seen them before, but not here." Mary was walking back toward the house as Miriam was heading in the opposite direction.

"So you do know what's going on?" Miriam asked as the two women's paths intersected.

"Whatever it is can't be good. Those are government buses used to transport the military and mercenaries." Mary's statement finished louder as she reached the front door.

Miriam barely listened to anything that Mary said, determined and decided as she was about getting to the bus beside Isaac and finding out what was happening.

9:58 P.M.–10:03 P.M.

The screeching halt jumbled everyone around on the shuttle bus. After the long ride from the airport, Rachel was ready to jump off the shuttle and into her bed. The ride had been uncomfortable and curious from start to end. When the shuttle bus pulled up in front of the terminal, Rachel was unsure if it was the correct transportation. The small group was hurried onto the long retrofitted school bus. Along with the unfamiliar shuttle bus, Rachel did not recognize the driver either. Exhausted from travel and desperate to get back to their Herzlton residences, the small group didn't ask any questions. Rachel, like the rest of the group, decided to board and save the questions.

Once aboard the shuttle, Rachel could tell that everyone was uncomfortable. The shuttle bus was simply not up to par with their usual accommodations. The seats were old and tattered, with broken springs nudging their way through the patent leather seats. Every bump and pothole reverberated throughout the bus, lifting and pushing around the passengers who moaned and groaned their discomfort along the way. Rachel was unfamiliar with the driver, the route he was taking to Herzlton, and wondered why the airport security guard was aboard. When the shuttle bus made a pit stop in what appeared to be the middle of nowhere, the passengers were all confused. Before anyone could ask about the sudden stop and its purpose, two men appeared out of thin air and boarded the shuttle bus, taking a seat next to the security guard in the row just behind the driver.

Rachel whispered to her fellow passengers, inquiring about the driver, the route, and the bus. From the time she boarded the shuttle bus, Rachel felt something was off. This was only Rachel's second time on the shuttle bus that traveled between Herzlton and Entebbe International Airport. Unlike her fellow passengers, Rachel was not able to stay quiet about her questions and discomfort. When the bus would bounce and bump around, Rachel made sure to be very vocal about the experience. She let out highly audible ouches and sighs along the way, which it seemed most everyone found more humorous than alarming. Rachel was unsure if her fellow passengers were used to this ride and route, thus making her behavior appear more ridiculous. Rachel began asking others she thought may be more familiar with the drivers and route. She asked if people knew the driver's name, to which the answer was a resounding no. Rachel questioned the route taken and the time and length of the trip, to which her fellow passengers confirmed similar perspectives that all echoed her concerns.

The only two men in the group of predominantly women passengers sat beside each other, seemingly content with staying put and quiet for the duration of the journey. An hour into the journey, Rachel decided she would walk forward to the row where the two men were seated and ask them similar questions. As Rachel stood, the shuttle bus hit a hard pothole, and she fell to her knees and slid forward. When Rachel pulled herself up, she had slid right next to the row where the two men were seated. She noticed the men were secretly holding hands underneath a trench coat that was strategically draped across their laps.

"Ma'am, I need you to take your seat." The driver's voice was polite though commanding—not at all the customer service tone that the shuttle drivers and staff used with Herzlton residents.

Rachel shot a look of frustration at the driver who was looking at her through the rearview mirror. Once Rachel was sure her look had been registered with the driver, she squeezed next to the two men to begin her interrogation.

"Do either of you know what's going on?" Rachel queried the two men.

"What do you mean?" the man nearest to Rachel responded as both men kept their heads facing forward.

"I mean this bus and this driver. This is strange, no?" Rachel tried her best to whisper-talk even though she was sure that everyone behind her could hear their discussion.

"I don't know why we are not on our usual transport. Could be that the bus broke down and this is what they had available. We arrived later than scheduled, and so the usual driver could have been unavailable. I really don't know. I will say they are taking the long way home. Fortunately, they are heading in the right direction." The man kept his face forward.

Rachel found his answers reasonable and decided she would leave them alone and head back to her seat. Sneaking back a few rows to her seat, Rachel thought perhaps she was pouring worry somewhere it was not needed. Arriving at her seat, Rachel decided that a short nap would calm her nerves. A nap would at the very least make the ride feel shorter and relieve her of the deep observation duties she began when the shuttle pulled up at the airport terminal.

Rachel was a few minutes into waking up when the brakes screeched their way to a full stop in the middle of the block. Rachel looked around and noticed others had also fallen asleep during the ride. The grinding halt jolted everyone's heads forward and jerked them back when the bus finally came to a complete stop. Whatever concerns or questions Rachel had dissipated when she saw that they were in Herzlton. The dimly lit street was a sight for her very sore eyes. Rachel and the other passengers began to gather their personal items and awaited the sound of the doors opening as their cue to get off. A few minutes passed and still, the doors had not been opened nor had the driver addressed the passengers. Rachel decided to break the silence and ask that they be let off the shuttle bus. To ensure that her voiced demand was heard fully, Rachel stood. And as she stood, she noticed Isaac walking up and then alongside the bus toward the door. Figuring that the driver was simply awaiting Isaac's arrival, Rachel sat back down and didn't say anything. When Rachel sat down, she could hear two things that perturbed her: the sighs of relief from her fellow passengers who just hoped she'd stay quiet, and what sounded like a loud warning being issued by Isaac. Rachel couldn't quite make out exactly everything Isaac said. But then for just a moment, the bus was still and quiet enough that Rachel could hear Isaac through the padded bus walls. Isaac was mid-statement when

Rachel heard him exclaim: "This is not a drill!" His voice boomed with concern and alarm, and Rachel saw several people who were watching from porches go inside their houses, and others peered from their windows.

10:03 P.M.—10:10 P.M.

"What's going on out there?" Daniel asked Mary as he watched from the window.

"I am not sure. But from the looks of it, nothing good." Mary was tugging at Daniel's shirt to encourage him to move away from the window.

"Do government buses usually ride into Herzlton?" Daniel asked as he looked around for a radio with the hopes of getting some sense of what might be happening.

"Very unusual to say the least. What are you looking for?!?" Mary was growing testy and felt the tension and anxiety rising in her body.

"A radio! There must be some kind of report going on that could give us some insight." Daniel spoke with his back turned as he scrounged around for a radio.

In response, Mary went into the broom closet. Using the step ladder inside the closet, Mary reached up and grabbed a radio. She closed the closet swiftly so as to make the sound of its shutting audible. The sudden shutting noise made Daniel stand straight up and run to the window.

"What was that?" Daniel sounded panicked.

"It was the closet door. And here is your radio." Mary held the radio out to draw Daniel away from the window and out of the front of the house.

Daniel grabbed the radio. He began fumbling around with the antenna and tried to locate the proper station that provided twenty-four-hour news.

"Can we do this in another room, please? Isaac is the head of Herzlton security, and if you heard the way his voice trembled, you would know that something is not right with that bus." Mary tried luring Daniel out of the kitchen and into the family room. Daniel's curiosity was fully piqued, which made it difficult to change his gaze elsewhere.

"Daniel, we must get out of this room. Now!" Mary's raised and emphatic tone made the hairs on Daniel's neck stand up. When he turned to her, Daniel finally noticed Mary's panic.

"Okay. Okay. I just want to make sure everything is all right before we leave the room." Daniel took one last look out the window. Mary made a loud groan to voice her frustration in response.

Daniel watched as Isaac raised his hands above his head to indicate he didn't have any weapons. Daniel thought that gesture was odd, if not concerning, but was too entranced by the scene not to watch a little longer. After a few minutes, the bus door squeaked open.

Through the opened door, Daniel could hear that there were people on board yelling for help and other sounds of discontent. A man dressed in a security guard uniform strolled off the bus, and the door squeaked closed behind him. The uniformed man then pushed Isaac to the sidewalk. He patted Isaac down and checked for any weapons. After a thorough search, the uniformed man pulled out a gun and stuck the nose of the gun into the arch of Isaac's back, instructing him to put his hands on his head. The uniformed man then hollered, "Clear!" After a few beats, the bus door opened. The uniformed man grabbed Isaac by his collar and pushed him up the steps and onto the bus. Isaac walked up the stairs obediently with his hands above his head.

"Mary, I think you're right! Something is going on. They just took Isaac up on the bus. A security guard pulled a gun on him and checked him for weapons. And the white lady you were talking to outside from next door is heading toward the bus." Daniel sounded more fascinated than fearful.

"What?!? A gun! A security guard! Miriam is still walking out there like a fool! This is dangerous!" Mary ran over to the window, pushed Daniel back, and cracked it just enough to make sure she could be heard.

"Ms. Miriam, you get back inside! Now! It is not safe." Mary was clear and emphatic, and Miriam immediately heard her. Miriam stood halfway between her house and the bus, looking as though she didn't know what to do.

"Ms. Miriam! Get back in your house now! Follow the emergency protocols!" Mary pleaded with Miriam, who stood frozen for at least another minute.

Daniel tried to get back to the window as Mary pleaded with Miriam.

"Daniel, stop! Go into the family room now!" Mary swatted Daniel back. Daniel muttered something inaudible to voice his dismay, but soon enough, he was out of the kitchen. Relieved that Daniel was out of sight, Mary made one last plea to Miriam, who had finally turned back and was walking slowly without urgency.

"Ms. Miriam, please go inside. Listen to Isaac! This is serious!" Mary watched as Miriam quickened her pace. Before shutting the window and leaving the kitchen, Mary wanted to be sure that Miriam was back inside. As Mary looked down the block, everyone else was already inside, leaving Miriam the only visible person from her vantage point.

Miriam walked with an increasing speed but still not with the urgency that was aligned with Mary's warnings. And then, just as Mary was closing the window and watching Miriam reach the porch, she heard a series of terrifying sounds. First, there was the unmistakable loudness of a gunshot. Then there was a second shot fired. The echo of the second shot was accompanied by the sounds of breaking glass. In rapid fashion, there was an unforgettable bloodcurdling scream from inside the bus. The sounds chilled Mary to the bone. Mary felt her feet become like cement as she watched Miriam race inside the house.

Daniel raced into the kitchen with the radio in hand to see about Mary, who was stuck in place.

"Hit the button, Daniel." Mary sounded numb as she offered her husband the instructions.

"What button? Huh?" Daniel was pulling at Mary and trying to get her out of the kitchen.

Mary, finally able to move, pointed Daniel toward the emergency button she'd found earlier behind the wallpaper.

Pulling up the wallpaper exposed a large red button that had the word "Emergency" written in bold red letters around its circumference. Mary pushed the button. The button lit up in a bright red that filled the broom closet. Within seconds, red light poured into the windows from outside. Daniel looked out and was amazed to see that all the streetlights lining the neighborhood had changed from dim white to bright red. The red streetlights were followed by the blare of a siren. The siren boomed like thunder, rolling through the walls of the house and the streets of Herzlton.

2:00 A.M.—4:00 A.M.

In the bunker, Daniel watched with great awe and fright as the video cameras showed what was happening aboveground. He watched as two mercenaries walked off of the bus and kicked down doors. Entering and leaving house after house, the men searched for residents. After several hours of searching, the men returned to the bus.

"Come out now and no one else will get hurt. We just want what is ours, what we are owed!" A man's voice blared from a megaphone attached to the top of the bus. The booming sirens shifted to intermittent loud beeps, like a dispatch signal. A few hours later, the two men came back off of the bus. They then ran up to several homes and unloaded automatic rifles into the residences. Glass shattered, wood splintered, and the sound and sight made many of the adults in the bunker tremble and fall to their knees in prayer. As the men fired round after round into the homes, the megaphone on the bus roared.

"Come out now! We are prepared to kill everyone on this bus! Come out . . . Come out . . . Come out!" The tone of the voice behind the demands was eerie. As the person on the megaphone continued to repeat

"Come out" over and over again, the two men fired more rounds into additional homes. When no one revealed themselves or came out, the men began running inside each of the homes they hadn't shot up and grabbing perceived valuables. Vases, artwork, money, china, and even a few safes had been discovered, acquired, and taken onto the bus.

"Come out . . . Come out . . . Come out!"

"We are safe down here." Miriam placed her hand on Daniel's shoulder as she joined him watching the closed-circuit surveillance. Daniel, so engrossed with what he was watching on the cameras, didn't notice that anyone had come into the video room of the bunker.

"Safe for now. Maama and a few of the other women are with the children and managed to get them to sleep. But how long can we keep this up?" Mary entered behind Miriam, expressing her concern about the men and whether or not they would eventually leave.

"This bunker was built to sustain the community for several months if need be. And that would be for all two-hundred-plus families. There is enough food to feed hundreds of people for months. And the bathroom facilities and plumbing can only be accessed from this area." Miriam's confidence belied her own worries, which were chiefly about Isaac's well-being.

5:45 A.M.–6:00 A.M.

Mary, Daniel, and Miriam were fast asleep in the video surveillance room when Martha walked into the room to check in. Martha looked at all three of them and softly whispered a prayer of gratitude that her family and most everyone was safe. As Martha looked over them with loving eyes, she saw them transform from the adults of the present to the children of the past. She could see their innocence and vulnerability.

Martha took a deep breath. She was not sure how long they would have to be sequestered in the subterranean bunker, but she knew that the founding families built it to be protective, sustaining, and virtually impenetrable. She also recalled that somewhere within the structure, there was also an allegedly hidden vault of sorts containing a large sum of money. Until the moment she was standing in the bunker, which she had never actually seen even while it was being constructed, Martha believed the whole thing to be a myth that the founders made up.

Realizing that she was becoming lost in her thoughts, Martha snapped out of her mindful imagination and looked to the cameras to see if anything was visible. Most all of the fifteen cameras were visible save for two of them. Mary was asleep on one. Miriam was asleep on the other. Both women faced each other and slept in similar positions and postures. Martha was astonished. It was as though the two women were mirrors of each other, and for the first time in twenty-five years, she saw their father's face. Martha peered in closer, amazed by the resemblance. Nearby, Mary jumped awake and startled Martha. Martha's quick gasp awoke Miriam. When both women peeled themselves back from the cameras, new information was revealed. In the cameras, they could see Isaac waving in distress. They could see that he was holding his side and looked wounded. Miriam, who was immediately concerned, reached to the microphone and turned on the audio option that had been turned off to prevent hearing the ominous "Come out!" refrain.

"Isaac, is that you?" Miriam's voice dispatched through the microphone.

Upon hearing Miriam's voice, Isaac waved hard with all of his strength to signal it was indeed him. "Call the medics and the police. I have been shot. Everyone else is safe. Bumps and bruises are all. I have been shot." Isaac fell hard to the ground.

Miriam was shaken by seeing and hearing Isaac in distress. She tried to move but was frozen.

"We have to save him. We have a baby on the way . . ." was all Miriam could muster.

While Mary and Martha tried to coax Miriam into more meaningful action, Daniel assessed the room, located the phone line, and made the call.

7:47 A.M.—8:00 A.M.

"Breaking news. Tanzanian military has taken Kampala, and Idi Amin is no longer president of Uganda. Former president Amin, whose whereabouts are unknown, is expected to give a public address later today." The newscaster's voice over the radio made its way into Aaron's ears, disrupting the series of nightmares he'd endured from the moment he fell asleep.

After such a long and mysterious day at work, Aaron was exhausted. Soon after eating dinner and kissing his children on their heads as they slept, Aaron joined his sleeping wife in bed. As he lay down, Aaron racked his mind trying to figure out the purpose of the plan in which he had participated. He wondered if the flight crew ever left the airport and if the passengers made it back to Herzlton safely.

Each time he replayed the sequence of events in his head, Aaron kept coming back to the sly look on the security guard's face when he left the terminal and hopped onto the shuttle bus. Eventually, Aaron was able to fall asleep, only to find that his dream space was replete with scenes and faces from the day. Hypothetical scenarios played out in a nightmarish fashion. At one point, Aaron was able to see the bus riding on the road, and the passengers were handcuffed and crying for help and mercy. That sequence made Aaron jump out of his sleep, sweat beads extended across his forehead. On the third occasion where Aaron jumped out of his sleep, his wife checked in with him to ensure that everything was okay.

"Everything okay?" Aaron's wife asked, half-asleep and half-awake.

"Yes, baby. Everything is okay. Having a weird dream is all."

Aaron sounded reassuring enough that his wife returned to sleep.

Soon enough, Aaron too was back asleep, only to find that the dream sequence awaiting him was more terrifying and escalated to a horrific scene where he was bound and gagged at the back of the bus. He couldn't move or speak. When he tried to get up for some assistance from one of the passengers on the bus, the security guard's sly look returned. With a gun in his hand, the security guard approached the back of the bus. After shooting one of the passengers in the chest, Aaron was hit in the head with the back of the gun. Aaron saw and felt paralyzed with fear and pain as he squirmed around trying to free himself. It was there, in that place of a nightmare feeling so real, that Aaron heard the radio.

"Breaking news . . . Idi Amin is no longer president of Uganda."

The outside voice helped break his sleep paralysis, and he awoke drenched in sweat. His wife was already awake amidst her morning routine of preparing breakfast for the children while listening to the news broadcast on the radio. Grateful that the dream was not real, Aaron quickly jumped from the soaked sheets and ran into the kitchen.

"Turn that up, please," Aaron asked his wife as he pointed to the radio.

Aaron's wife obliged, turning up the radio and returning to cooking the breakfast meats.

"After eight years, Idi Amin is president no more. Reports have come in from across the country of raids by mercenaries owed by former president Amin. The Tanzanian military has taken hold of Kampala. We have been advised to inform our listeners to stay home. School and other official functions have been canceled. Again, please stay within the safety of your home."

Both Aaron and his wife looked at each other, stupefied by the broadcaster's announcement.

"School is canceled?" one of the children asked, sitting at the kitchen table.

"Apparently, yes. School is canceled," Aaron's wife answered.

"Yes! Yes! Yes! No school today!" The children began to cheer and dance with excitement.

Aaron, dazed by the combination of the news about the president and his seemingly endless nightmares, was stuck.

"Did he know?" Aaron said to himself, unaware that his words were heard loudly by everyone in the kitchen.

"Did who know what?" Aaron's wife asked while also signaling to the children to get quiet.

Just as Aaron was figuring out exactly how to respond to his wife's question, the news broadcaster's voice rose from its rapid, subdued pace.

"We have just received additional breaking news. Authorities are investigating and interviewing victims of an apparent hostage crisis in Herzlton. Several mercenaries seeking an outstanding debt from former president Amin infiltrated the small private Jewish community located between Kampala and Entebbe. Disguised as transportation staff, three men are said to have terrorized the community throughout the night into the early morning. There was a subsequent scuffle between the men and head of Herzlton security Isaac Maliyamungu, first cousin of former president Idi Amin, where all three disguised mercenaries were also killed. Mr. Isaac Maliyamungu, who survived a gunshot wound, is believed to have fled to Zaire. We are told most members of the Herzlton community remain in Israel and only a few were present at the time of the attack. We will continue to track this story. In the meantime, please obey the stay-at-home order until authorities determine it is safe."

Aaron fell to his knees and began to cry and pray as his wife and children looked on. The children left the table to comfort their father.

"My goodness. How lucky we are that you are home with us. You worked that charter all day yesterday." Aaron's wife rubbed his shoulders, kneeling beside him. Encouraging the kids to kneel beside their father, Aaron's wife joined in prayer as the radio report played in the background.

Initially, Aaron kept his prayer quiet for fear of revealing his shame to his family. He knew something was awry the entire time he was at work, and he felt ashamed he had in any way participated in bringing harm to anyone. He hoped that God would forgive him and that his prayers would signal that he was seeking repentance. Aaron felt foolish and also couldn't believe how much had transpired between the time he left work and when he woke up. He had not always been the most prayerful person and began to believe that perhaps this ordeal was a lesson to him about losing sight of his personal relationship with Jesus Christ. Aaron worked through his mind, thinking through and trying to recover any meaningful scripture from his many years of Bible study camp to assist him in this time of crisis. Searching and searching for something that he could recite, he thought back to when he was a teenager.

Arriving at the memory, Aaron was transported ten years into the past, when he was in summer Bible study camp. He could see the amber face of the older woman, the camp supervisor, leading them in daily prayer. Aaron's turmoil began to subside as he remembered her kind but stoic face and dutiful commitment to God. Aaron remembered how she noticed he would only mouth the words and wouldn't speak them. On the last day of camp, she pulled him aside and directly spoke with him and gave him a prayer that he could utilize whenever he felt lost or just needed support.

"God is always with you," Aaron could hear her reminding him before she taught him the prayer and they recited it together.

Recalling the prayer he was taught, Aaron began to recite it aloud as his wife and children accompanied him. "Our father who art in Heaven, hallowed be thy name. Thy kingdom come. Thy will be done. On Earth, as it is in Heaven. Give us this day our daily bread. And forgive us our trespasses as we forgive those who trespass against us. And lead us not into temptation, but deliver us from evil. For thine is the kingdom and the power and the glory. Forever. Amen."

"Amen!" the family shouted in support of Aaron's prayer.

Aaron looked at his family with gratitude, the prayer having lifted his spirits and reminded him that he and they survived and were safe. "Thank you, Ms. Martha," Aaron susurrated as he rose to his feet with relief.

4

THE PARABLE OF THE PEOPLE'S REPUBLIC OF SOUTH AFRICA

1827

When Olufemi jumped to escape capture, his father Babawale was armed with two blades on the family boat in the Oba River surrounded by a mysterious group of armed, garbed men. Olufemi swam furiously in the middle of the river, afraid to look back. Before the raid, Olufemi and his father were concluding two days of fishing. As Babawale pulled and reeled the anchor in, their boat and four others were suddenly encircled by eight small boats of armed, red-garbed men.

Engraved with the British flag on both sides, the small boats were familiar to Babawale because British slave traders used them to regularly police, raid, and rob fishing boats. The small boats were also used to survey the rivers and towns nearby to develop regional maps for British soldiers and missionaries. It had been at least twenty years since Babawale recalled seeing these small, ominous boats. Unable to see or make out the men's faces further alarmed Babawale and Olufemi. As familiar as Babawale was with the old British police boats, he was equally unfamiliar with the layered red linen garb adorning the bandits. Where Babawale had become accustomed to pale-faced English men aboard the small boats in search of easy pickings, these raiders, however, were a dangerous combination of unrecognizable and ominous.

As Babawale attempted to steer the boat and escape downriver toward their home and dock in Olumoye, he and Olufemi noticed there were armed, garbed men awaiting in the distance. At the sight of the trap, Olufemi saw his father's face was not lined with the look of dread he felt. Instead, Babawale's face looked like that of a deadly warrior. Olufemi froze, terrified by both the men in the river and his father's expression. Olufemi tried making his face contort and align with his father's, but he couldn't.

Without a word, Babawale reached for his sharpest knives and instructed Olufemi to ring the emergency bell to alert the other fishermen. First, Olufemi was to ring the bell as hard and as rapidly as he could to ensure the other fisherman could hear and that those perhaps down the river could as well. Next, after sounding the alarm, Olufemi was to jump overboard and swim at Babawale's signaling.

Before Babawale became a family man, his life involved criminal activities such as robbing or stealing valuables from someone at knifepoint. When Babawale became a father, he turned over a new leaf and dedicated himself to providing for his family through legitimate and nonviolent means. Even still, a brutal warrior and ace with a knife and machete resided deep inside of Babawale. Olufemi frequently watched in amazement as his father cleaned and filleted pounds of fresh fish within minutes.

When three men leaped onto the boat, Babawale gave Olufemi the cue to jump and swim away. Olufemi looked back before he jumped, witnessing his father cut one man's throat clean from his neck and then lunge the same blade into the eye socket of the second man approaching from behind.

Olufemi's heartbeat boomed as he swam as hard and fast as he could. He heard the groans and yells of men in the background. He also saw the other fishing boats were under siege. Olufemi swam directionless in a confused and hurried diagonal. He looked back just as two people familiar to him jumped into the water. Olufemi searched for the current underneath that would help lead him out of harm's way and out of sight. He closed his eyes to feel for the downstream current. No sooner than he closed his eyes, Olufemi felt a tug at his leg and began splashing about vulnerably, like freshly caught trout. Olufemi assumed the tug, which was now a grip, on his ankle was one or more of the raiders. To Olufemi's surprise, however, the two people were a father and son he knew well.

The father, Oluwatobi, was well-known as the Oba River's best fisherman. Oluwatobi was his father's greatest fishing rival. When Olufemi first met Oluwatobi's son, Ireoluwa, they did not get along. Ireoluwa had become a proxy rival for Olufemi, given the contentious back and forth of their fathers for the crown of top fisherman of the Oba River.

Oluwatobi's catches were always bountiful and the talk of the town. Oluwatobi was also a generous man. Rather than just turn his bounty of fish into all profit, he sold just enough to cover his overhead and save for a bigger house and better boat one day. Oluwatobi would salt and smoke cure the surplus fish. After the curing process was complete, he provided the smoked fish to those in the greatest need. Oluwatobi was incredibly attentive to provisions for orphaned children, grandmothers who were head of household, and women widowed due to the terrible and continuous clashes between Yoruba forces and the British slavers and colonizers.

Over the years, Olufemi's father Babawale became Oluwatobi's biggest rival. Olufemi listened on many occasions to how badly his father desired to beat out Oluwatobi. Babawale tried going out earlier than Oluwatobi, only to return home with less fish than his rival. Discovering that the spot that Oluwatobi had selected seemed to be where the fish flocked, Babawale dragged Olufemi along as he tried fishing at the same spot. Oluwatobi, being the gregarious man he was, often extended an offer for him and Babawale to fish jointly. "Oh! No need for your help," Babawale always indignantly declined. Babawale's pride would not allow him to collaborate, as he believed the rest of the village would just credit Oluwatobi with whatever had been caught. This rivalry went on for so many years that pretending to entertain Babawale's strategies to outwit his fishing nemesis had become routine for Olufemi. What had also become routine in recent months was noticing, swimming with, and getting to know Ireoluwa, Oluwatobi's son. As the only young boys on any fishing boat, Olufemi and Ireoluwa saw each other a lot. Despite initially being at odds, the two boy became fast friends.

Olufemi and Ireoluwa were only a few months apart. And while Olufemi was the oldest of his parents six children, Ireoluwa was an only child. Oluwatobi was a single father and his son, Ireoluwa, was never far behind. Through the years, Olufemi and Ireoluwa would find each other during the times they were allowed to swim. They would each swap stories. Olufemi would share his angst and woes of being stuck on the boat with his father for days at a time sometimes. Ireoluwa would offer some solace by sharing that life on the boat of the greatest fisherman was pretty mundane and not always as successful as everyone believed. Both Olufemi and Ireoluwa shared their dreams of becoming anything other than fishermen.

Ireoluwa would listen intently as Olufemi bemoaned the expectations and duties of being the firstborn child, son, and oldest sibling. Olufemi would in turn offer encouragement when Ireoluwa confessed fears of disappointing his father by not wanting to be a fisherman. Ireoluwa told Olufemi in great detail how Oluwatobi was painstaking in his intention of ensuring that the secrets and traditions of fishing he'd learned from his father, who learned from his father and his father before him, remained in the family.

Olufemi learned from Ireoluwa why he and his father were so close. Oluwatobi always wanted a son, especially as his first child. Oluwatobi and his wife, Ife, were so delighted when they heard the baby's cries as he exited his mother's body and entered into the world. Looking at the little brown baby cooing at her, Ife knew exactly what she would name him. After a difficult pregnancy, Ife felt so much gratitude when laying eyes upon her bundle of joy. Because the pregnancy had been so hard and both she and Oluwatobi feared the outcome, the couple agreed that they would provide a name for the child immediately. Although the naming ceremony would still be scheduled and heeded, the fear that the child might perish without a name was too much of a risk. The idea of the baby's spirit swirling in the atmosphere unsure of where to go without a name greatly troubled the couple. And so the expecting couple selected a name and agreed they would bless it upon the child as soon as it entered the world. Oluwatobi was sure the baby would be a boy though there were two names selected depending on the child's gender.

During labor, the chief midwife and her team of doulas reported to Oluwatobi that they feared the worst. There was a very strong likelihood that neither the mother nor the baby would survive delivery. Oluwatobi cared not for their concerns, believing that if he gave the negative outcomes any energy they would become true. Praying outside and anxiously awaiting better news, Oluwatobi refused to accept this outcome. Although Ife had been bedridden for the final months of her pregnancy, Oluwatobi only ever saw her as the strong and fierce woman that it took him a year to get the courage to speak to and another year to convince to marry him.

After a few hours of waiting, Oluwatobi's faith had been rewarded. When Oluwatobi went into the room to greet his wife and new child, both the mother and newborn looked at him with adoration.

"Aren't we the fortunate ones, Tobi? Olodumare has smiled upon us with all of his goodness."

They both stared at the baby who was feeding at her breast, eyes closed and relaxed.

"Oh yes! God has been so good to us." Oluwatobi kissed Ife gratefully.

Pulling the baby from feeding, Ife placed him into Oluwatobi's arms. "Here is your son. Tobi, you were right. Ireoluwa. God is good."

Oluwatobi just stared at Ireoluwa. The sight of his son made Oluwatobi feel as though the world had stopped. As in love with Ife as Oluwatobi was, cradling little Ireoluwa gave him a newfound sense of love. Oluwatobi had never felt a love like that before. Overwhelmed by the instant love for Ireoluwa, Oluwatobi was brought to tears. Oluwatobi began to hum a sweet-sounding melody learned in his youth, passed down in his family for generations.

The humming melody was a family secret. It was based on a technique his great-great-grandfather had used to encourage the fish to his rod or net. The hum sounded like a call to easy waters. "The fisherman's lullaby" was the name for the family's secret, effective, rhythmic sound. For generations, the fisherman's lullaby worked like a charm, producing an impressive yield even during droughts. For many years, Oluwatobi's great-great-grandfather had been frustrated with the unpredictable nature of fish. "There you are as the fisherman. Oh. Atop a boat that the fish can clearly see and sense. You are trying to lure them out of their world and into your belly. Fish must be coaxed." His great-great-grandfather, after whom Oluwatobi was named, taught and shared the fisherman's lullaby to his firstborn son, who taught it to his firstborn son, and so on.

Oluwatobi hadn't realized that he had begun humming the fisherman's lullaby until his wife looked up and said, "Oh. Why are you singing to our son like you do the fish? He is a boy. Eh. Not trout." Ife laughed, watching joyously as the bond forged between father and son.

Oluwatobi began noticing that Ife was no longer sweating and was instead becoming cold. Ife's face turned from gentle and aware to hazy and feeble.

"Something is not right. You must get help!" Ife implored Oluwatobi.

Oluwatobi became frantic when he saw her hand reach from underneath her robe fully soaked in blood. "Help! We need help in here!" Oluwatobi shouted.

Oluwatobi paced back and forth with Ireoluwa, whose ear-piercing screams filled the air. The shouting disturbed little Ireoluwa, who began crying with the same frenetic pace as Oluwatobi. Oluwatobi paced back and forth, noticing Ife's lips were rapidly turning blue.

"Please be calm. The baby can tell you are upset," Ife requested.

By the time the chief midwife and team of doulas arrived, Oluwatobi was sure something was horribly wrong. "Where have you been?"

Oluwatobi was distraught and frustrated. The baby's cries reached an ascending screech that made all the adults grab and cover their ears.

"We are here now," the chief midwife tried to speak calmly. She gestured for Oluwatobi to exit and allow her and her team to attend to Ife.

"This is not something for a new father to see. Unfortunately, she is losing a lot of blood. We must attend to her right now. Okay. Please go. Time is of the essence. Someone will fetch you when the matter has been resolved." The chief midwife pointed to the door down the hall where Oluwatobi was to wait with Ireoluwa.

"Please, please. You must do all that you can. She and my son, they are all that I have," Oluwatobi pleaded.

"We will do all in our power to save her," the chief midwife spoke solemnly but not confidently.

"Save her?" Oluwatobi said aloud, expressing his confusion and growing fear.

Oluwatobi's question received no answer. The doulas swiftly ushered him outside where he could wait. As he waited, he prayed and asked that Olodumare show them favor once more and save Ife. He cradled Ireoluwa, who was becoming aggravated as though he too was aware that his mother's life was hanging in the balance. Oluwatobi rocked him gently and hummed the fisherman's lullaby, walking back and forth.

Eventually, Oluwatobi managed to quiet Ireoluwa. With Ireoluwa sleeping at his chest, Oluwatobi took a seat and tried to relax. To pass the time and generate positive thoughts, Oluwatobi tried filling his mind with images and scenes of the life awaiting him after they left the hospital. Oluwatobi closed his eyes and fantasized to calm his mind. He pictured the big catch he would pull in when he got back on his boat. He imagined how delighted his wife and baby would be when he revealed his big catch. Oluwatobi envisioned their collective joy when Ife revealed they were expecting another child. This time it was a girl. Oluwatobi pictured them laughing and jumping up and down with excitement. These images continued until Oluwatobi saw all seven of his and Ife's children—three boys and four girls. Oluwatobi imagined the family dinners, the ceremonies, the weddings, and all the everyday things that would transpire over their marriage. He saw himself on the large fishing boat of his dreams with a small crew that worked for him to supply fish for several villages. He saw his business expanding and his children growing. He imagined himself teaching Ireoluwa the family's secret—the fisherman's lullaby. Oluwatobi could see Ireoluwa practicing the pitch and register of the fisherman's lullaby day and night until he had it right. He saw them debating about whose was better until the time came for Ireoluwa to finally do it without any support. Tears rolled from Oluwatobi's eyes as he pictured his daughters, all four—different weights, sizes, heights, and shades of black, blue-black, and brown. Oluwatobi saw himself seated at the front of each of their weddings, sitting with a smile that could block out the sun with its brightness. Imagining his many grandchildren, Oluwatobi saw himself sitting on the front porch with Ife, hair streaked with grey, watching their grandchildren play. Ife was laughing and smiling and looked so beautiful. Oluwatobi just stared at Ife and watched her face move; her cheeks rose and fell with the laughter, revealing the deep dimples she had on each side. Suddenly, Ife began fading from his view. First, Ife's hands faded, then her arms, and then her body dissolved into thin air. Stunned, Oluwatobi looked around to find that their grandchildren were gone too. Then the house was gone too. When Oluwatobi opened his eyes, the chief midwife was before him.

"Sir, I have some very unfortunate news," the chief midwife spoke as she approached Oluwatobi, who had been moving between sleeping, dreaming, and a wakeful dread.

"Un . . . unfortunate news," Oluwatobi stuttered.

"I am sorry. But she, your wife, did not make it. There was just too much blood lost. I am very sorry that we were not able to save her." Tears streamed down the chief midwife's face even though her tone was measured. Seeing that Oluwatobi, who was large and tall, was about to buckle, the chief midwife grabbed the baby from his hands. Oluwatobi fell to the ground. As the chief midwife rocked Ireoluwa, Oluwatobi wept.

When Olufemi learned Ireoluwa's story, they both cried.

"I am a bad person. I killed my mother," Ireoluwa confessed his shame and guilt.

"No. You are one of the most clever and kindest people I know. We are brothers now. Eh." Olufemi gave Ireoluwa the warmest hug he could muster. Olufemi looked confidently at Ireoluwa, who was on the verge of being lost in the pain of the story. Olufemi saw that his confidence and affirmation were soothing Ireoluwa, whose look of confession and sorrow shifted to a broad, invigorated smile.

"Brothers. Yes. Brothers we shall be." Ireoluwa felt the pain leave his heart and float into the river as they swam back to each of their respective fishing boats.

Olufemi and Ireoluwa's brotherhood had only been a few months old when the harrowing siege arrived. Amidst all of the chaos and panic, what Ireoluwa or Oluwatobi were up to hadn't occurred to Olufemi much at all. To be sure, Olufemi knew they had to be as surprised as he and his father were and likely jumped to action when they heard the emergency bell ring. Splashing with closed eyes, hoping for a down current, Olufemi felt the grip at his ankle tighten. Afraid he was captured, Olufemi's body went limp. Olufemi opened his eyes to face his captors. Relief, however, came upon Olufemi when he opened his eyes. The grip at his ankle was that of Oluwatobi. He and Ireoluwa were directly beside Olufemi and had escaped the men too. Oluwatobi pointed toward a small patch of dry land.

Unfortunately, when Olufemi, Ireoluwa, and Oluwatobi reached the dry patch, they were greeted by a man whom the men called "sheik" with great deference. Accompanied by five heavily armed men, the sheik didn't make a sound. His eyes, outlined in charcoal, conveyed commands and a great fearsomeness. As Olufemi, Ireoluwa, and Oluwatobi were tied up, bells rang sounds of victory from all five fishing boats.

The raiders waved in the distance from each of the five boats, signaling to the sheik that their mission was successful. Olufemi watched as a man hopped from his family's boat onto a small dinghy and sailed in their direction. Olufemi looked at Ireoluwa; they were both confused and terrified. Oluwatobi was wiggling around, appearing to loosen the knots tied at his hands and feet. At first, Oluwatobi's movements had gone unnoticed, and one of the knots at his feet nearly came loose. Just as the knot started to break apart, Olufemi heard the sheik speak in a language he had never heard before: *"Injilziun!"* As suddenly as the sheik had made the command, Oluwatobi was hit in the back of the head twice with the butt of a sword. Oluwatobi fell unconscious.

The sight of an unconscious Oluwatobi terrified Olufemi and Ireoluwa even more. The near thirteen-year-old boys cried as toddlers and pleaded for the men to let them go. Their pleas were met with the sharp edge of a sword to their faces. Olufemi and Ireoluwa went as silent as they could. To prevent them from any further sound, the raiders filled their mouths with the moist soil and another rope was placed between their teeth and tied tightly at the back of their heads.

When the dinghy reached them, Olufemi and Ireoluwa were lifted and placed on the small boat and escorted back toward the fishing boats. Olufemi and Ireoluwa leaned on each other at the back of the dinghy. They kept as quiet as they could and tried not to move, though the terror they felt inside was itching at their throats for sound.

Olufemi and Ireoluwa watched as the fishing boats pulled alongside each other and turned around in the opposite direction of their home, Olumoye. Just as the dinghy they were forced upon traveled the short distance back toward the congregated fishing boats, another dinghy passed by them to fetch the sheik and the two men who stayed behind. When Oluwatobi landed on the boat, there was a loud thud.

"AHH!" The hard landing seemed to awaken Oluwatobi.

The sound of Oluwatobi's voice offered a small comfort to Olufemi and Ireoluwa. Perhaps all had not been lost.

Olufemi was eased some by the sound of Oluwatobi's voice, and it made him wonder where his father was. Olufemi wondered if Babawale managed to escape. If Babawale had escaped, Olufemi was sure he was swimming home furiously to seek reinforcements. The thought of his father seeking rescue and support helped calm Olufemi's chest-pounding heartbeat. As Olufemi's heart calmed at the thought of being saved, the wet soil in his mouth slid down his throat and caused him to involuntarily cough. Ireoluwa, thinking that this was perhaps a plan of Olufemi's, followed suit. Ireoluwa coughed, and the soil shot forward. The immediate relief they both felt from removing the dirt from their mouth was short-lived, as one of the men turned to them both and smacked both boys across the face. The smack was so hard that Olufemi heard a ringing sound in his ears for weeks.

Dazed and slightly injured, Olufemi and Ireoluwa stayed quiet as the dinghy pulled alongside the fishing boat. Three men reached down to help pull Ireoluwa up. After Ireoluwa was pulled on board, Olufemi was lifted and placed next to Ireoluwa. The deck was blood-soaked. Fish, some dead, some alive, were scattered about the boat. When the men pulled Olufemi up next to Ireoluwa, he looked around to see if his father was aboard. Nothing—just blood, fish, and no sight of Babawale.

Olufemi saw the two men his father fended off as the raiders pulled the bound captives, which included several other fishermen, along the deck. One man's throat lay beside him, arms clenched as though he died trying to put his Adam's apple back in place. The other man whom Babawale had stabbed in the eye sat on the deck bleeding heavily, screaming in excruciating pain while tearing away the fabric covering his face. The removal of the fabrics revealed the man was not white or even pale-faced. He was brown—not as brown as Olufemi, but unmistakably brown. Olufemi was astonished.

The men aboard pushed Olufemi and Ireoluwa to the left rail of the fishing boat as they attended to the man blinded by Babawale, knife still engorged in his face. Olufemi felt sick from the man's bloodcurdling groans. While one man attended to his blinded colleague, the other dragged the dead man's body out of sight. Combined with the boat's rocking and the man's grunting, Olufemi's seasickness reemerged, and he began puking. One of the men noticed and cut at Olufemi's rope and pushed his head over the rail to prevent the vomit from landing on board.

Olufemi's profuse vomiting made his vision blurry and threw off his equilibrium. His body rocked, and the man held his back straight and pushed his head over the edge until it seemed Olufemi's seasickness subsided. As Olufemi finished, he felt his stomach emptied and his vision returned. When Olufemi looked down into the Oba River, his heart broke into a thousand pieces. Babawale's bleeding, lifeless body was floating aimlessly. Olufemi realized then that these men were not merely river pirates. Olufemi understood that the armed, garbed raiders were something else altogether. After Oluwatobi was thrown aboard, the sheik approached Olufemi, who was fighting with the men to get to his father.

"If you do not stop, you will be killed like that man there"—he pointed to Babawale's body—"And all those in the village." The sheik pointed dispassionately in the direction of Olumoye.

Olufemi grew still and numb at hearing that everyone in his village was dead too. Olufemi relented, and the raiders placed him beside the remaining captives in the fishing boats. Each dinghy was drenched in petrol and burned as the raiders set sail up the Oba River. Soon after, Olufemi, Ireoluwa, Oluwatobi, and the six captured fishermen learned that they were now slaves headed to somewhere in the great desert. Using Union Jack–embossed maps, the captured fishing boats sailed up the Oba River. Olufemi cried himself to sleep each of the four nights on the fishing boat.

A month into their capture, the sheik-led crew had doubled in size. After the fishing boats reached the end of the river, they were joined by more men who had captured women and girls. Eventually, they reached a great lake that the maps called Lake Chad. When they arrived at Lake Chad, the captives were rearranged by age, language, and sex. The captors also revealed that they spoke at least three languages. There was the language that united them—Arabic, which was used during their prayer time and also to coordinate any plans. Then, there was also French, another language foreign to Olufemi. He heard it for the first time when the new captives, women and girls, had been added. Olufemi's captors used English and French interchangeably to communicate commands.

Usually, they used English and French to say "Move!" or "Stop!" or "Quiet!" or other short demands of that nature. It was at that time that Olufemi became aware of Black Africans who spoke French, being as he was from the part of Africa where English had become common.

Olufemi was also intrigued by the evening prayers that the men participated in. While the captives would be huddled into bounded encircled groups, near or around sunset, the men would roll out small rugs. The ritual always began with the men removing the fabric from their faces. Then the sheik would stand before them. From a book Olufemi had never seen before, the sheik would speak passionately before his men. The usually fearsome and silent leader became talkative as he passionately delivered his message from the great book. After some discussion, the men would all join in a chorus of prayer, repeating and chanting in unison.

Olufemi always watched the prayer ritual with deep intensity. He was taken by the men's obedience. He was enraptured by how the messages from the great book moved the men to reveal their humanity and humility. Even the sheik would assume similar obedience. The prayer ritual was the only time the sheik did as the other men did, even though he spoke and prayed at the front. Although Olufemi was still not proficient in Arabic, he was certain that the men were communing with God. He would listen intently to their rhythmic calls to "Allah" and wondered if anyone was praying for him with the same obedience and rhythm.

After a few days at Lake Chad, the campsite was packed up, and the captives were tied up to camels in a web of ropes and chains. Olufemi found that the large camels made the men seem even more imposing. He also found that he missed the scent of the river. He missed the way the Oba River converged into the Osun River. He missed seeing the women and girls adorned in all white. He missed seeing Oshogbo in the distance. He missed how the offerings rolled and traversed up the river and rode alongside the current and up against the boats. And even though he was prone to seasickness, he even missed that feeling too. Olufemi desperately missed home. The farther the journey and the deeper into the endless sands and dunes of the Sahara Desert they traveled, the more home became a figment of his imagination—a fragment of a life that had been suddenly and forever taken away without his permission.

Olufemi was now on a persistent journey into unknown areas and parts of Africa he'd only heard of in stories the elders told to keep children from traveling too far from home. Rarely ever did the captors allow the men near the boys or the women near the girls. Therefore, Olufemi and Ireoluwa would go for days without directly seeing Oluwatobi. The captives were grouped by the language they could be directed and controlled with, by height, and either as a child or as an adult. At night when the captors slept, Olufemi would whisper to nearby Ireoluwa, sharing his fears and hopes of salvation. Meanwhile, the adult captives had developed a very clever system to communicate with the children by circulating short messages during prayer time, when the captors were enraptured in their routine, until all were informed. Through this method, Olufemi learned that Oluwatobi was well and shared the news with an increasingly despondent Ireoluwa. Olufemi also learned and picked up a few French and Arabic phrases and words.

From Lake Chad, the captives were taken on the long, arduous journey into and through the Sahara Desert. At first, Olufemi was amazed at the sight of the great sands. Olufemi found it especially fascinating how the green of the forest ended and suddenly there was only sand. A few miles into the Sahara, Olufemi looked around and saw all the green was gone, replaced by the white, yellow, and golden dusty sand. He found it hard to keep proper balance on the sand.

Olufemi found it extremely difficult to keep his footing in the sand that was as hot as burning coals. Ireoluwa even tried helping him, whispering tips and tricks he had used to learn how to master walking the great sands. Ireoluwa told Olufemi that it was easier if you pictured it like river water. After a week or so of trying, Olufemi found Ireoluwa's advice helped a great deal. So when they began their second week of walking through the sand, Olufemi imagined that they were in the water and that, like the river, the sand had currents and waves. As Olufemi tried imagining himself rocking in the boat along the Oba River, he suddenly felt a sharp, searing, throbbing pain in his left foot. Olufemi opened his eyes to discover that he had accidentally stepped on something very sharp. Olufemi felt a large gash bleeding from the ball of his right foot. The weeks of travel across the hot sand had already made his feet both callused and fragile. Without thinking, Olufemi let out a loud and painful sound: "OH! OW!" Once the sound of Olufemi's groans reached the front of the line, the slow procession came to an abrupt halt.

As soon as the movement of the camels fully stopped, the captors looked around, worried the sound was that of nearby thieves. The sheik could be overheard commanding his camel to kneel down and allow him to hop off. He, along with a few other men, surveyed the area to find the source of the abrupt sound. The sheik also peered into the distance to ensure they were not being followed or targeted by desert pirates or wandering opportunistic nomads. Then, he walked up to his men and began talking quietly.

Olufemi was scared he'd be punished or even killed for causing the procession and journey to pause. Just a week earlier, a terrible fate befell a boy who looked to be Olufemi's age. During one of the long afternoons of walking, a boy was bitten by a snake on his big toe. The bite alone was pretty gruesome and frightening. In a matter of minutes, the boy's toe turned from brown to red and then green. When the sheik and his men stopped and assessed the damage the boy had endured, they had a short discussion amongst themselves. When they didn't want the captives to know what they were saying, the men spoke in Arabic. One man stood before the young boy who was crying and pleading for help. Without making a sound, the man pulled the jagged sword from behind his back and cut the boy's head off right there. Then, the boy's decapitated body was unchained and left in the desert. Olufemi was horrified. A woman who looked as though she could have been the boy's mother or aunt or relative let out a big gasp and began to cry uncontrollably as they journeyed on. When the men were unable by way of whipping and slapping to get her to stop crying, they cut her head off too.

"Take this as a lesson. No noise. No talking. No questions. No injuries," the sheik spoke with a cold, menacing tone.

Fearing for his own life, Olufemi recalled that horrific event. Olufemi, always a quick study, picked up on their actions that day. He was mindful and clear that a huddle with the leader and his crew could result in death. Even though he couldn't fully understand Arabic just yet, Olufemi did learn then that there was nothing that a captive could do to prevent the brutal discipline that usually followed these pow-wows. Speaking only exacerbated and worsened the punishment.

Crew members walked down the line once more, looking to identify the source of the disruption. The sheik grew impatient and directed the men to abandon the search.

"Water! *L'eau!*" the sheik directed his men to hydrate the prisoners.

When the water command was given, the captives experienced two types of hydration: one was where a half cup was splashed upon them to offer respite from the harsh sun and sand; the second was a half a cup into their mouths. The skilled had figured out how to hold and take in the water with several small swallows, not letting a single drop miss their mouths. Others, however, were not as fortunate or skilled. This was especially true of the young girls and young boys who were both unable to hide their confusion and whose mouths were still too small to handle the sudden, more-than-a-mouthful amount of water. So while some water was fully absorbed by the captives, much of the impatiently poured water fell from parched lips and mouths onto the sand, where it quickly dissipated.

Olufemi watched as water was poured into the women's and girls' mouths. One girl, who looked to be no more than eight years old, tried to lift her head high and open her mouth as wide as she could. Despite those efforts, the water made her cough and choke. Before the little girl could do anything about it, water had sprayed forward onto the backs of those in front of her and onto the hot sand beneath her feet. As a natural instinct, she began to cry. She didn't make a sound, but those who were paying attention could tell that she was crying and terribly dehydrated.

Rather than attempt to bring her more water, the men laughed, and then one man smacked her hard across the face.

Olufemi's foot was bleeding pretty badly by the time the water was poured over his head and then into his mouth. Although Olufemi's skills at conserving and retaining the water they received had improved during his month in bondage, he still wasn't as skilled as others with holding on to all of the water in his mouth. So instead of just simply trying to swallow down all of the water, Olufemi leaned forward as much as he could and turned over his foot slightly, releasing any extra water onto the area where he felt the cut on his foot. Some of the water was from his mouth, while the rest was a combination of sweat and water poured over his head.

When Olufemi saw his foot turn, he noticed a small white fragment in his foot. As painful as it was, Olufemi knew better than to make a further fuss or draw attention. Olufemi's foot throbbed, but he pressed on and dared not make another sound as the trek recommenced. The rhythm of the procession resumed, and a sudden burst of wind rolled through the desert, kicking up sand. When the wind settled, Olufemi was mortified. The rush of wind exposed human skulls and bones for miles in both directions. Olufemi realized he had been cut by the bones of the dead hiding underneath a thin layer of sand. Several of the captives tried to jump over some of the bones, superstitious and fearful that they would anger the dead by walking directly upon their bones.

The crew was unmoved by the discovery and pulled the lines of captives forward. They whipped at the sides of the camels that made them move even swifter, forcing the lines of captives to begin jogging to keep pace. As they jogged forward, each attempted to meet the eyes of the others to affirm they too had seen and been shaken by the terrible secrets of the desert. Seeing the bones in the sand triggered another feeling of sorrow within Olufemi. When the group reached their resting space for the evening, Olufemi allowed the sorrow to come up. Small tears fell along the sides of his face as he watched the crew put up the tents they used to provide temporary shelter during the journey. As Olufemi cried in silence, he heard his best friend, Ireoluwa, whisper out to him in Yoruba that they would survive and be victorious.

At the outset of Olufemi, Ireoluwa, and Oluwatobi's capture, there were others from his village held with them. As the journey proceeded, however, those individuals had been sold and sent away with other groups. When the time for separation came, many pleaded and protested, offering their homes and inheritances to try and stop the trades.

The separations that came along the journey were a startling sight to witness. There was no certain rhythm to it. Captives could be sold at the beginning of the day, the middle of the day, while eating, and even while sleeping. The process all seemed to depend upon what kind of deal had been presented to the leader, whether it be money or supplies or exchange of an adult for a child or vice versa. Olufemi also took notice of how girls who were just sprouting into maturity and young women were the most likely to shift in and out. That was unless those girls and women hadn't already been taken into the men's tents at night. Some of the men treated the younger women and girls with some level of noticeable affection. They would give them more food or water, tend to any injuries, and sometimes even remove their chains at night. Sometimes the sudden arrivals and departures might be one woman and two boys. Other times it was five men and a girl. There wasn't a way to really predict who would be next. And that lack of predictability made the journey through the desert, especially a month in, even more difficult.

Olufemi hadn't realized how observant he had become until Oluwatobi communicated a message to them one evening. From the circle next to them, they received a message from Oluwatobi: "Keep learning all you can." When the message arrived, Olufemi saw Oluwatobi was watching him and Ireoluwa at all times. That realization gave him great comfort. Even though Babawale had perished in the fishing boat siege, Oluwatobi's survival made Olufemi feel as though his father was still alive, living on through his great rival's resilience.

Olufemi ran with Oluwatobi's encouragement. He began practicing late into the night with Ireoluwa the foreign phrases they overheard.

The prayer ritual proved an ideal time for Olufemi to practice and also pick up additional phrases and words. While Ireoluwa concentrated on overhearing the words spoken during the transactions, Olufemi tried to engage the other captives that spoke French and other African languages unfamiliar to him. Together, Olufemi and Ireoluwa had grown proficient in the ways and words of their captors.

Olufemi was especially dutiful, being that he was unsure of the final destination and if he would be separated from the group. He followed orders and never asked questions. Olufemi slept and ate when directed. Olufemi even made it so that he got used to the bone fragment in his foot. After his skin healed around it, Olufemi found that he could manage and appear like he was on equal footing with the rest as they traveled through the desert.

Olufemi, however, was nervous when two things happened back to back—a challenge and an attempted escape. One evening after prayers had concluded, one of the men went to take a resistant young woman into his tent for the evening. The young woman had only been with the larger group for a few days when this occurred, having been traded from another group for supplies such as water, cured beef, and lamb. For those supplies, the sheik received new captives and also a few gold coins as part of the trade. The woman, like so many Olufemi watched the men take at night, was young and dark-skinned. When the man came to take her, one of the male captives who had been traded alongside her stood up in defiant protest. He spoke in an African language unfamiliar to Olufemi and apparently also to the man who was attempting to take the woman to his tent. Initially, the defiance was ignored. But when the woman was snatched up to be taken for the evening, the defiance turned into more than words. The challenger threw several rocks and then sand. Soon enough, the two men were scuffling. Punches were thrown, landing along with kicks to the face and chest. This went on for some time.

Meanwhile, the young woman, who was initially terrified, was now looking for a potential exit. No longer the center of attention, she looked into the vast darkness of the moonlit desert. Unsure whether to stay or leave, she waited until she could make eye contact with her defender. Olufemi could see in her eyes an awareness that this was her best opportunity to get away for good. Her eyes moved between looking at the fight and at the moon above, hoping for guidance. Then, the captor was knocked to the ground, his face in the sand. His red garb was unraveled, revealing his legs and later his head, face, and chest. Some of the captives couldn't help but snicker and savor this beatdown.

"*Bori!* Fatou, *bori,*" the challenger commanded when their eyes finally met. Without hesitation, Fatou ran into the darkness with the swift elegance of a gazelle. Olufemi could hear her first few steps swish in the sand beneath her feet. But soon enough, her body and sound disappeared into the night.

Then the tide turned in the fight. What was once a back and forth between an armed captor and an unarmed challenger shifted. The captive was summarily beating upon the captor, who was now pleading for his life. As the man pleaded, the challenger stripped the man's clothes, showing the captor's full humanness. The mystique of terror used against the captives fell away as the captor's clothes fell to the ground, exposing a thin, average-size man.

Several women encouraged the challenger to kill the man. The challenger, heeding their call, looked around and grabbed a stake from the end of a nearby tent. As he was reaching for the stake, the nearly nude captor wrestled to prevent the use of the stake. Both men reached for the stake with one hand, using the other hand to tear at one another's face. And though the challenger had been victorious thus far, the attempt to get the stake made it so he was losing his advantage. The captor, fearing for his life, tapped into a well of reserve energy, fighting with renewed vigor.

As spectacle of the melee continued, Olufemi watched as one woman jumped to action, kicking the captor in the face. With the swift kick, the man let out a loud groan that echoed. Until that point, the scuffle had been surprisingly quiet, not reaching a volume higher than the sounds of the fire crackling, winds, and howls of the night desert. But when the kick landed, sound escaped the area and sailed into the tents of the rest of the captors and their leader. Like an expected, though still sudden, strike of lightning, the captives were surrounded by the sheik and his men. The women who had been inside their tents were dragged back to the group, some by their arms, others by their heads, and chained and tied up with different groups of captured women.

Some of the captors were fully clothed, others were without their tops or face coverings. By the time the sheik came forward, the challenger was about to thrust the stake into the man's heart. The sheik kicked the challenger to the side and began barking orders at all of his men. The sheik, whose face was also exposed, looked over his defeated and nearly killed colleague with disappointment and disgust. He commanded everyone into silence and quietly surveyed the captives. As he scanned the group, many of the captives trembled in fear, waving their hands in subtle pleas for mercy. The sheik whistled; the sound traveled into the distance and then stopped. When the sound stopped, he grabbed one of the men and pointed into the distance. The man immediately ran in the direction where the whistle had fallen dead.

Meanwhile, the challenger was being held down by five men. The challenger was unafraid. As they held him down, his daze and rage had turned into a deep belly laugh. *"Je m'en fiche. Tue-moi!"* The challenger bellowed at the sheik with cynical laughter.

Olufemi, who had become somewhat proficient in French, whispered to Ireoluwa the challenger's message. "Luwa, that man just told them to kill him. He doesn't care."

Ireoluwa's eyes grew large as he digested the message. After everything they'd seen, it wouldn't be surprising for the challenger to be killed immediately.

"Tue-toi?" The sheik responded with his own laughter. Unlike the challenger, the sheik's laughter was creepy.

Olufemi was afraid to whisper, as he might get caught speaking. Instead, Olufemi looked back to Ireoluwa, shaking his head and closing his eyes to convey that a worse fate was in store for the challenger. Olufemi saw Ireoluwa looking around for a glimpse of Oluwatobi.

The sheik looked down at the challenger, who was no longer struggling to get free but laughing hysterically. The sheik grimaced and walked over to his defeated colleague who was attempting to place his tattered garb back upon his body and achieve some semblance of recovery. The sheik spat upon his colleague, then he snapped his fingers. On cue, several men grabbed their desperate colleague and dragged him toward the sheik's tent. As they dragged him, he pleaded with the leader, who acted as though he couldn't hear. The sheik walked back to the challenger and snapped his fingers, and he too was dragged off to his tent.

As the challenger's hysteria grew fainter, the man returned from the distant darkness with Fatou in his arms. She was unconscious and badly bleeding from her ankle. There was a knot at the back of her head and a sizeable cut in her right calf. Fatou's legs were retied tightly. All the captives watched with great silence, shocked by her sudden and efficient recapture. Some of the young girls and boys began to cry without sound as though their dreams of escape had been destroyed at the sight of Fatou's unsuccessful attempt.

The sheik looked around at all of the captives with rageful eyes. "Sleep! *Dormez!*" he commanded.

Like toppling dominoes, each of the captives lay on the ground and closed their eyes. Some, who were already exhausted from the long walk and eventful evening, fell asleep immediately. Others, including Olufemi and Ireoluwa, pretended to be asleep until it was clear that their captors were no longer in earshot. Ireoluwa tapped Olufemi. Olufemi looked again to Ireoluwa and noticed a small, shiny object. Ireoluwa had a dagger. Olufemi was surprised and confused about how he'd missed Ireoluwa's attaining a knife.

The next day, the journey through the sand seemed to be going as usual. The heat combined with the sand was unforgiving and relentless. Fatou was still bleeding, and only a small bandage covered her. Fatou's defender was placed in front of Olufemi, who kept bumping up against him due to his constant stumbling. Olufemi was frustrated with the man; he did not want to get in any trouble because he had been unable to keep pace. In an effort to temper his frustrations, Olufemi practiced Arabic and French words while praying for a sign that he would survive.

Olufemi quietly rehearsed lines he'd heard during the prayer ritual and continued to look into the distance when a sparkling light reflected back at him. As Olufemi squinted for a precise view, he saw an oasis just a few miles ahead. Olufemi had heard a great deal about these mysterious locations in the desert where communities existed, operating as a lively, ephemeral port for wanderers, nomads, and travelers making their way through the desert.

The sight of the oasis filled Olufemi's mind with so many thoughts. For the first time since being captured, he felt a sense of excitement racing around in his chest. Just as Olufemi began to speculate to himself what the oasis would look like and how it would sound, he bumped again into the man in front of him. This time, however, the man fell to the ground. Olufemi was surprised. As with any disruption in the rhythm of the procession, the crewmen flew from atop the kneeling camels to determine the problem. When the halt arrived, Olufemi noticed that the man's short pants were blood-soaked. Olufemi had also noticed the brown sack that had been dragged at the end of their chain. It was odd, but Olufemi didn't know what to think about it. Olufemi leaned over to try and help the man up, but he was too heavy, too big. Olufemi's attempt to assist had also meant that now his pants and part of his body were covered in the man's blood.

Two of the captors, noticing the man on the ground, ran to him. Two other men walked along the line of women and girls to see if there had been any issues there as well. Pushing Olufemi aside, they turned the man over and pulled away. As they turned and pulled the former challenger away, Olufemi saw that the man was dead, and their dragging of him made his short pants roll down, exposing intensely mutilated genitals. It took all of Olufemi's discipline not to faint or vomit at the sight.

The two men called to the sheik. The sheik did not look back, raising his hand in command. In response, one of the men pulled a sack from his bag. After being placed into the sack, the dead man was tied to a rope attached to the back of the sheik's camel.

Fatou went from shrieking to violently sobbing. Fatou then gave words to her sudden grief in a shrilling call to the sky above. *"Mon mari est mort!"*

Fatou's scream caused everyone to cover their ears. The two crewmen surveilling the women and girls rushed over to try and subdue Fatou, who fought with them. The nearby women and girls tried to get out of the way. The two men rolled around with Fatou in the sand. The men were unaware that during the struggle, Fatou had gotten hold of a dagger tucked at one of their waists. As suddenly as she had begun struggling, Fatou gave in and returned to her feet. The crewmen put Fatou back in position. Set in between her bound hands, Fatou took the dagger and pulled it furiously from the left side of her neck to the right side, and blood burst forward as she fell to the ground dead.

By the time the sheik and his entourage arrived at the oasis, Fatou's lifeless body had been dragged in a sack alongside her dead husband for several miles. When the sheik entered, he was greeted like a great warrior king, and his men were welcomed like faithful soldiers. The three brown sacks were pulled forward. The captives were escorted to slave quarters. Olufemi was passing by just as the contents of the first of the three brown sacks were being revealed. Unable to look away, Olufemi saw the face exposed was the man Fatou's defender had beaten and nearly killed. He was wrapped tightly in white linens. Olufemi remembered these linens, as they were similar to those placed upon the man his father had killed on the fishing boat. A few days into their journey up the river, Olufemi recalled how the men had found a plot of dirt just off shore, and the sheik led and oversaw the funeral at the Oba River. At the time of the impromptu funeral, Olufemi was still too shocked and confused to really care about how the man Babawale killed was treated by the red-garbed men. Now keen on studying his captors in search of the ultimate advantage, Olufemi connected several things at once. Olufemi understood that the white dressing was a key part of the death ritual in the religion he watched them studiously and obediently practice.

After everything Olufemi had witnessed, he had now finally figured out that the gold and red of the sheik's head were a crown of sorts; for everywhere they went, he commanded an expectation of fealty, sovereignty, and loyalty. Back in Olumoye, only chiefs and high priests were treated in such a manner. The way the sheik was greeted time and again was like that of the big bosses of the underground from Babawale's stories of his past criminal life.

As Olufemi came to deduce these clues about his captors and their sheik, for the first time since his capture, Olufemi was no longer afraid, no longer terrified. Instead, Olufemi was even more determined to escape the clutches of the sheik. Olufemi believed he would live to tell the tale of his survival of the cruel sheik. It was then, in this overwhelming feeling of strength and fire, that Olufemi also realized Babawale was still with him. Certain that his father did not perish in that river, Olufemi was convinced that his father's spirit had been following overhead as he, Ireoluwa, and Oluwatobi made the arduous journey. Olufemi was sure that Babawale's spirit had been protecting him the entire time and that explained why he hadn't been separated or sold or killed. Olufemi's face cracked with his first smile in ages, when he realized his father was still protecting him. The fishing boat, the rivalry—they were not just a vocation or unimportant trivialities. His father had used the fish, the river, his stories of fallen criminals, and even his relentless discussion of how to beat Oluwatobi as a special classroom for Olufemi, his firstborn son. Olufemi's time with his father had been full of master lessons. And as Olufemi traveled to the slave quarters, his smile was met by a grinning, reunited Oluwatobi and Ireoluwa.

1847

Just above Ireoluwa's head, the sun was setting in a beautiful mashup of violet and red hues. The purplish-red streaks stretched across the sky wrapped around Table Mountain, adding an undeniable glow to the wedding ceremony. Cape Town looked so round, large, and beautiful below. Ireoluwa took the colors as confirmation that the mighty Spirit in the sky was watching with great approval and encouragement as he took the big leap into marriage. The sun and, in particular, the sunset had been a trusted guide and friend to Ireoluwa as he found himself in distant lands, shores, and horizons. As a young boy in the desert, Ireoluwa noticed the sun's seeming guidance and support as they journeyed through the wilderness of worlds, languages, and unknown customs. And so, when the sunset appeared with such an unexpected and spectacular combined hue of violet-breathing-red flourishes, Ireoluwa was especially taken. He took a moment to stare at the sunset and offer up his eternal gratitude for the sun's protection and guidance.

After Ireoluwa believed he had captured the sunset's essence in his heart and mind, he closed his eyes. This sudden pause did not go unnoticed. The minister stopped and stared as did the rest of the bridal party. They too understood the power of this moment for Ireoluwa. An unspoken agreement emerged whereby a generosity of patience took over so as to allow Ireoluwa to absorb and bask in the impressive and beautiful colors of the setting sun. Ireoluwa's big heart had been bruised and battered, though it still managed to pour love into others.

Though Ireoluwa hadn't anticipated being so taken with the colorful sunset, he felt it was important that he took it all in. He didn't ask permission, taken as he was with the inviting vibration of the sunset. Ireoluwa felt a powerful frequency emanating from the mountain into his body and outward toward the sunset. Everyone watched patiently and lovingly as Ireoluwa experienced this vibrating sensation of color, earth, and sun. Ireoluwa took in a few long, deliberate, deep breaths and held them in until they filled his belly. He then allowed the air to swirl around as if it were meant to find and attach to something he no longer needed. As the air settled and attached, Ireoluwa released each breath with slow and warm gratitude. His eyes closed, and the luscious sunset in his belly filled him so that he felt he might burst through his ceremonial garments.

And so he released the air he'd captured inside one last time. While Ireoluwa did so, he placed his hand over the key along with his beaded necklace. Ireoluwa pulled the key past the scar on his chest and over his heart. The stiff warmth of the iron key passed over onto his heart, and Ireoluwa felt his father Oluwatobi standing beside him with pride. Feeling the pride emanating from Oluwatobi, Ireoluwa began to see again the key events that led him to this moment, guided him to Cape Town, and prepared him for this sacred ritual atop Table Mountain, all of it coming together in a wondrous prism of remembrance. As the light rose up from his heart into his mind's eye, everything he had endured played in rapid recall.

Anger anchored the first memories Ireoluwa recalled. Ireoluwa remembered how angry he was with his father the day they were all captured. Ireoluwa thought back to him and his father on the fishing boat in the Oba River. He recalled how they had been arguing just before their fishing boat was attacked and ransacked. After being on the Oba River for two straight days, Ireoluwa was frustrated with his father's incessant rivalry with the other fishermen, especially Olufemi's father Babawale. Oluwatobi was a very kind and generous man but also very competitive.

In fact, Ireoluwa felt that one of his father's great talents and secrets was his quiet competitiveness. Oluwatobi was always determined to outwit and outfish anyone who tried to beat him out or dare challenge him. The truth, however, was that Oluwatobi was extremely gifted at hiding his competitiveness under a veil of being seemingly unbothered by the presence of a challenge. Oluwatobi was so effective at this performance that his success often came due to the fact that his unbothered disposition would madden his competitors, leading them to acts of self-sabotage. In their quest to defeat the seemingly unbothered Oluwatobi, competitors would usually make a serious error of judgment or mistake, like breaking a fishing pole or making too much noise and thus scaring off the fish. The spooked fish would usually end up directly in Oluwatobi's nets or hooked to his fishing lines.

Whereas the other fishermen had children and large families to provide food for in addition to selling them at the market, in Ireoluwa's case, it was just he and his father. Ireoluwa's grandparents had all ascended into the great beyond by the time he was ten years old. One set, his father's parents, died from an illness that swept through the village. Everyone was sure that the British missionaries traveling the Oba River on small dinghies were the source of the disease that killed dozens of families.

The other set of grandparents, his mother Ife's parents, had passed on from the suffering and grief brought upon them by the sudden loss of their prized, precious only child and daughter, Ireoluwa's mother. Ireoluwa's extended family made him feel and believe he was cursed, contending that any proximity to Ireoluwa was life-threatening if not fatal. Ireoluwa's relatives on his mother's side often declined the fish his father offered. Once Oluwatobi's parents succumbed to illness, the rest of the family believed that being near the father and son was like inviting death to lie beside you. Ireoluwa once overheard his aunt telling his father that not having a proper naming ceremony had been the reason behind his wife's death and had resulted in Ireoluwa being cursed.

Ireoluwa, however, didn't need much help to be convinced that he was cursed. He had long believed that his birth had killed his mother. As a child, when Ireoluwa played outside, he noticed how all the other children had a young woman watching over their every move and how he did not have that. At first, Ireoluwa thought that one day his woman protector might appear. Ireoluwa was around five when he got up the courage to ask his father about the missing woman in his life. When Ireoluwa asked Oluwatobi, he could tell from the pain in his father's eyes that something terrible had transpired. Over the next year, his father provided answers in small doses. Oluwatobi recounted, a piece at a time, the romance he and Ife shared, the excitement of her pregnancy, and the unexpected tragedy in the birthing room. Even though Ireoluwa knew he could not help being born and would never want to have hurt his mother, he believed that had he not been born, his parents would be a happily married couple.

By the time Ireoluwa finally found the courage to tell Olufemi the story of his birth and mother's death, he believed his being cursed was permanent. What began initially as proto-rivalry emulating their fathers transformed into a budding friendship between two twelve-year-old boys bored on fishing boats and mutually dreading a shared destiny as fishermen. Ireoluwa was so nervous and caught up in the telling of the story, blurting it out as they both dried in the sun, he hadn't been looking at Olufemi's face as he spoke. So when Olufemi held on to him, embraced him, and called him brother, it was a total shock. Up until that moment, Ireoluwa had never been hugged by anyone other than his father. Olufemi's words were confident and sure. "We are brothers!" The phrase cycled around Ireoluwa's mind several times before he was able to digest it.

Ireoluwa felt something break inside when Olufemi shouted, "We are brothers!" Ireoluwa felt Olufemi's affirmation releasing him from the so-called curse. Even if only in words, they were to be brothers, and Olufemi's confidence convinced Ireoluwa that neither his life nor Oluwatobi's was cursed.

For the next two months, Ireoluwa prodded Oluwatobi about ending the rivalry with Olufemi's father, Babawale. At the beginning of his campaign for reconciliation, Ireoluwa would bring up the issue in small doses, dropping remarks in random spots between baiting hooks and pulling in lines. Ireoluwa tended to the bait and exclaimed: "Oh look! Olufemi and his father are having a good time. Should we wave?" or "Father, my swim with Olufemi was fun. I think he is my friend. Do you think you and his father could be friends too?"

Each time, though, Ireoluwa was quickly rebuffed and dismissed. Oluwatobi would scrunch up his face, look at Ireoluwa, and reply: "Falling for their clever tricks. Eh?" or "Son, you are the only friend I need or desire. Now tend to the line!" Months into this failed attempt at compelling Oluwatobi to reconciliation, Ireoluwa was deeply frustrated and grew angry with his father.

It was their argument about ending the rivalry that had made both Ireoluwa and Oluwatobi deaf to the sounds of the raiders approaching the fishing boats. Ireoluwa was yelling at his father, telling him how terribly unfair he was: "You want me to be lonely my whole life!" Ireoluwa had just barked at his father when they both heard the bell sounding an emergency from Babawale and Olufemi's boat. With the rattling of the bell, Oluwatobi quickly ran to Ireoluwa. He felt his father grab his shoulder.

Oluwatobi grabbed Ireoluwa, and the two of them ran to the edge of the boat to see what was happening. As they neared the back of the fishing boat, they saw Olufemi jump into the water. When Ireoluwa looked to the front of their boat, two men were aboard and charging with swords aimed in their direction.

"Trust me, son." Oluwatobi looked to Ireoluwa and grabbed his hand as they both jumped off the boat. They began swimming furiously toward the small patch of dry land a few yards in the distance. Oluwatobi noticed Olufemi splashing directionless and confused. Afraid Olufemi might drown, Oluwatobi grabbed his leg and pulled him. Although Ireoluwa had imagined Oluwatobi's embrace of Olufemi would be under different circumstances, when they were captured, he appreciated it had come to pass no matter the context.

By the time the journey had reached Lake Chad, Ireoluwa's depression had grown. Ireoluwa was also mad that he was taken without his consent. Letting his mind wander during the trek, Ireoluwa was sad at the thought that perhaps the captors knew that no one would look for him and his father. Ireoluwa was sure that someone must have betrayed him and Oluwatobi to ensure that they would never return to Olumoye ever again. Ireoluwa's depression made it so that he was growing more disconnected from his body, numb and withdrawn.

Whereas Olufemi seemed to be looking for a way out at all times and consumed with the prayer rituals of their captors, Ireoluwa was hopeless. So many of the captives were killed, sold, and traded, which sometimes made Ireoluwa jealous and even more depressed. It was not until Ireoluwa noticed a map the captors used during their time at the great lake that he began to feel something different than depression consuming him. Even still, Ireoluwa began to take note of the various transactions that had occurred. Ireoluwa made mental notes of the chain of command amongst his captors and the various languages used.

Then, when the captors dismembered a boy right in front of him, Ireoluwa felt something inside him change. Over his life, Ireoluwa was very sensitive to the pain of others. Even when his father would clean and cut the fish, he would feel a little wrenching in his abdomen. When the boy's head fell to the ground, Ireoluwa awoke from the spell of darkness and apathy that had been overwhelming him. As the captors dispatched similar barbaric measures on the boy's mother, Ireoluwa compelled his spirit to reintegrate and rejoin his body. Ireoluwa knew if he allowed his spirit to continue to hover away from his body, he would never be able to help Oluwatobi, Olufemi, or himself get away from this walking prison.

Little by little, Ireoluwa gained an understanding of French and some Arabic. He figured out that the materials the men were using to capture people and plot their way through the wilderness were based on British and French maps of the areas. Then came the messages from Oluwatobi, which uplifted his spirits.

The sight and sound of Olufemi bleeding and in pain also helped Ireoluwa break free of his disassociation. Even though Ireoluwa couldn't control what the captors did, he began to believe that he was not without control. Ireoluwa still had power; it was just hidden underneath the turmoil and pain. Ireoluwa recognized that he could and did have power over himself. That newfound sense of self-control became the foundation of Ireoluwa's search for a new purpose, compelling him to draw upon his inner power. Ireoluwa could not allow or abide by Olufemi's sudden death. Ireoluwa's mind sorted through a variety of scenarios to determine how to help Olufemi when a guiding voice told him to look up to the sun. The voice was confident yet gentle, quiet while also being clear. Though Ireoluwa had never heard the voice before, it felt familiar and safe. Ireoluwa knew he had to trust it. So Ireoluwa looked up at the beaming orb overhead, squinting and squeezing his eyes so that he could make out the sun's circumference.

In response to the intensity of the sunlight and heat, Ireoluwa's eyes shut. The inner voice returned, instructing Ireoluwa to trust and call upon the help of the wind to aid his friend and fellow captives. Again with great obedience, Ireoluwa did as he was instructed.

"Mighty winds please save us. Please help my brother," Ireoluwa whispered as the captors searched to locate the rule breaker.

When the wind didn't come, Ireoluwa worried that he hadn't asked correctly or with enough belief. Ireoluwa listened harder for directions from the guiding voice. The voice rose up again, directing him: "Call the wind."

"Wind," Ireoluwa whispered his command.

A sudden powerful wind came across the desert and saved Olufemi. When the sands shifted to reveal the carcasses and bones beneath their feet, Ireoluwa knew he had tapped into a power that resided deep within. Later that evening, Ireoluwa and Olufemi tried tending to his wound and pulling the bone fragment from the ball of his foot. Their attempts caused Olufemi more pain than leaving it in place. Ireoluwa thought about telling Olufemi then about the voice he heard, but he changed his mind, figuring there would come a time when he was supposed to share it.

Ireoluwa remembered how anxious he was when he noticed the small knife in the torn garb. The night before the fight over Fatou at the fire had broken out, Ireoluwa had revealed to Olufemi his notes on the sheik, the crewmen, and his recent discerning of the Wolof language. It was Ireoluwa who had told Olufemi that Fatou had been instructed to run. Even if it had not been clear to everyone else, Ireoluwa was sure that Fatou's defender was her husband.

Before the melee began, Ireoluwa heard the voice again. The voice hadn't come to him since the winds blew and saved Olufemi. Ireoluwa had thought it a fluke and was glad that he had not shared the information with Olufemi. But just before the man came to take Fatou, he heard the voice: "Eyes open. Opportunity strikes."

Again, the voice came from inside Ireoluwa just as the captor suddenly appeared and unlocked Fatou's chains. As Fatou pulled away and the challenger rose, Ireoluwa closed his mouth. He could feel a swirling again, like that which came when Olufemi was injured. The voice spoke again: "Look for the shine in the torn clothes."

Pretending to watch the fight like everyone else, Ireoluwa scanned the ripped fabrics for a shiny object. In looking at the torn fabric, he observed Oluwatobi sneakily grabbing and hiding something in his pants. It happened quickly, and Oluwatobi hadn't noticed Ireoluwa watching. As his father leaned back and returned to spectating, Ireoluwa noticed a shiny object that looked as though it was glowing from the light cast by the fire. The torn garments were too far to reach with his hand. They were close enough to reach with his foot. When Ireoluwa leaned his foot into the pile of fabric, he felt a sharp object and knew that the shiny object was a knife. Ireoluwa worked his foot to the handle. Ireoluwa coaxed the knife from inside the fabric and used all of his toes to pull it toward him.

As Ireoluwa began remembering the desert oasis, the lights of the memories faded. A misty fog roiled Ireoluwa's mind as he tried to return to the scene, attempting to recapture the moment when he and his father reunited and shared their tools of escape with Olufemi. Ireoluwa pulled and pushed, sorting through his mind's library of his life. Just as the memory of Olufemi's look of surprise in the oasis grew more vivid, it dissipated again. Ireoluwa began to conclude that perhaps it was time that he opened his eyes and returned himself to the wedding ceremony when the inner voice returned: "Remember me." The voice beckoned Ireoluwa. Before he could question what was or who was to be remembered, the last twenty years replayed as though they were on an unhinged wheel racing and spinning into the present. Ireoluwa's three escapes from captivity flashed in sequence.

As though it was a play happening before him, Ireoluwa watched a projection of his younger self as the guiding voice grew louder: "Remember me. Remember it all."

Ireoluwa saw the moment when he pulled the knife out in the slave quarters under the full moon in the desert oasis. Cutting the rope on the second night, Oluwatobi moved briskly and immediately as the bandits partying grew louder and more raucous.

Ireoluwa cut everyone nearby free from the large ropes that entangled them together. After cutting away the ropes of those nearby, Ireoluwa handed the knife down the line so that those out of reach could use it to free themselves. Each person passed the blade down until the entirety of the rope had been cut away. At the same time, Oluwatobi tried the key on the lock that bound him, and when it popped open, everyone was shocked. The popped lock amazed everyone. To the ears of the captives, many of whom had been in bondage for several weeks, the sound of the lock opening was like the roar of a mighty lion and that of answered prayers. Some cried when they heard their own locks pop open and release, while others jumped, danced, and moved around as they regained their freedom of movement.

The releasing of the locks also provided the choice to escape alone or as a collective. Olufemi tried translating with what little words he'd picked up in Arabic, English, French, Ibo, and Wolof. Olufemi stood tall, emulating the posture of the sheik. All the captives, including Ireoluwa, found Olufemi's performance a combination of eerily familiar, hilarious, and compelling. They were amazed at Olufemi's linguistic dexterity and his ability to soothe the anxieties many felt as the chains and ropes were released from their bodies, falling to the ground in piles. Oluwatobi's key made the rotation through the slave quarters, and for a few moments, people just stood still with gratitude.

Olufemi tried giving everyone a sense of the safest direction out of the quarters and oasis and into the darkness of the desert. Ireoluwa wrote a compass into the sand, mapping out east, west, north, and south. But as Ireoluwa was finishing his compass in the sand, impatience disrupted the harmony, and some began to go their own way. Some of the women and girls had decided their path was through the captors. After the treatment they'd endured, they left to rescue their sisters, nieces, aunts, cousins, and mothers stuck with the oblivious celebratory captors. The women and girls grabbed anything they could fashion into a weapon to rescue the other women and girls. Olufemi tried to call them back, but they refused, and some of the men went along with the women and girls. Others awaiting further direction looked to Ireoluwa to point the way southwest, as they all knew that their homes had to be southwest of the great desert. When Ireoluwa finally pointed southwest, the group of fifty captives was completely disbanded. People were running east and west, northwest and southwest. The captors, who were partying in the center of the oasis, had thought the group of captives so obedient and fearful they'd forgotten to assign an overseer for the evening.

As Ireoluwa, Oluwatobi, and Olufemi ventured southwesterly, they noticed they were alone. Despite all of their directions and the compass, folks had decided to take their own path. Then came the loud thuds and screams from the center of the oasis. The three of them looked at one another, knowing that the slaughtering had begun. And from the sounds in the distance, the armed women and girls were getting the best of their captors. Ireoluwa's memory spun seamlessly to the second escape.

Following a few weeks of traveling southwest, the trio was fooled by a nomad who promised to help them to a shortcut out of the Sahara Desert and back toward the great lake. Before they knew it, the trio was surrounded and tied up by men in green garb. A week later, all of their progress seemed erased when Ireoluwa could see the oasis they'd escaped in the distance. As they approached, the oasis wreaked of the stench of death. After a scout went inside to check it out, it was clear that there were no living people inside, and they continued to the oasis. Other than the bodies of dead men and women, valuables looked to have been removed. A night later, they were traded to a different group of men in black garb and told they were going to be sent to a place across the seas called India. Before they were to board the vessel, the men revealed a final cruelty. Adult captives were to stay behind, and the young boys were to be castrated to prevent them from procreating.

Ireoluwa and Olufemi were screaming when the sharp knife pierced the skin of their scrotums. Ireoluwa could feel the blood flow down his leg and onto the dusty table. He turned his head to see Olufemi, who was on the verge of passing out from the terror and pain. Oluwatobi stormed in and began stabbing the men just before the boys were fully cut. Ireoluwa didn't know how Oluwatobi had gotten free or how he managed to get inside the room. He grabbed loincloths and pulled Olufemi up from the table. The two young boys hugged each other as they watched Oluwatobi's prowess with amazement.

"Run, my sons! You must go now!" Oluwatobi commanded them.

Ireoluwa looked at Olufemi, who understood what was about to happen, as it was reminiscent of the last words of his father during the Oba River siege. Ireoluwa was reluctant and hesitant.

"Go now! Go to the ship." Oluwatobi was now standing in front of the two boys and fending off two more men who had come into the room upon hearing the noise of the scuffle.

The third escape was the final one. Whereas the first two had been weeks apart, the last one took nearly twenty years and much more planning. Believed to be fully castrated, Ireoluwa and Olufemi were assigned and made to be eunuchs. They were informed that upon arrival, they would be working at the behest of the Guptas, a very powerful family in India. The journey on the ship was long and rocky. And because the new place was across an ocean neither had ever seen nor heard of, escaping would not be as simple as it was when they were in Africa.

In addition to several properties across India, Ireoluwa learned that the Guptas oversaw several large ships that traveled between England and South Africa exporting and importing rooibos, sugar, and a host of spices and fabrics. Ireoluwa and Olufemi were kept in a series of homes where wealthy men held and hid their concubines. Ireoluwa and Olufemi were shown to a room they would share for the entirety of their time and told the rules, obligations, and potential punishments for disobedience.

Most often, Ireoluwa and Olufemi were responsible for overseeing the day-to-day activities of the hidden harem. They cooked and cleaned. They took turns regaling the trapped women with wondrous stories of Africa they'd learned as small children. Isolated in slum quarters in New Delhi alongside numerous young Black African girls and women, Ireoluwa and Olufemi did their best to encourage and protect their charges; it was terrible and difficult work. Many nights, they were forced to listen as older men took the women to their beds for sex and other acts.

After fifteen years of captivity, Ireoluwa and Olufemi became prized possessions. As true as it was that the duo had become of great value, there were still times, however, when they were harshly disciplined. This was especially the case when, from time to time, a young woman would run off or commit suicide. In those cases, Ireoluwa and Olufemi would be lashed and placed into a dark cell for weeks at a time. During those times in the quiet darkness, Ireoluwa and Olufemi practiced and taught each other the language of their newest captors, prayed, and further developed their plans to return back to Africa.

Over the years, their duties grew from just cooking, cleaning, and watching after the concubines and their children to training new boys who had been mutilated and reduced to eunuch status. Olufemi, who had been quickly identified for his penchant for languages, was also responsible for translating for the women. Ireoluwa was also very good at interpreting and understanding the languages, but he and Olufemi thought it wise if one portrayed proficiency in certain areas while the other pretended to lack proficiency in that same area. The scheme proved highly effective, so that by the time they were nearing twenty-eight years old, Ireoluwa and Olufemi had not been separated. Both young men watched as others were separated and moved in covered wagons to other properties where eunuchs were needed. It was never a good feeling to see the young boys shipped off elsewhere into the darkest corners of the city's underground world.

Olufemi had also become quite religious, self-converting to Islam. "Allah shall provide a way for us, my brother. We will survive this," Olufemi would often console Ireoluwa in times of great despair.

By the time the boys had matured into adults, they had developed a keen sense of the patterns of their captors and were implementing gradual plans of escape. Ireoluwa and Olufemi would over time get enough money to pay for a place in the cargo of a ship back to Africa. There were several ships a year that went to and from South Africa. Being that the place was called South Africa, Ireoluwa and Olufemi thought it made sense to try and use that as the place to either return to their homes or start a new life and move forward. After all, being in India for fifteen years had brought them to the belief that all of Africa was home no matter the location. Having managed to live through so many nightmares, Ireoluwa was sure that an ideal scenario for escape would soon emerge.

It was during these years that Ireoluwa finally shared with Olufemi that an inner voice offered and provided him guidance in times of great need. Ireoluwa told Olufemi that it had helped him bring forth the wind and played a key role in each of their previous escapes. Olufemi believed and trusted Ireoluwa, so he did not question the existence of the inner voice. They were both happy to receive any help that they could.

Ireoluwa and Olufemi's plans for escape hinged on deploying a small fortune they had managed to accrue and hide over the years. Some of the coins and jewelry came off of some of the men who died inside the quarters of natural and mysterious causes. When incredibly brutal men tried to make their way through the residences and torture the women, Ireoluwa had developed an extremely effective slow-acting potion that would gradually kill even the strongest man. To avoid being caught, Ireoluwa had to be discerning about when and to whom he fed the mixture of mashed oleander and arsenic in food and tea. The first time Ireoluwa used the tea, it was on an Englishman who had relentlessly raped a young girl for several days. The back and forth between screams of anguish and menacing silence that came from the room roiled Ireoluwa and Olufemi. Unable to handle the idea that this Englishman would be able to get away with such barbarism, Ireoluwa and Olufemi concocted a way to get the man to drink the poisoned tea and even take several bags with him to ensure that he received the full dose. Believing the two Black eunuchs were offering a great service with their tea, the man tipped them several silver coins. Ireoluwa later learned the man died aboard a ship on the way back to England along with two other men who shared the tea. No one knew why or how, and because men dying at sea was a rather frequent occurrence, the deaths carried little suspicion. Years later, the tips and tricks had developed into quite the stash for Ireoluwa and Olufemi. Trusted as they were after so many years of service, their belongings were not checked or surveilled, which made it easy enough to store and hide their contraband. Ireoluwa had learned that living in a den of evil with thieves, rapists, and liars was quite fertile ground for exacting a plan that required backstabbing and betrayal.

Fifteen years was a lifetime, and they'd been pretending to be castrated and obedient for all of that time. While they knew they would leave soon, when to pull the trigger on the plan had to be well-timed with the ship traveling to South Africa. The objective was to pay a few men to carry them onto the ship as cargo and stow them away until they reached a place they had heard of called Cape Town. Ireoluwa had learned that slavery was outlawed there just ten years earlier, and a community of freed slaves had settled in a district in Cape Town. While the duo agreed they would leave in a few weeks, that timeline was shortened when a young girl from Cape Town arrived at the residence as a new concubine. Her name was Gugu, and Olufemi thought she was the most beautiful woman he'd ever seen. And from what Ireoluwa could make out from how Gugu looked at Olufemi, the feeling was mutual.

About two days after Gugu's arrival, a wealthy Indian man and relative of the elder Gupta came to make his usual rounds through the new girls. When he arrived, Ireoluwa could tell Olufemi's blood was boiling watching the man scan Gugu's body with desire. The man pointed at Gugu, a sign that she was to go up to her quarters and await his arrival. Olufemi panicked, and Ireoluwa was concerned about hastiness. Anticipating this situation might come to pass, Ireoluwa had bargained with two of the men whose loyalty he knew was to money above all things. They'd agreed that they would help him, his friend, and Gugu stow away on the last ship of the year to Cape Town. The voyage would be uncomfortable, but they would be placed where they would not be caught. Ireoluwa enhanced a survival package that had initially only been enough for him and Olufemi and did his best to build it up to sustain the three of them, even if it meant he would go some days without food. To Ireoluwa, the sacrifice was worth it.

Ireoluwa tried calming Olufemi as they watched the older man head up the stairs and heard the door to Gugu's room close. "Hold on," Ireoluwa's inner voice returned for the first time since their second capture. Ireoluwa half understood and even tried humming the fisherman's lullaby to Olufemi to calm him as he often did in times when they were under great duress.

"Luwa, he is going to rape Gugu. The humming won't stop that!" Olufemi was enraged.

"Femi, the wagon is nearly here, and I have given the man a heavy dose of the tea." Ireoluwa spoke with deep patience and understanding.

Then they heard rocking and a muffled sound. Olufemi couldn't contain himself. He grabbed a knife.

"I will meet you in the wagon. I promise, brother." Olufemi was scarily calm, holding on tightly to the long knife he retrieved from the kitchen.

Ireoluwa knew that he would lose precious time if he didn't hurry.

Soon enough, Ireoluwa was hiding inside the wagon. Ireoluwa handed over the tidy sum. After counting and sorting through the payment, the men winked at Ireoluwa and started to pull off. Ireoluwa asked the paid men to wait just a few more moments, as the two others were on their way.

"If they are not here in two minutes, you will have to decide if you stay or go. We have to get this cargo to the ship before it leaves in an hour."

In half that time, Olufemi arrived carrying Gugu, who was passed out. Everyone ignored Olufemi's bloody hands, and the wagon proceeded to the dock. Hidden in a large trunk of fabric, the trio made it onto the boat. The trunk was placed in the bowels of the ship, remaining at the bottom of the boat until they arrived in Cape Town. Having arrived just as the moon replaced the sun in the sky, the chest containing the trio was pulled off the ship. The three of them bounced around inside, making little noise as the chest along with others was taken on a wagon into the heart of Cape Town. They felt a great thud when the chests were dropped to the ground and placed at a receiving dock of a garment factory.

Ireoluwa's wheel of memories spun forward. There was the birth of Gugu's first baby, born of her harrowing experience in India. He and Olufemi feeling on top of the world after acquiring the deed to their own fishing boat and a multifamily residential building in Cape Town's District Six. Ireoluwa recalled Olufemi and Gugu's beautiful wedding. Then there was Olufemi's shining, joy-filled face at the birth of he and Gugu's second child, a boy, whom they named Babawale after his fallen father.

Ireoluwa recalled his exuberance at meeting Gugu's sister, Mlambo, for the first time. His memory flashed forward to the moment of Ireoluwa's proposal of marriage to Mlambo and her acceptance. Then, as Ireoluwa's visions seemed to pull him forward to just before the beautiful sunset over Table Mountain, all of the memories merged and formed into a wheel. The wheel spun so quickly, it appeared still. Each of the escapes, the fears, the new beginnings, and endings were pulled into the spinning wheel. When Ireoluwa tried to open his eyes, he couldn't.

The wheel became a clock just as Ireoluwa was beginning to feel trapped in the furious rotation of his thoughts, feelings, and experiences. The clock ticked one second forward and wound backward. Then another flash of light appeared, and Ireoluwa was standing behind two people who were holding hands with their backs turned to him. The inner voice spoke again: "You are loved."

When the figures turned, Ireoluwa was stunned. Ireoluwa's mother and father were standing before him with youthful vigor. They approached him and showered him with kisses, hugs, and words of affirmation. Ireoluwa began to cry. As he cried, his mother wiped his tears and kissed him upon his head. "Son, we are with you always. Our pride is as bright as the sun and as wide as the seas." Oluwatobi rubbed his shoulders. Then Ireoluwa's mother looked at him as tears streamed from his eyes. Ireoluwa couldn't believe it had been Ife's voice and that he could know and trust her without any memory of his mother.

"Open your eyes." Ife's voice was as gentle and as sure as it had always been. As he had done in the desert and all his life, Ireoluwa did as the voice instructed.

"Luwa's back from his journey," Olufemi exclaimed to the audience captivated by his short and peaceful pause. Olufemi, who was beside Ireoluwa, smiled at his wife, Gugu, who was standing next to her sister. Both Gugu and Mlambo were adorned in beautiful body-length bracelets of blues, reds, and oranges.

Ireoluwa's eyes smiled as they reopened.

"Welcome back, my love." Mlambo's smile was wide as she rubbed her pregnant belly. The minister, who was no stranger to the comings and goings of the Great Spirit, was moved by Ireoluwa's expression of relief and release. Having just relived and rewitnessed his life in such sudden fashion, Ireoluwa thought that he had been standing for days or weeks. Instead, his remembering had happened in a matter of seconds. The sunset was still blazing purples and reds across the sky. The ceremony was still underway. Ireoluwa looked around at all of the guests and his family with gratitude. Reaching for Mlambo's hand, he looked toward the Indian Ocean that had brought them to the shores of South Africa with renewed appreciation.

"I accept and receive you as my wife, in this life and for always." Ireoluwa's tears streamed, dripping at his chin.

The minister joined Ireoluwa's and Mlambo's hands together. As the minister held their hands, he spoke a prayer over their hands. When the prayer was finished, he gave Ireoluwa and Mlambo a loving look. After a few beats, the minister addressed the adoring audience. "And so it is, that Ireoluwa and Mlambo have been joined as one. Let us all rejoice and embrace their marital and sacred bond."

As the reddish-violet sky gave way to the rising light of the moon, the children and teenagers in attendance formed two lines extending from the bride and groom. After the lines were formed, the young people began to dance. The brass cymbals and bells at their ankles and waists rang with a celebratory rhythmic harmony. Then Olufemi and Gugu joined in, dancing and singing their way down the line. Praise lifted into the air, announcing the newly married couple to the Great Spirit in the sky above.

As Ireoluwa looked at Mlambo, he wanted to tell her how he had met his mother. He wanted to tell her how happy his parents were. Ireoluwa wanted to tell her that he had learned that true lovers always find each other, even in the great beyond. He wanted to tell Olufemi how Oluwatobi gleamed with majesty and that his spirit survived and lived on. He wanted to tell Olufemi that the inner voice of protection and guidance was his mother the whole time. Ireoluwa wanted to tell everyone in attendance how he never knew how he would survive being stolen, captured, nearly castrated, humiliated, escaped, and returned. He wanted to tell little Babawale how fearsome and strong his grandfather was and how he had protected them all even after his death.

Ireoluwa wanted to speak aloud to the setting sun with the gratitude he held in his heart. He wanted to thank the moon for rising and casting light even when he and Olufemi had been trapped in the darkness of a cell in India or inside a chest of fabrics at the bottom of a boat in the ocean. There were so many things Ireoluwa wanted to say and express. When Ireoluwa began to try and communicate all of these things, his mouth shut, and his eyes opened wider than they had ever been. And it was in that moment that Ireoluwa knew all that needed to be said had been. All that he had lived had to be. If not, he wouldn't have found Mlambo and his purpose. He wouldn't have a child to inherit the fisherman's lullaby. He would be free without knowing how freedom truly felt. And so, Ireoluwa kissed Mlambo on her forehead and then on her belly. He reached his hand out to hers, and the two of them jumped and danced down the line as the sun fell below the mountain.

1927

"Speech! Speech! Speech!" the intimate crowd of Cape Town's Black and Coloured elite called and shouted as they held champagne flutes high in the air. Babawale, who was preparing to check on the children, hadn't anticipated that there would be a speech requested. A few hours earlier, he had regaled the room of the many escapades of his father and uncle as they created and sustained the family's businesses. Starting with a small fishing boat off the coast and a multifamily residence, Two Brothers Enterprises emerged as a District Six staple. Babawale looked to Oluwatobi, hoping that he might rescue him from the calls for more discussion or a grand speech. Oluwatobi, the more bashful of the two, looked back at Babawale with eyes that confirmed that he would not be making the speech. Babawale took a deep breath and walked back to the front of the group.

"Speech! Speech! Speech!" The group, drunk with celebratory drinks and exuberance, chanted in unison.

"Alright, Alright!" An exasperated Babawale stepped forward, motioning with his hands for the crowd to simmer down.

"Remember the little ones are upstairs, and I have finally gotten them from restlessness to sleepiness with our ritual nighttime story."

"We are sorry, Wale. We are just so excited that the business has made it to its eightieth anniversary," someone spoke aloud in response to Babawale's reluctance and caution.

Babawale nodded his head, accepting the unexpected request and spotlight.

"I will be brief. The building is everything. Founded by our fathers Olufemi Abdullahi and Ireoluwa Adeyemi in 1847, Two Brothers Enterprises was born right here in this very room that we stand in together this evening. When he was alive, my father would regularly say the story of Two Brothers is evidence of one of Allah's greatest miracles. My father, Olufemi Abdullahi, lost his father, was enslaved, and almost rendered unable to have children. Yet he and his dearest friend and brother, Ireoluwa, persisted. The love and brotherhood they shared created all of this. The fish market and the childcare service center. Twenty of the best rental flats in all of Cape Town. Together with our beautiful mothers, they took an empty shell of a building and made a new life. In one year, they created a storefront to sell the fresh fish they caught. Within the next year, all twenty flats were rented and occupied. And within another ten years, a successful childcare service center was flourishing. This has not been without struggle. But they endured. We endured. And let us always remember that as we have conquered one struggle, others continue. Every day, our sisters and brothers are being sorted, beaten, and killed by police because of their skin color—the Africa that is in their blood. This discrimination and treatment are an affront to our shared humanity. It pervades not just South Africa, but all of Africa and all of the world, for that matter. Tomorrow morning, we return to a world where our children have been sorted by color and tribe, increasingly surveilled and unable to play in peace. We must draw on the lessons of the past and the courage of our ancestors. We must be vigilant here in South Africa where every day the scales are tipping in favor of racism and repression. We are already seeing it across the district. Let these eighty years mark victory and renewed purpose for all of us.

"This night, in this room, floating in our energy and spirit, is our fathers' legacy. The legacy of Two Brothers Enterprises runs parallel with our community and neighborhood. Oluwatobi and I, who are descended from stolen West African children and the daughters of Xhosa people, are here, alive, and able to commune on the occasion of eighty years of success. This is our fathers' legacy, our legacy. A district founded by formerly enslaved people is a powerful place to headquarter your dreams.

"Thank you, everyone, for coming tonight and celebrating eighty years of Two Brothers Enterprises. Tobi and I are fortunate to have inherited this business from our fathers, Ireoluwa and Olufemi. As I look around the room and see how this business, family, community, and circle of friends has grown, my heart is full. On behalf of myself and Tobi, we first thank our ancestors. I hope they are pleased with us. I also want to express our deepest gratitude to our wives and children. We also thank our friends and loyal customers. We thank the longtime and new residents of the building. The building is everything!" Babawale's chest slowly emptied of air as his words moved rhythmically across the room.

Babawale's words had proven powerful enough to generate a commanding pause after he spoke. Then the audience swelled into impassioned applause that shook the walls and vibrated with an unmistakable, enthusiastic endorsement.

"Here, here!"

"Asé!"

"Amen!"

"Hamdullah!"

The glasses clanged, and affirmations and applause rang harmoniously. As Babawale looked around, he noticed that people looked both delighted and sobered by his message. Resistance members in the gathering raised fists in salute to his message. Though Babawale had not planned to make a call to celebrate and resist, he was glad that he did. He looked to Oluwatobi who had a long stream of tears running down his face. Babawale could see so much of his beloved uncle Ireoluwa in Oluwatobi's eyes and face, and for a moment, the similarity made him feel at ease despite all the difficulties they'd endured and those ahead. Now both old men, Babawale and Oluwatobi could only relish the fact that they were living out their fathers' wildest dreams. Before heading up the stairs to check in on the children, Babawale went to Oluwatobi, as moved as he was, as evidenced by the tears rolling down his cheeks.

"Tobi, our fathers would be amazed, don't you think?"

"Indeed they would, dear brother. Make sure that you continue your entries in the journals as I have. It is important that we keep my father's practice of capturing our stories and lives going. Something tells me some day our family's story will make an even bigger difference."

Oluwatobi, who was shy and soft-spoken, was more comfortable writing than speaking. When his father, Ireoluwa, first revealed his journey books, it was to help Oluwatobi become comfortable speaking and perhaps break him out of his shyness. Instead, the books gave him a refuge of expression and purpose, and he interviewed and recorded the recollections of every member of the family he could.

Since they were children, Oluwatobi made sure Babawale kept a journal and that those left behind by their fathers were kept in safe storage. Having kept track of the details of the family history, Oluwatobi was especially sensitive to the moment of triumph the eightieth anniversary meant. When Babawale and Oluwatobi hugged, the room erupted into raucous and joyous applause. Unaware that their moment had been watched, Babawale was caught off guard. So as to not spoil the energy, Babawale just turned to the group and smiled.

"Now I am pretty sure the children are up, and off I go to story time duties." Babawale folded his hands and bowed with gratitude to the guests.

"I will join you, as it is time to present the children with their journey books." Oluwatobi grinned, revealing two brown leather-bound books he hid inside a drawer in the sitting room.

Approaching the door to the bedroom, Babawale could hear the children whispering and scurrying from their ear hustling at the base of the door. He could hear them shuffling back toward their beds and whisper-talking to each other to pretend to be asleep. Even though they were first cousins, Femi and Ife were treated as siblings and even twins at times. Ife and Femi were born on the same day at nearly the same time, and although they did not resemble each other, their similarities in all the other areas made it so their family ignored the differences.

"I think Baba's coming!"

He could hear the coy voice as the door opened. The bedroom was still dark, save for a small candle that burned to provide a small light and allay any fears of the dark the children may have.

"Is that you, Femi, that I heard? I thought we all agreed that you would both go to bed." Babawale looked at both beds where each child had pulled the covers above their head so as to appear to sleep and avoid his gaze.

There was a pause and a little quiet, as the children were determining whether or not their act was convincing.

"I can see you both squirming around under the covers. Now I may be old, but I am not blind. Pull those covers back so Baba can see your beautiful brown little faces." Amused by their youthful innocence, Babawale smiled as they reminded him of he and Oluwatobi when they were the same age.

"Baba, tell us another story," Femi politely demanded of his grandfather.

"Please, Baba, please. I promise me and Ife will go to sleep after one more story." Femi pleaded using the sweetest part of his innocent voice to coax his grandfather to sit back down. Femi pulled the covers just above his mouth, as he tried to hide his smile. When his grandfather turned around and placed his walking staff back against the bedroom door, that was Femi's signal that another story was on the way.

Femi, however, did not want just any story. Femi wanted his grandfather to confirm for Ife that he was not making up stories when he told her earlier that they were also Nigerian. Ife sucked her teeth at the notion, believing that Femi was fibbing again. Femi always had a way of fooling her and convincing her of the most incredulous stories. Femi couldn't blame Ife for being suspicious, as he knew that his penchant for playing with the truth was not always as fun for the listener as it was for him. But this time, Femi had been telling the truth, and he needed his grandfather to back him up.

Unbeknownst to the adults, Femi and Ife were locked in a wordless conflict. The two who were usually as thick as thieves hadn't spoken to each other for several hours by the time they began arguing again. As the moon began peaking, they were each sent to bed and given their nighttime story rituals. Normally, they would have both listened to the story, pretended to fall asleep, and then told each other about their day or the dreams they had the night before. However, the two were not on good terms following an abrupt and increasingly common police encounter. A few hours before the anniversary party, Femi and Ife were playing in front of the family building when a police officer interrupted the fun.

Both Femi and Ife spent most of their waking hours somewhere inside their family's building. If they were not at home inside one of the flats, they were chatting it up while they watched one of the adults clean the fresh fish and wrap it up for customers. If they were not in the fish market, then they were in the child center where they would learn words and stories, color, and draw pictures. There, Femi and Ife spent time with other children from District Six and other parts of Cape Town. Most often, their days at the child center, though activity-centered, meant that Femi and Ife were around adults every hour of their day.

While Femi enjoyed minding the business of adults, Ife preferred to be around other five-year-olds or kids her size. She found adults serious and self-involved. As a result, the best part of the day for Ife was the thirty minutes when they were allowed to play outside in front of the building. Femi enjoyed it too, mostly because he really liked how Ife became so free and allowed herself to have fun. For the last few weeks though, those thirty minutes had become less and less fun for Ife. She couldn't exactly remember which day it started, but at some point, there were two new white police officers patrolling the neighborhood. Everything would be going well until one of the police officers began interrogating the children, holding up his large baton, red-faced as he questioned and disrupted playtime. The kids were always frightened when he appeared, and that fear usually killed all the fun.

"At least before they used to leave kids alone," Ife had said aloud as the short, stocky officer intimidated her friends with his baton waving. With only a few hours before the adult party, Ife was really looking forward to playtime. When the police officer interrupted, she had officially reached her limit with this new disruption. More than just a police officer, the man came to symbolize for Ife how adults took all her time. And now the thirty minutes she cherished were being taken away without her permission.

The group of children was playing a guessing game when the police officer appeared. Ife was just about to take her turn when the officer began harassing them. Divided into two teams of four, the goal of the game was for each person to guess which adult was being imitated. The winning team would get the lion's share of the candy that they'd accumulated. The kids were frightened when the police officers appeared, questioning if the bag of candy was stolen. Ife, never one to back down from anything or anyone, tried letting the officer know that they were just kids playing and that it was all of their candy.

"I am only interested in hearing from the Blacks here. Coloured girl, stay out!"

Ife was angered as she watched the officer harass her friends, and she certainly did not like being silenced. Unsure what to say and afraid any words would escalate the situation further, Ife looked to Femi.

"Tell the policeman one of your fancy stories, Femi!"

And so Femi did. He told the police officer that all the children were a part of the same family, which was not true. He went on to say that the family who owned the building descended from the powerful Gupta family and that they were more than Coloured. They were Nigerian as well. Femi's storytelling abilities were very powerful, stopping most adults in their tracks.

The police officer was at first primed to beat Femi over the head with his baton but soon was mesmerized by this little brown boy's story of the building and his family origins. Femi wasn't sure if his story was effective at first, and so he did offer flourishes. A little exaggeration here about one thing, and a little playing up of the success of his family's business enterprises there. Meanwhile, the other children, who had been playing with their cousins, scattered when they sensed the police officer was caught up in Femi's storytelling exercise. Soon enough, the police officer was too confused to remember why he'd stopped in the first place. Then the officer's partner arrived, and after a brief exchange, the two strolled down the block continuing their daily patrol.

"You see. They ran off, Femi! You always go too far with your stories! Why did you have to lie?!?" Ife was annoyed with her cousin, feeling as though he allowed himself once again to get carried away and ruin the fun they were having.

"Exaggerating and lying are not the same. I did not lie. We are Nigerian, and we are related to the Guptas. Baba told me a few days ago. I overheard part and asked a question, and he told me the story of how our family got to Cape Town from India by sneaking and hiding on a ship in a trunk full of fabric."

"Are you sure? I have never heard anything like that before, Femi! And why would Baba tell you now?" Ife was even more frustrated with Femi and even more convinced that he was lying again.

"I don't know why adults tell kids things they do when they do. That's anybody's guess! I know they were talking about the eightieth anniversary party for the family business, and so maybe that's why." Femi revealed his feelings of insult, recounting his source as the two of them headed inside to prepare for the big event.

Meanwhile, Ife wasn't buying it—not one bit of it. She was already upset at being distinguished from her friends as "Coloured." Ife didn't like it when they said that about her or people in her family. She didn't like the way it made her feel. She didn't like that it was used to make her Black friends run away or separate from her. Ife especially didn't like it that Femi seemed so casual about playing around with the terms when she was certain that he knew how violent and cruel the police were as they ran around enforcing some nonexistent rules about skin color. In any case, all she wanted to do was play and eat some candy. And Ife thought that was what Femi wanted too.

Femi shared with Ife that his grandfather told him a story about a place called Nigeria where their ancestors originated. Femi really wanted more information and not so much a nighttime story meant to put children to sleep.

Babawale grabbed a book from the top of the nightstand. The book contained a collection of folklore and fables that Babawale would use to encourage the children to sleep while also teaching them the ways of the natural world. Babawale especially loved to read them the stories where elephants were central characters.

"Baba, no not those stories." Femi was now pleading with his grandfather, who seemed to be content with just picking up where he left off in the great book of folklore and fables. "Please tell us about Nigeria. I overheard you talking about it with Mother and Father while they were decorating for the party downstairs." Femi hoped his honest confession combined with his plea would compel Babawale to share.

"Femi, I am not sure what you believe you heard," Babawale asked-answered.

"See, Femi. I knew you were making things up again!" Ife's annoyance with Femi returned, now accompanied by disappointment as well.

"Ife, do not be upset with your cousin. I do not know what he shared with you or what he overheard, but your great-grandfathers were both from a village in Nigeria called Olumoye." Babawale kneeled down between the two twin beds and looked at both Femi and Ife. He hoped that his posture and presence might help ease the clear tension that had presented itself between the two cousins.

Babawale looked at both children with eyes that glimmered with strength and truth in the candlelight. There was a light knock at the door.

"And guess what? Here comes your surprise," Babawale exclaimed as he stood tall and walked to the door to open it.

"Grandfather!" Ife was ecstatic when she saw Oluwatobi's face enter the room. She jumped up and ran to him. Hugging him at the knees, Ife like Femi loved and adored her grandfather so.

AFTER THE EMBRACE, OLUWATOBI KISSED Ife on the forehead and pointed her back to her bed. Oluwatobi then walked over to Femi and kissed him on the forehead too. Following his warm embrace of the two children, Oluwatobi presented them each with the brown leather journey books. At the same time, Babawale grabbed a second sitting chair and placed it next to his. Babawale took his seat while Oluwatobi placed the two books on each of the children's beds.

Once Oluwatobi was seated, he gave Babawale a look that indicated that he knew the time had come to give the children a small doses of their family history. Understanding the message Oluwatobi was communicating without words, Babawale nodded. Now in agreement, the two grandfathers turned to their grandchildren prepared to give them their start for their journey books. Femi and Ife hadn't looked at each other or their grandfathers, taken as they were with the beautiful journals, each with their names engraved at the bottom.

The candle began to flicker and crackle with unmistakable timeliness.

"You two hear that candle?" Oluwatobi inquired.

"Huh?" Both Femi and Ife responded puzzled, unaware of the candle or much of anything else and mesmerized by the journey books' sudden arrival at their beds.

"Listen, and you will hear it," Babawale confirmed Oluwatobi's observation and called for the children to redirect their attention.

The candle flickered even more, waving back and forth. The flame was elongated. Then the wick sizzled, and the candle let off a few crackles.

"What does that mean?" Femi asked curiously.

"It means that our ancestors are present and accounted for. They are with us." Babawale's tone was inviting, even if matter-of-fact.

"Which means that it is your time to know who they are and begin to understand your heritage." Oluwatobi's words were tinged with urgency and immediately followed Babawale's insight, giving further credence to Femi and Ife that they were going to learn something very important and significant.

"Tobi, just before you arrived, the children informed me that Femi overheard my discussion and learned of a place called Nigeria." Babawale's confession surprised Femi, who'd expected that his listening in would have been perceived as a mischievous and lightly punishable offense.

Oluwatobi and Babawale chuckled together for a few seconds. After their moment of shared laughter, they both turned to their grandchildren with smiles that could warm and brighten even the coldest and darkest space.

"You see, we are laughing because it has occurred to us that we were both your age when we first overheard the name Nigeria ourselves. Five years old and minding the business of the grownups. It's clearly in the blood."

Oluwatobi and Babawale laughed again. The laugh was so loving and alluring, soon Femi and Ife were laughing as well. The children did not know exactly what they were laughing about or why they were laughing, but the shared laughter made them both feel good, feel better.

While Ife's laughter made her feel cleared of the police harassment, Femi's made him relinquish his upset that his story had been considered all lies. Ife and Femi had been in such tension all day after their encounter with the scary and mean police officer, laughing with their grandfathers lifted the uneasiness. And as the children felt a new easiness take hold, the tension dissipated from their bodies. The sizzling wick was accompanied by a flurrying flicker of the candle.

"The books you have been presented with are called journey books." His laughter subsiding, Babawale returned to the matter at hand of explaining the leather-bound gifts the children hadn't expected to receive.

"Now you may open your books," Oluwatobi instructed.

Ife was first to pull the strap that closed the book from the loop and open the cover. Femi, looking over at Ife, followed her lead, releasing the strap and opening the cover as well. When they pulled the cover back, both of their eyes widened. Ife and Femi were enthralled by the curious map at the back of their journey book's cover.

"Now we begin with the fisherman's lullaby." Oluwatobi cleared his throat before beginning.

"Lullaby?!? That will put us to sleep. Those are for babies," Ife expressed her confused impatience.

"Lullabies are for babies!" Femi reflected Ife's disconcerted looks, glancing in her direction as he spoke.

"Now the only reward for impatience is more waiting. Listen and do not speak until Tobi has shared what he means to share with you." Babawale's voice was stern, and the children's postures quickly moved upright and obedient.

Babawale looked at Oluwatobi and winked, a sign that the children were willing and ready to learn and listen. Oluwatobi began the soft hum of the fisherman's lullaby. As the humming progressed, Babawale joined in. Once fully accompanied by Babawale, the two hummed through one full round of the fisherman's lullaby. As Babawale began the second progression, Oluwatobi broke from the chant and began to tell the children of its origin. Oluwatobi gave the children the best first dose of their family's history he could. Babawale kept the soundtrack low and engaged rolling with the story as Oluwatobi unfolded it for the children.

After fifteen minutes or so, Oluwatobi stopped his narration, and Babawale finished humming the tune. Both he and Babawale promised Femi and Ife that they would bring their journey books next time and continue where they left off. The children were grateful, and their quiet was a signal of their appreciation to their grandfathers for entrusting them. Oluwatobi and Babawale could see the children's eyes lowering as they laid their heads to their pillows, holding their journey books beside them.

"One day, I will have a successful fashion business, and the clothes I sell will celebrate our family's history," Ife confessed with quiet confidence as her eyes drifted closed.

And soon enough, full and drunk on the unbelievable but true stories of their great-grandfathers, Femi and Ife were sound asleep. Babawale and Oluwatobi looked over their grandchildren with great pride. Each longing for and missing their fathers, Babawale and Oluwatobi realized that they were everywhere in everything: hanging on Ife's dimples, in the rise and fall of their grandchildren's chins, and in the deepest black of their eyelashes.

"You feel that too, right?" Babawale asked Oluwatobi as a vibration rose from his foot up through to his forehead.

"I do. They are so pleased." Oluwatobi's smile widened with knowing surety.

"The building is everything." Babawale hugged Oluwatobi and affirmed as they exited the bedroom.

"Indeed. The building is everything," Babawale conferred as he closed the door to allow the sleeping grandchildren's dreams to unfold.

1957

Ife's bed was surrounded by mountains of papers. Newspaper and magazine clippings of the family business's rise and fall were strewn around the floor of her bedroom. Denied applications lined the walls of the bedroom.

All of Ife's many attempts to repeal the evictions of her tenants, the sudden closing of the childcare center, and the shuttering of the fish market were painful reminders of how quickly and swiftly everything her family had built had been taken under the apartheid regime. Each appeal was at least one hundred pages long, accompanied by the large poster with the word "Eviction" in bold red.

Most days, she couldn't bring herself to read through the documents nor throw them away. When she would examine the large stacks and the sheer volume of paper that she had managed to hoard, Ife would walk over to one of the piles and try and begin to downsize. But each time she would pull out a letter or quickly scan one of the sheets, the idea of throwing everything out or even moving things around felt like an act of cowardice. Ife refused to let the government take her family's livelihood and destroy their beautiful, diverse community and neighborhood without documenting her persistent battle to retrieve what had been taken and stolen. The mountains of papers both haunted and encouraged her.

Even more, on some nights, especially when her husband's commute from Cape Town went long after midnight, the piles would call her in her sleep, whispering messages of resistance and failure, longing and enduring, survival and sacrifice. Ife was afraid to tell anyone, especially her family, of the ghostly powers of the mounds of paperwork. Ife feared that were she to tell anyone of this persistent quality, it would be conflated with her depressive state and could lead to being placed into a mental asylum for the rest of her life. And though Ife understood that she was struck with a severe case of depressive blues, she knew she was not crazy. As these thoughts spiraled around in her head, Ife's anger would spike. A fit of rage would take over, and she would channel those fits into new appeals, new strategies to reclaim her family's possessions.

Over the last eight years, what started as a small hill of papers and eviction notices had transformed into a chain of mountainous piles of denials, obituaries, missing-person notices, forced removals, racist threats, and unpaid notices. Prison letters stacked atop one another in paper mountains and paper valleys. Beginning as court-appearance notices for participation in political resistance efforts for family members involved, there were now separate volumes for cousins and uncles, aunts and sisters, brothers and nephews.

The largest and tallest accounted for Femi, who had been arrested, convicted, and imprisoned on a fifteen-year sentence with false evidence purporting that his leadership of a local resistance movement in District Six amounted to terrorism. Weeks of back and forth, the sham trial, and legal paperwork filled the middle of Femi's paper mountain. Atop it were letters from Femi encouraging Ife, asking about the well-being of her children, and an expression that soon freedom shall come. At the end of each letter, Femi would conclude: "Amandla!" Ife was sure he was unaware that either the prison or post office ensured that the word appeared with the strikethrough "~~Amandla!~~" and that his continued resistance would likely increase his prison time. Even still, Ife was sure to continue to file appeals on Femi's behalf, especially once he became the only one alive of the ten members of the family jailed within the first eight years of apartheid's legalization and implementation.

In the beginning, all of the money for these expenses came through a bank loan leveraging the family's property and fishing boats. But once most of the family was behind on the bills and behind bars, Ife was the only one left to manage the fallout. Without her permission, it had become Ife's responsibility to keep up with the children left behind, fight the forced evictions, and salvage whatever personal effects she and her husband and children were able to carry during the long, excruciating, painful, and humiliating involuntary migration to inhospitable and underdeveloped land miles outside of Cape Town.

Within an eight-year period, a fortune that had taken one hundred years to accrue disappeared. Lawyer fees and court fees saw to it that whatever remained of the family's wealth was long gone, now replaced by debts that would take at least two generations to pay off. On most days, Ife was depressed and angry, her childhood dreams of fashion design indefinitely deferred. Outside of feeding her children and looking after them when she had the capacity, most of her time was spent in court, at a police station, traveling for prison visits, and doing everything she could to reclaim the life that had been stolen from her and her family.

Ife scanned around the bedroom, her hair undone, and her face scrunched. As Ife mentally climbed each of the paper mountains, she would recategorize each pile using her memories as a guide. Without having to pull a sheet, she could recall what each mound included, when it started, and the most recent notice regarding the matter. The tallest of the piles was dedicated to the violent eviction that she and her family experienced seven years prior. The first set of evictions was not directly targeted at her or her family per se. Rather, all of the tenants had been evicted. Unaware that these notices had been sent to her tenants via mail, Ife was preoccupied with the South African government's sudden seizure of the family's fishing boats. When one of the tenants knocked at her door, she was in the midst of trying to find a lawyer to help her get the boats back and hold the government accountable. The tenant, believing that Ife was aware of the eviction notice, cursed her so badly that the scar of the words lingered in her ears on days where her depression was most severe.

As Ife felt the darkness opening up, the tallest mountain began to lean and speak to her.

"Save us. Save us," the large leaning tower of papers requested. Ife pretended not to hear and looked elsewhere to a smaller stack.

"Save us. Save us." The voice grew louder and more demanding.

"What do you think I am doing?!? Huh! What am I doing?!?" Ife screamed until her voice cracked and her throat strained.

There was no response. No voice emerged in reply. Instead, the pile began to lean further forward. Now appearing on the verge of collapse, Ife was becoming more fearful that the pile would not only crumble but also, like dominoes, knock all the rest into a mess of disconnected information surrounding her bed.

Ife threw the bedsheets to the side and placed her feet on the floor. As she tried to pull herself upright, her body wouldn't move. She tried to move her hand, but it would not budge. She tried turning her head forward, but her neck would not let her face turn away from the leaning tower. The leaning continued, and as it persisted, sheets of paper began sliding forward as though they might fall to the floor or onto her bed. Were Ife not so worried about the pillars falling, she might have been more terrified than she felt. The collapse would confirm her worst suspicions that the world of her childhood and young adult life was forever gone and that her family's works had been permanently destroyed never to return. And while Ife had given in to feelings of grief, she refused to believe that her past was a fantasy never to be lived again, never to be experienced by her children.

Unable to shift her face or turn, Ife's neck grew sore. Her arms, set forward to lift her from the bed, began to go limp, falling asleep as her feet grew numb. It was in these times of severely reduced movement when Ife did her very best to breathe, to try and grab new air from outside, command it, and pull that new direction into her body. Ife tried first taking a deep swallow of air with her mouth, but nothing moved. She tried again, and her mouth opened, but nothing came in. Her throat was strained from screaming with the paper ghosts, so it was too swollen and hurt to assist. Panicking that she might be found dead from self-suffocating in an air-filled room, Ife tried once more to get her mouth and throat to cooperate. Still nothing, and now with seconds left before she would feel herself dying, Ife reminded her nose that it too was a source. Ife pulled a sliver of air through her awakened nostrils. The crisp slice of air slowly reinvigorated her face and then her neck. She took a few more breaths through her nose, each one larger in size and effect than the one prior. Soon enough, she was back on her feet, pressing her body against the leaning tower of papers.

Ife pressed with as much precision as she could, hoping that even if something fell off, it would be in easily sorted chunks. As she leaned into the papers, she felt the foundation restabilize. She took a deep sigh of relief. And as she let out the air, several sheets of paper slid forward, and like little razors, their edges cut her face. The sharp, painful sensation gave way to a loud and painful plea.

"Humph. Please don't fall. Please don't fall." Ife was now unsure if she could get these piles back against the wall without help. She called for her six children sleeping in the room next door. "Children, come now! Help me, please!"

Ife usually kept the children out of the bedroom and the door closed so as not to frighten them or feel the humiliation that might come if she made them a witness to her hoarding. But if she ever beckoned, the children were swift and dutiful to their mother's call. When no one came, Ife made her call louder.

"Children, come and assist me!"

Still, no one came. Stuck with the decision between holding up the paper mountain or going to see where her children were, Ife felt powerless. The powerlessness made Ife sob. As she sobbed, she slowly walked away from the leaning pile, letting it fall as she approached the door to see about the children. Expecting to hear a thud behind her as she walked, Ife was caught off guard when the paper mountain did not crumble. Instead, she heard it begin to hum a familiar tune. In disbelief, Ife turned around to find the papers moving in rhythm and fluttering as they performed the fisherman's lullaby. Rather than feeling scared or afraid, Ife was enchanted. The tears that had flooded her eyes began rolling off her face, her body rocking in harmony with the soothing sounds.

"Grandfather, is that you? Has it been you all this time?" Ife asked, as she was now standing and swaying before the xylophonic paper mountain. Although she did not hear a response back to her query, the humming continued until Ife found herself in a full-on embrace of the pile of harmonic papers. This time though, when Ife felt the papers, they did not feel like thin razors. Rather, the paper mountain was warm and tall like her uncle Babawale during story time when she was a child; it was comforting like her grandfather Oluwatobi when he would console her during her difficult teen years whenever she felt different or forgotten.

These sensations and memories shifted Ife's energy, and soon enough, she was dancing around the room from the stack to the pile to the mountain and back. No longer in the confines of a bedroom with hoarded paperwork documenting her failed attempts at defeating apartheid, Ife was now back in dance class moving with the eclectic improvisation of a jazz piano.

In a trance, Ife felt her feet and arms moving with natural control for the first time in what felt like forever. A certain joy had begun to fill her heart. The wetness of sadness and sobbing had transformed into that of pulsating heat and sweating. In feeling the vibration of her beloved ancestors, Ife felt alive again. Just as Ife's feeling of great aliveness escalated, she began to spin and twirl around with a wild abandon. Her feet reverberated her passion, and papers began to find themselves back in the obedience of the stack. Loose sheets flew into place as she pointed and directed them to their proper location. The humming grew, extending from the original source.

All of the more than fifty paper hills and paper mountains were now an orchestra performing the fisherman's lullaby with fantastical whimsy yet extreme precision. All the things in the room were under her control. The sheets of the usually unmade bed began unfolding and remaking themselves until the bedding was flat and refreshed. The dust that had accrued along the floors and walls moved into the air, gathered like a small whirlwind, and with one flick of Ife's wrist, the dust flew out of the window up into the sky. Ife looked to her dresser and commanded the comb and brush to her head.

As directed, the brush and comb flew up into the air and began styling her hair into a beautiful, curly, twisty afro. Clothes then pulled themselves from underneath the bed and began folding themselves. A beautiful gown, which Ife had forgotten existed, appeared before her. Floating in the air, the gown swayed back and forth like a gifted young child trying to get their parent's attention as they perform the most difficult of feats. The purples and yellows of the gown were glowing, making the dress even more stupendous than Ife remembered from when she made it. Her eyes widened with confirmation that she agreed to be adorned in its majesty. As Ife twirled, her house clothes were seamlessly replaced with the gown. Renewed and refreshed, Ife felt all of her troubles melting away, giving way to an impassioned redness that illuminated her skin.

Looking for a handheld mirror to mark the occasion of her magical beauty, Ife began pointing at drawers to open until a mirror appeared or revealed itself. Unable to find one, she whisked her left hand upward toward the ceiling, and the bed lifted, revealing a small mirror. Ife commanded the mirror to her as the paper piles continued playing in symmetrical mellifluence. As the small mirror made its way to her, Ife saw that its small size would not allow for a full view. Upon this realization, Ife blew air into the levitating small handheld mirror until it transformed into a full-length, gloriously clear pane of glass. Before gazing at herself, Ife felt around her body to make sure that everything was in place. She wanted to ensure that she would see the outcome and not the process.

Once her double-checks had been concluded, she called the newly formed full-length mirror forward. As the mirror stood before her, everything looked as it had felt. The room was more than tidy—it was clear and shining. Rather than its usual elegiac posture, Ife's body was regal and sophisticated. The gown and her skin were luminescent, glowing in reds, violets, and yellows. The paper mountains were neat while flittering with the sounds of wind and brass instruments.

Amazed by the wonder of it all, Ife closed her eyes and took a deep breath. She wanted to be sure to let the occasion into her heart so that she could store it for safekeeping as a memory of comfort and healing. When she opened her eyes, the music began to slow. The mirror began to gyrate. Ife noticed and grew disturbed as the flicks of her hands and wrists were now having the opposite effect. The mirror began to shake and move side to side. The music that she had been conducting without trouble was now growing slower and more disharmonious. What were once the pleasant sounds of hums and lulls were now sounding like harrowing screeches and cries.

To stop this impending disorder, Ife used both hands to issue an unmistakable command to all things in the room to obey her. The use of both hands initially appeared to have halted the regression, as everything became entirely still. A palpable silence accompanied the stillness. No longer panicked, Ife let out a small sigh of relief. As Ife released her relief, the mirror cracked straight down the middle. The paper stacks began to slide over onto the floor again. The largest of the paper mountains rumbled with the sound of impending doom and chaos. Unsure of how to stop what was happening, Ife pointed north and south, east and west. She looked up and down, right and left. Nothing seemed to be working, and even worse, every new move she made seemed to be undoing all the progress she had accomplished. Her masterpiece was unraveling. Ife's glowing red skin shifted from soothing warmth to inflamed and fiery, and the gown she adorned began to singe and burn from the inside out.

Helpless and increasingly angered by the sudden devolution of her magical surroundings, Ife went to her last resort. She began to hum the melodious sounds of the fisherman's lullaby. As she did so, the crack in the mirror healed. As the mirror showed her singing the tune, she noticed that the paper mountains stayed still. Completing her first round of the lullaby, Ife's skin calmed and began to soothe. So Ife continued with the lullaby. Feeling her fury subside, she began to sing, vibrating the harmony with more confidence. Without warning, the mirror shattered into a thousand pieces but not before it showed her that all of the papers behind her had begun toppling and melting.

The shattered glass fell to the floor. The papers flooded to the ground. In a last-ditch effort to save everything, Ife threw herself to the ground, hoping that her body could lessen the collapse of her surroundings. Her attempt was unsuccessful. Not only had all of the papers morphed into a mess—scattered and blended together—but her hands were cut on the mirrored glass shards. Now as she pulled her arms in, her blood streaked across papers. Lifting herself from underneath the piles of papers, Ife looked for the brown leather journey books that she and Femi had kept through their childhood. Of all the things stacked around her, those were most important.

Ife flipped through the stacks of lawyer bills, prison letters, obituaries for her father and grandfather, missing-person notices for her sisters and several nephews, and the numerous eviction-stamped notices and appeals in search of the leather-bound memories and thoughts. Exasperated by her search and the sheer volume of papers everywhere, Ife was about to give up when she recalled that the journey books were in a chest separate from the piles of paperwork. The chest, which had not been opened or involved in her dancing and singing, sat unbothered by the whirlwind of papers, brushes, combs, and shattered glass. Ife raced to the chest, slipping, sliding, and trekking over the papers that flooded the room like high and rolling ocean tides.

Relieved at the sight of the untouched and unaffected stacks of family journey books, she looked around for a lock to make sure that nothing could escape the chest and no one could easily access it. Her spontaneous and disorganized search for a small lock in this valley of crumpled paper mountains was futile. Ife's blood was now everywhere, streaked and striped across everything. Wiping her hands on the soiled gown, Ife ripped the dress off of herself to discover that her house clothes were underneath.

Feeling confused, she dug through more stacks and piles in search of the small lock. As she threw bank statements and bills into the air from one part of the room, new paper mountains formed from the disparate documents thrown aside. Ife looked more and more, searching beneath and underneath everything, and still came up empty-handed. Her hair, which she tugged and pulled as she searched, was patchy and unkempt by the end. Finally defeated by the ordeal, Ife tried to make noise, but nothing would come out. She wanted to cry, but the numbing sensation that took hold of her body wouldn't let tears emerge. Then there was a knock at the bedroom door. Ife couldn't move or speak. Then there was another knock. Ife still couldn't move. She tried everything she could to get herself off the ground, as she was sure it was one or all of her children coming to check on her.

"Everything is okay. Is everything okay?" Embarrassed at the state of disrepair in the room and hoping to avoid the humiliation of being discovered in such a state, Ife mustered up enough strength to speak and beat back the numbness. There was no response on the other side, which Ife interpreted as a sign that her answer sufficed. A few seconds went by in silence, and just as Ife began looking around at the room in shambles, the door began opening. She tried to pull her body from the ground and race to close the door, but she was unable. As the door opened, a blinding light came through until standing before her was her youngest child, Ireoluwa.

"Mama, a letter from Uncle Femi has just arrived."

Ife tried to reply and brace herself for the emotional toll of being exposed.

"Mama, Mama . . . Mama . . . Mama," Ireoluwa's voice echoed around in Ife's head.

"I'm sorry, Ireoluwa. I believe it was not a good idea for you to come today after all."

Ife heard the voice that, while familiar, was not that of her young son who had been standing before her.

"Wait." Ife opened her eyes, her voice finally pushing its way through her throat and up out of her cracked lips.

When Ife looked around, she was shocked. Ife did not understand where she was. No longer surrounded by papers and blood and hiding in her bedroom, she was in a sterile room. Her house clothes were replaced with a white hospital gown. Her bedroom was replaced with the chairs and tables of the visiting room of a mental institution. Her seven-year-old baby boy, Ireoluwa, was a young man of sixteen.

"She said to wait," she heard Ireoluwa say to the white nurse who was standing in observation.

"Mama, I am here. I love you and I am here." Ireoluwa reached out for Ife's hand, which recoiled at his touch.

Ife wanted to jump up and hug her son and tell him she loved him. She wanted to ask how he had grown so fast. She wanted to tell him how the drugs they gave her made her heart hurt, her body rejecting her control even as she was still present and alive somewhere inside. Ife wanted to do and say so many things, but she couldn't control her body anymore. Her body was working against her, attacking her when she tried to take control. And so no sooner than she pulled her hand away from Ireoluwa was he escorted in tears from the waiting room.

"Please call ahead next time, and we will let you know when and if she is having a good day. No need to have you travel for hours. It is not good for either of your health when she is in this condition," the white woman nurse instructed an obviously inconsolable Ireoluwa as he was taken through double doors out of Ife's view.

1977

The chest filled with the family's journey books and records scuffed and scraped a long line across the floor as Ireoluwa brought it from the back to the front of the house. The chest was one of the few items Ireoluwa was able to recover before his family's home was bulldozed by the South African government. Without notice or much time, Ireoluwa and his siblings had to quickly gather what they could and find a new place to live. The flattening of their home led to a long migration from home to home and also had split Ireoluwa and his siblings up, scattered as they became across different places and couches in Soweto, Johannesburg, and King William's Town.

Ireoluwa carried a lot of guilt for the bulldozing of the home, as he knew that it was a consequence of his journalistic efforts to inform the public of the brutality and corruption of the South African government inherent in the apartheid regime. All the authorities needed to do to take away someone's freedom, property, or even separate families was to claim suspicion of conspiring against the South African government. Even if unfounded, the process of interrogation, handcuffing, and jail left many dead, permanently injured, or missing.

After watching his mother, Ife, mentally deteriorate at the loss of her community, neighborhood, and family business, Ireoluwa made it his life's purpose to investigate and report on the misdeeds of the South African government. Oftentimes, Ireoluwa's stories began with a simple enough premise—apartheid was racist, immoral, and a new formation of slavery. To demonstrate this premise, Ireoluwa's stories tended to begin with some of the smaller things the government seized using the premise of suspicion or suspicious behavior. The first story, which drew the attention of the editor of *Drum* magazine, was a mystery of sorts based upon the sudden disappearance and reappearance of four goats over four days in two townships.

The families had attempted to report the goats as stolen, but no one would listen or take them seriously. The notion that livestock went missing or could be stolen was not uncommon nor of much interest to anyone. But when Ireoluwa heard of the situation, he went and interviewed all four families. The process was arduous and required him to travel by foot, bicycle, and bus, and hitchhike into various townships to make his inquiries. At first, his investigation seemed to confirm the disposition of the authorities that the goats were taken and, given the issues of extreme poverty and starvation, such was not unusual. Then he discovered that, unbeknownst to the families, each had a relative imprisoned at Robben Island.

Even more curious was Ireoluwa's discovery that the four relatives were cellmates on the same prison block as Nelson Mandela. All were originally incarcerated for so-called acts of treason and for resisting and organizing against apartheid. It had been a few weeks into his investigation when Ireoluwa discovered the Robben Island connection between the families. So moved and sure that the connection was meaningful, Ireoluwa made his way to each of the families to share his discovery and query their thoughts on the potential connections with the missing goats.

To Ireoluwa's great surprise, upon his arrival, each family's goat had miraculously reappeared. Each family's story was the same regarding the goats: late one evening, the goat came running back to the family quarters as though nothing had happened. Each family had put a small brand on their goats and were sure that it was the missing goat. Ireoluwa tried to convey the Robben Island connection, but in all of the cases, the family was so relieved to have their goat back that they were no longer interested in Ireoluwa's pursuit. Even more, now with the goats returned to the families, all requested that Ireoluwa stop his investigation for fear of inquisition or harm at the hands of authorities in the government.

Rather than become more invested because of Ireoluwa's Robben Island discovery, the families were resistant, reluctant, and even recalcitrant. "Stop this now!" was a refrain and command that echoed in Ireoluwa's head as he walked the long way home from each of the residences where the goats had suspiciously returned.

Not one to fade away when a story had begun to feed his voracious appetite for the truth and exposing the apartheid government, Ireoluwa kept quiet though he followed the story each day and kept his investigation alive. A little over a month later, his request to see one of the relatives imprisoned at Robben Island had finally been honored. When he received the letter notifying him that the visit had been approved, Ireoluwa was anxiously excited. Because he had been approved, Ireoluwa knew that the authorities would be watching his every move if not already surveilling him. He also knew that the imprisoned relative had to agree since they were not related, making Ireoluwa feel like a real journalist for the first time. As Ireoluwa boarded the ferry to Robben Island, he felt a sense of real accomplishment and couldn't wait to share and send the printed story to his mother. Upon arrival, Ireoluwa was sent back and told that the person he was scheduled to visit was no longer available.

Ireoluwa's pride turned to sour confusion. It was unwise to argue with the prison officials, and so he rode back on the ferry. During the ride back, the feeling of dejection made Ireoluwa's wheels turn in his mind, greasing the gears of sleuthing that had been in motion since the missing goats first came into his purview.

Over the next few weeks, Ireoluwa attempted to send letters to the inmate, all of which were returned with an abrupt reply from the prison: "Inmate unavailable." Then came the mysterious illness that one by one gripped the families of the returned goats. In two of the four families, an elder had come down with what authorities determined was pneumonia and died. In the other two families, two children were determined to have died from a similar illness. Ireoluwa knew this could not be accidental and encouraged the families to have the goats examined. The examination found that each of the four goats had been injected with a hormone that caused the milk, if drunk, and their flesh, if eaten, to be highly toxic for human consumption.

It took Ireoluwa five months to get the story and sleuth out the issues. In the end, he was able to convincingly show that the South African government was disappearing and poisoning livestock as a tactic to gain further leverage against inmates imprisoned for their continued participation in the resistance movements. Ireoluwa's story, "Apartheid in the Milk," ran in Drum magazine that winter. Having spent the advance and some of his own money on the medical examination of the goats, the article cost Ireoluwa all the money he had. But it was worth it, especially after Ireoluwa was offered a continued arrangement with and partial ownership of Drum magazine. During the process, the editor was so impressed with Ireoluwa's persistence, cleverness, and rigor that he was offered an agreement where he would be paid to investigate and publish the experiences of aggressive suppression at the hands of the South African government. No sooner had Ireoluwa's story been published, than the bulldozer came. He and his family were awakened by its menacing roar at dawn, and within minutes, the whole structure was gone.

The ordeal and watching the demolishing of the home was painful. Had it not been for his uncle Femi, who'd recently been released from prison in Johannesburg, the entire family may have been killed by the bulldozer that morning. Femi heard the sound of the approaching bulldozer when it was a mile or so away and woke everyone up. He instructed everyone inside to grab essential items, gather the children, and hurry outside, as the bulldozers were known for pulverizing a home even with people still inside. At the time, Ireoluwa was hungover from celebrating his article's publication. Femi pulled him up from the bed and gave him a shake to bring him back into the present moment and instructed Ireoluwa to grab the locked chest his mother kept.

While the matter of the key would be resolved later, Femi required

Ireoluwa's help pulling the heavy chest out of the house, or it too would perish. Ireoluwa did as he was instructed, and the two men carried the heavy chest out of the house just as the bulldozer was approaching. As Ireoluwa carried the heavy chest with his uncle, he realized that he hadn't grabbed the issue of *Drum* magazine with his newly printed article. For a few seconds, Ireoluwa considered dropping the chest and racing back to his room to retrieve the magazine. But when the roar of the bulldozer grew so loud it sounded as if it was already in the kitchen, Ireoluwa let the notion go and determined he would get another copy somewhere at some point.

Ireoluwa and his family all held each other as they watched the small but mighty structure fall to the ground. The bulldozer rolled over the heap for good measure. Meanwhile, Femi watched the bulldozer with great control. Whispering some sort of chant under his breath, Femi kept his eyes focused on the driver of the bulldozer and the police who accompanied him. Even as disorienting as the sounds of the children crying were for the others, Femi held a hawk-like focus on the individuals who had mercilessly annihilated the home. Femi also stood strong and steadfast, as he knew in these circumstances it was common for the victims of the bulldozer to appear humiliated and embarrassed as their neighbors watched, having been awoken by the ruckus.

As family members' heads began to bow in the atmosphere of destruction, Femi went to each of them and pulled their heads up. "Watch or look up at the sky. Do not look down. You do not deserve this!" Femi was emphatic, and his courageous energy infected each family member until they all watched with fomenting righteousness.

Ireoluwa, however, was not quite able to stand as strong and defiant as the rest. Ireoluwa blamed himself for the bulldozing. Once the bulldozer rode atop the hill of debris, broken glass, and splintered wood, Ireoluwa did everything he could not to scream, cry, or fall to his knees with apologies to his siblings, nieces, and nephews for the ordeal. Ireoluwa discovered he wasn't alone in that sentiment that he was to blame, as his siblings revealed such with angered comments directed at him over the sudden loss of shelter. Femi was quick and precise in communicating his thoughts about the source and cause of the bulldozer.

"No one deserves to have their home taken from them without notice or cause. And if there is any possible reason for this, blame me. Say to yourself, it was because of my uncle's continued involvement in the resistance. If it was because of Luwa's article, they would have already done so well before it was published." Femi's insights rang with solemn confidence that was at once sure and apologetic.

"All this time you have been with the resistance and watched me struggle to get that story together?" Ireoluwa found himself unexpectedly upset with his uncle whom he loved and adored. Although Ireoluwa had meant to keep his words inside, they somehow broke out of his head and exited straight out of his mouth aloud.

"How do you think you were able to get that approval for Robben Island? Of course I helped you. The leadership inside the resistance is small, and we all know each other." Femi looked at Ireoluwa's face move from that of a confused inquisitor to that of an impressed detective.

"Look, there are safe places that we can all go. It will unfortunately mean that we will all have to split up. This will ensure the children are safe and that you each are able to move out of the government's crosshairs," Femi informed the group as he gave four of his cousin Ife's children an address and some money to get them to safety. Ireoluwa was befuddled as his sisters and brothers, nieces and nephews began heading in the direction of the addresses Femi provided.

"Luwa, you will be with me." Femi tugged at the chest, directing Ireoluwa to pick up the other end. Ireoluwa followed his uncle as they headed up the road.

The bulldozing scene was seven years ago. Over those years, Ireoluwa conducted more investigations and published more stories. Five years into his agreement, Ireoluwa eventually became a permanent contributor for *Drum* magazine. Most often, Ireoluwa's stories were the product of his connections to insider reports from resistance members about government suppression. To aid in keeping their identities protected, Ireoluwa had a common angle that anchored all of his pieces.

For Ireoluwa, his stories amounted to tracking, assessing, and keeping a record of the peoples and places lost and created by the forced involuntary brutal evictions from Cape Town's District Six. In particular, Ireoluwa was most interested in documenting the afterlives of District Six residents and families following their forced eviction and migration to South African slum areas. The chest that he and Femi rescued proved an invaluable resource. Unaware of its contents until his uncle broke the lock and opened it up, Ireoluwa was amazed by the numerous journey books, letters, diaries, and other family ephemera it contained. Alongside tips from Femi, who was also a key resource, the chest helped Ireoluwa gather contacts and facts. During those years, Ireoluwa and Femi also had developed a system wherein his published articles contained short coded messages decipherable only to those in the resistance.

Now living in a small home in Soweto with his wife, Nonhle, and two daughters, Fatou and Gugu, Ireoluwa was a respected figure in the journalist and justice communities. Ireoluwa also became the family griot and historian as well. When he and his siblings gathered for festivals or holidays, Ireoluwa would regale the family with a story pulled from his great-grandfather's or his mother's journey book.

While for the listener it appeared as though Ireoluwa was randomly pulling a book and page from the plain chest, none of it was random. Ireoluwa spent many days and nights combing through them and indexing the materials. As he did so, Ireoluwa found himself amazed, saddened, empowered, motivated, and humbled by the extraordinary stories captured and told in the books. Indeed, Ireoluwa hadn't realized that he was named for his great-grandfather until he scoured the books. So moved was he by his family history, Ireoluwa insisted to his wife Nonhle that their children receive names that reflected important names from his family's history. Having followed the unfolding stories over their courtship and marriage, Nonhle was easily convinced.

Along the way, Ireoluwa's reading, assessing, and organizing of the materials within the chest incorporated with his journalistic pursuits had created a daily ritual. Ireoluwa began each morning by waking just before dawn and sipping a hot cup of fresh rooibos tea while reading and indexing a portion of one of the family's journals. Ireoluwa had organized the materials in a linear progression related to year and relative—beginning with the elder Ireoluwa and Babawale, making it easy to begin where he last left off. Following his reading, he would attend to his own journey book, which he obtained shortly after he and Femi made it to Soweto.

In his journal, Ireoluwa would make a daily entry comprised of his thoughts and experiences and then annotate clippings of the day's important news stories. Ireoluwa's journey book looked more like some combination of treasure map meets ransom note. Of late, Ireoluwa's descriptions and details were often questions concerning the potential collaboration of the Black Consciousness Movement and the Unity Party.

Underneath the selection, Ireoluwa would indicate his understanding of the players involved and any suspicions he held about the South African government's involvement. By mid-September, the news clippings as of late had been tracking the events following the arrest of his hero Steve Biko, leader of the Black Consciousness Movement. Biko had been on detention order, disallowed from leaving the town.

As was his practice, after finishing his tea, Ireoluwa retrieved the newspaper and discovered a headline that was close to home and devastating:

13 September 1977

Steve Biko, the controversial leader of the Black Consciousness
Movement, dead at age 30. Having violated his detention
order, Biko was arrested on August 18 by police officers at a
roadblock just outside of Cape Town. Biko was immediately
taken into custody and questioned by authorities as to the
violation of his order of detention. Two men, Peter Jones and
Femi Abdullahi, who were accompanying Biko were also taken
into custody and questioned. Biko died in hospital of natural

causes. Authorities are still in search of Femi Abdullahi who
is believed to have tipped Biko off about the police awaiting
his arrival in Cape Town. Police are requesting that any person
who knows of Abdullahi's whereabouts immediately contact
them so that he may be brought in for questioning.

Ireoluwa cried and prayed as he clipped the story from the newspaper and placed it into his journey book. Ireoluwa was aware that Femi
had brokered the meeting for Biko in Cape Town to meet with Neville
Alexander of the Unity Party so that they might amplify the efforts of
collective resistance to apartheid.

Even though Ireoluwa knew of the barbaric tactics and brutality resistance members endured at the hands of the police, he had been confident
that Biko would find a way out. Biko always found a way out. That was part
of what made him so incredible to Ireoluwa. As he clipped the article out
of the front page, Ireoluwa couldn't believe that Biko had died. Pasting the
article into his journey book, Ireoluwa was heartbroken. Ireoluwa promised
himself his next story would certainly demonstrate that Steve Biko had
been killed.

In the meantime, Ireoluwa knew he would have to tell Nonhle and his
children when they awoke, and they too would be devastated. Ireoluwa
closed his eyes, which were flooded with tears. Ireoluwa visualized his
uncle and prayed for Femi's survival. As Ireoluwa opened his eyes, little
Fatou was standing before him.

1997

Dear Mr. Ireoluwa Makeba:
We have received your letters and calls of inquiry regarding your
mother, Mrs. Ife Makeba. We are sorry to report that Mrs. Ife

Makeba died two nights ago from an apparent heart attack. She was discovered unresponsive in her quarters near midnight. Shortly after being resuscitated, Mrs. Makeba fell into a coma. After falling into a coma, doctors and nurses worked around the clock to assist Mrs. Makeba. Unfortunately, our attempts at saving her proved unsuccessful. She was pronounced dead at 4:04 a.m. Monday morning. We expect that this loss will come as shock and can only imagine the grief that you and your family will feel at this unfortunate news. To assist in this time of grief, we have gathered and packed Mrs. Makeba's personal effects and will make those available within a week's time.

We are so very sorry for your loss. To arrange your time to retrieve her personal effects, please call ahead to ensure a staff member is available to assist you upon arrival.

2001

The excitement of the day was gone. In its place was indescribable and palpable grief. When Ireoluwa, his remaining siblings, and family arrived at Cape Town, they all recalled how long it had been since they'd even stepped foot in District Six. Before arriving, Ireoluwa had instructed everyone that it was important that they all gathered at the spot where their family's building and businesses once stood. Having been torn down in the early 1960s, the lot where the building once stood was empty. The emptiness of the lot was both saddening and inviting. For older family members like Ireoluwa, the building had always been this mythical place the elder members recalled with great, loving nostalgia. So to stand on the spot where all those memories had been born was moving and surreal. Ireoluwa looked at the emptiness and began to conjure the building back in his mind, cobbling together elements of each of its three floors from the journey books he'd read over the years.

As the building came together in his mind, he began to smell the fresh fish being sold at the market. He could hear children playing and adults chasing them around with playful games. He could, in his mind's eye, vividly see the youthful adolescence of his mother Ife and her favorite cousin Femi.

"This is where our family began. Right here on this spot, there was once a building and our family's businesses." Ireoluwa looked at his family who had been watching him and his wandering imagination with deep interest. And while many relatives were aware of the storied family businesses and the forced evictions under apartheid, Ireoluwa could sense the disbelief and disillusionment amongst his kin.

"On this very spot, two young Nigerian boys and their Xhosa wives created a beautiful life for themselves and their families. Today, on this day of great return, we honor them, their sacrifice, and the losses that our family has faced then and now." Ireoluwa's tone was of the temperature of a riveting minister who had brought his congregants through the valley and into the promised land. Using his large wooden walking staff, Ireoluwa traced out a large square in the dirt and then invited all fifty family members to stand within its boundaries. Once everyone, including the children, were inside the square, Ireoluwa instructed them all to close their eyes and imagine.

"We now stand together, hand in hand, and invite our ancestors to join us today. We, who have come for the return-of-land ceremony, thank you for your sacrifice. My beloved mother, Ife, may you rest in the sky knowing that we endure as does our loving memory of you."

Family members then went around the square and offered their own blessings and memories.

"My beautiful daughter Fatou has prepared some remarks for this occasion." Ireoluwa pulled Fatou to him and moved out of the center so that she could begin and share.

"This day marks the end of a long journey. May it also mark the beginning of a new one. Over my life, I have been able to witness many new endings and new beginnings. I experienced the last days of apartheid when its chokehold felt most unrelenting and as though it would kill us all on its way back into the pits of hell. I have lost many friends and loved ones as its ending, while inevitable, slowly dragged to its unmarked grave next to slavery, colonization, famine, and the Holocaust, and all the other human-created tragedies we have come to call history. And so that new ending came to pass. We all witnessed it. Just as the new ending concluded, a new beginning started. For me, as I am sure it is for us all, that start was watching Madiba, now president Nelson Mandela, walk out of Robben Island not with a grimace of agony but a wide smile of hope. It was the constitutional convention. It was the transformation of the prison which brutalized and tortured our sistren and brethren, including Great-Uncle Ancestor Femi, into the highest court in the land. It was the celebrations that followed, the hearings and testimonies. And yet, here we are standing atop the grave of our family's storied business, Two Brothers Enterprises. Here we are today on the precipice of receiving the land back that was taken from the beautiful community and people who called District Six home for over a hundred years before the great evictions. We, who have been chosen to survive, to witness this new beginning, have much to be thankful for and even more work ahead. Let us proclaim our gratitude to our ancestors and stay optimistic that a new South Africa may be the blueprint for a fresh and more loving world. I am happy to share my special announcement today. For my part, I shall be working to bring *Drum* magazine back to life as an internet resource with the eventual goal of publishing our family's history when the moment is right. Thanks to father's legacy share of the magazine, we have been able to negotiate a new beginning for this important international vehicle for sharing with the world the state of our conditions and struggle for freedom." Fatou beamed with so much light that her forehead appeared to be glowing and vibrating with a yellow halo crown.

Ireoluwa was so proud and in such deep admiration of his daughter, he'd felt transported across time and space into a place of great stillness.

As Fatou spoke, Ireoluwa felt as though the empty lot had been reconstituted into a life-size diorama where the building and people who once gathered and populated it were adorned in all white encircling the family. Afterward, everyone hugged, cried, and hugged some more.

Following the emotional embraces and family prayer, they all walked to the center of the district where the mayor would be presenting the land return to former residents and their descendants. Ireoluwa recognized and spoke with dozens of people he hadn't seen in many years during the journey through District Six to the center of the neighborhood where the ceremony took place. He heard stories of family members lost during the struggle against apartheid. Many people came up to him and his family to share their appreciation and love for Femi, who had been in the vanguard of the resistance against the government's mistreatment and subjugation of Black and Coloured South Africans. There was even a mention of Two Brothers Enterprises on the read-aloud list of thriving businesses shuttered under the apartheid regime.

That the family left empty-handed was a big blow—no land was actually returned that day. No new leases or mortgages or deeds were given or returned. It had all been a symbolic show of return. It was hard for the family to endure the ceremony when it became clear that even in the new South Africa, meaningful repair was not on the horizon, but stored away in a rabbit hole of confusion, pain, and suffering.

"To move forward, we must move forward," the mayor proclaimed as the ceremony concluded.

All the returned residents and their descendants cast eyes that communicated they all felt like fools. As had been the case with the testimonies during the Truth and Reconciliation process, no one had received their stolen livelihoods and possessions back. They merely were set up to show up, reveal their scars and the pain underneath to convince those in power of the horrors of apartheid.

Fatou, seeing her father's dismay and disappointment, rubbed his back with her optimism still intact. "It may not be today, Father. But we shall not be denied!"

Ireoluwa looked at his precocious and powerful daughter, recognizing in her the queen she had become. Fatou leaned her head on her father's shoulder as they walked toward the setting sun.

2027

From the time Fatou arrived in New York City, she had felt the whole experience to be a nearly overwhelming whirlwind of meetings, handshakes, photographs, and interviews. When she was able, Fatou scurried back to her hotel room to rehearse her remarks. Practicing her inflections and ensuring that there was the proper rise and fall where needed was especially important. Her parents were proud when the invitation to speak before the United Nations General Assembly arrived. The messenger was very official and initially made everyone nervous that his letter was of a dire nature. Reading the invitation aloud, Fatou couldn't believe that the series of articles she published online of her family's memories and histories managed to reach such a large and powerful international body. The letter informed her that the United Nations requested her presence and a speech to give insight and context to the calls for truth, healing, and reparations emanating from nearly every corner of the world.

Fatou was too excited to be nervous, and her parents were too proud to become worried. On the spot, they all decided along with her sister Gugu that the invitation would be accepted, and that the family would fly to New York City to all witness this extraordinary occasion. Before then, Fatou had never been outside of South Africa, let alone to New York City. The whole place was a wonder, and that she was being treated with such high esteem only added more glittery sparkle to Fatou's visit to the Big Apple.

The night before her speech, Fatou spoke with her husband and children who cheered her on and encouraged her with a bouquet of loving praise. She slept that night as though she were levitating, feeling lifted and carried into restfulness by her many ancestors who'd guided her to this very moment in time. Although she managed to get *Drum* magazine off the ground as a digital news magazine, it had been a hard and difficult road—one that she never truly shared with anyone for fear that it might encourage her to move on to other interests or purposes.

After many years of publishing new stories and cultural events, it had occurred to Fatou that her family's story could be meaningful and helpful. So when international news of the murders of Breonna Taylor and George Floyd reverberated through the world, Fatou returned to the chest of her family's history. Publishing the first of seven pieces, simply titled "1827," on the one-year anniversary of Floyd's death, Fatou saw the repeating of a history she'd already lived in South Africa. A new end had come to pass with the new beginning following it being hollowed out and transformed into an echo chamber of politics, disinterest, lies, and empty promises.

Fatou saw the publishing of her family's history as a tool to beat back the hollowing, to keep the light from being snuffed out by cynicism and the avoidance of publicizing and properly acknowledging the past. Fatou also thought her family's history might aid in the call for racial justice, equity, truth, and repair that had begun to fall into the cracks of the well-intentioned speeches of various world leaders in the aftermath of a pandemic and splintering calls for new laws, reforms, and policies.

Before Fatou knew it, she was before the United Nations in a room packed with representatives, ambassadors, celebrities, journalists, and activists. Just as she gathered the pages of her written speech, Fatou allowed her eyes to visit with as many of the onlookers as possible. She scanned the room until she found her parents and sister at the center. Fatou pulled a full breath into her chest, which provided her a measure of comfort and pride. She could feel all of her ancestors gathered, standing alongside her and lifting her up in the great moment of history. And so Fatou cleared her throat and began.

"I stand before you as a witness, as a descendant, as a journalist, as a historian, as a mother, as a daughter, as a niece, as a sister, as a proud South African woman whose unmistakable black skin color has been marked by slavery, colonization, apartheid, and the persistent false belief that all human beings are not of equal, mutual, and divine value. From the start, when I began to publish my family's histories, I recognized how fortunate I was that I had been able to inherit their stories in oral and written form. Otherwise, I may have considered them unbelievable. As I published them and then digitized them for South Africa's Archives for Racial and Cultural Healing, I was quite sure many of the readers likely questioned their veracity. And then I realized somewhere along the way that just because things are hard to believe or based upon dead matter does not mean they are not true and alive. Today, like many days, before walking into this powerful building, I looked up at the sun, a great fiery star roiling and warming our world with grand authority. How impossible, improbable, and unbelievable is the controlled power and existence of the sun? As a child, I once learned that the moon that greets us every evening is made up of dead matter that came together and created itself to offer balance to the power of the sun. How incredible is it that something that was once dead could come together to live again and guide the oceans and light the sky when the sun has retired for the day? How impossible, improbable, and unbelievable are the sun and the moon? Would we believe them or know the sun and moon to be true if we did not experience them or see them or have access to them?

"As these questions illustrate, the importance of experience and access to accepting and acknowledging the truth of a thing, the truth of a matter, are essential. It is quite easy to disbelieve what has not been shown or revealed and even easier to believe only what has been allowed to be accessed and shared. Where there is no light, there can reside darkness that makes things seem empty. This, I imagine, is the wisdom inherent to moonlight—to show us that darkness is also a form of light. It may be scarier and make things ahead less visible, but you can still see something if only yourself.

"Now many may wonder why I have begun by speaking about the sun and the moon when I have come before you all to talk about matters such as the legacy of slavery, human suffering, land dispossession, and South Africa in the decades following the end of the brutal regime of apartheid. It is because our human history is a collection of light and dark that has many times been hidden from us all while guiding our every step. When a light is placed upon slavery, it tends in the direction of the story of the West and how the ancestors of modern-day Europeans exported not just other human beings but a mindset of racism. By and before any Black person was stolen or bought or sold or transported across the Atlantic Ocean from Ghana, Sierra Leone, Nigeria, Benin, or Senegal, there was already a narrative spread that defamed and diminished the humanity of those Black people so that by the time of their arrival, other human beings saw not a mirror of their own humanity. Instead, they were CON-vinced that they shared no meaningful genetic, spiritual, biological, or binding connection to these dark others arriving on the shores of Barbados, Jamaica, Virginia, Massachusetts, Liverpool, or Brazil. As a result, Black people were and continue to be understood and viewed as subhuman or an entirely different species altogether—deserving and well-suited for slavery, subjugation, and suffering.

"We must remember that the narrative that equated melanin with being less human was a global script. Put simply, race is a con job, and racism is the art form that breathes continuous life into various CON-structions that distort the fact of our shared humanity. Against their permission, Indians were placed in a racial CON-tract whereby they were CON-structed as higher in the racial hierarchy than West Indians and Fijians, all the while situated beneath and within the CON-cept of white people and whiteness. Within these CON-structs, Arabs and Persians seemingly rose above Nubian or Yoruba or Ibo, Eastern European beneath Western, British and French above Italian and Irish, Afrikaans above Zulu and Xhosa, and so on. Therefore slavery, now referred to with the misleading and new age sounding name of 'human trafficking,' continues to be permitted. Europeans were not alone in the slave-trading business, as Arab slave traders took Black people from West Africa and trafficked them east, many dying in the hot desert plains of the Sahara or perishing from disease and blood loss from castration. We have been conned out of our dignity, humanity, land, happiness, dreams, and homes. And our fellow humans who look upon Indigenous, Native, Black, Asian, Aboriginal, and melanated peoples as somehow different, are conning themselves into a false belief that what has happened and continues to happen to your fellow human will not and shall not happen to you.

"We must no longer soothe ourselves with the convenient warmth of a lie. It is a lie that slavery ended. For example, in 1827 when the British formally ended their participation in the slave trade, my great-great-grandfather Ireoluwa Adeyemi was on a fishing boat with his father Oluwatobi. And they likely thought that while they still lived in the repressed condition of colonization, being captured, bought, stolen, or traded as property was over. Yet, Oluwatobi and Ireoluwa found themselves at the mercy of Arab slave traders who'd begun pilfering Black Africans from the same lands the United Kingdom and France abandoned. Nearly castrated at the hands of the slave traders, they were shipped away to India where they oversaw a tenement of sex work. Black women and girls, such as my great-great-grand-aunt Gugu, were forced against their will to become concubines and tools of sexual aggression and sexual desire. And while my great-great-grandparents were able to find their way to Cape Town, there are many others, many others who did not and could not. Trapped in a cycle of rape, unwanted pregnancy, and far away from their families and homes, these women and girls are but precursors to the systems of sex and human trafficking that have come before this powerful body of international government leaders in recent decades. Because slavery never ended, human trafficking exists, operates, and functions at a high and global level. If we continue to believe and state that slavery somehow ended, then we fortify the lie that humanity is a hierarchy discernable by skin color, religion, creed, gender, sexual orientation, tribe, or nation.

"Rather than new problems, the United Nations has been CON-fronted with residual and reimagined vestiges of patterns of human violation permitted and authorized by the global slave trade and the colonization of lands of the world. As many of you have likely read, before apartheid was legalized in South Africa, my family had a business that had been prospering for one hundred years. And while for much of the world apartheid seemed to be an overnight happening, I hope the story of my grandmother, Ife, shows that was certainly not the case. Apartheid crystalized in the law a social and political system of racial categorization that had already been in practice. My grandmother's story demonstrates that systems of racial inequity, systems of racism, take a psychological toll, a financial toll, and a spiritual toll on victims. Unfortunately, my grandmother, like so many Black and Coloured South Africans, never recovered from the great losses brought about by apartheid. My grandmother Ife and great-uncle Femi both died in state facilities, one a mental asylum and the other prison. My family has never recovered. And yes, there was a New Constitution and a Truth and Reconciliation Process.

"And yes, our Great Madiba was freed and elected president. But political and legal repairs have their limits and cannot be fully realized when financial, emotional, psychological, and spiritual repair are not manifested alongside. Still today, many of the townships suffer from the disease of poverty and lack of access to quality education and employment opportunities that allow for mobility. What was called new has begun to look and sound much like the old."

Fatou took a pause, her voice quivering with the painful memories brought about as she recollected her grandmother's unceremonious and preventable death, dying alone in and then cremated by a mental institution. Fatou took a sip of water and continued.

"I stand before you today despite all that has occurred and is happening in my country and across the world, and I remain optimistic. In fact, it was optimism masquerading in hopefulness that compelled me to publicly share my family history and revitalize *Drum* magazine as a digital resource. In 2001 when my family returned to the vacant lot where our business once stood proudly, we were all hopeful. We had hoped that the return-of-land ceremony may have actually meant some type of repair, only to realize it was all performance. No one intended to return anything. And as I marinated in what wasn't returned, I began to think about what might have happened if things like the family's land would have been returned. We may have been able to clear our debts, feel some measure of wholeness as we gathered together on holidays, and witness the community of District Six reestablish itself.

"That is what my family history taught me and the lesson that I hope has taken root as millions of people across the world have read and shared these stories. When slavery was ended by the Europeans, the United States kept its own version alive and even embedded its existence into its founding documents. And while we see in places like the United States and South Africa the practice of slavery ending in the 1800s, roughly 1837 in South Africa and 1865 in the US, soon after, a new distortion of the same condition of human subjugation took hold. Rather than thinking of the systems such as Jim Crow or apartheid as different, we must remember them as slavery's children allowed to flourish, nourished using the same legal apparatus that allegedly ended enslavement.

"I stand before you like a tuning fork for the reverberating global quests and calls for equity, truth, reparations, healing, and transformation. These quests, requests, and calls are all reflections of the shattered mirrors of our shared humanity. Refracted and fractured shards of glass that continue to draw blood and cut us distort a positive image of the collective until melded and repaired. We have created a world where we are made to spend most of our time persuading one another of our fundamental birthright to be happy. Happiness is not some sort of gift or privilege set aside by the Creator for an elite chosen few or those who are willing to sacrifice the collective for individual and personal gain.

"Happiness is a birthright. We must protest, activate, and organize within ourselves to proclaim before ourselves that our undeniable divine connection has been violated time and time and time again. It is time to break this cycle. It is time to look into the mirror and see not just your reflection but OUR reflection. You see, I have learned that this is what history is—a measure of time alchemized into a mirror that reflects back the truth, the lies, the secrets, the good, the bad, the ugly, and the indifference we have spread within and outside of ourselves.

"And when our divine obligations to each other have been unfulfilled, ignored, and cast aside, we find ourselves in a world where preventable suffering, death, and pain cover our news pages and strike our communities and consciousness into diseased pieces of emptiness and hopelessness. We begin to see in ourselves, and thus each other, the shame, fear, blame, and guilt reflected back in the mirrors of the past and present, shaping a void where our future is left to reside.

"Please look around the room. Look around at the names of the nations that adorn this room. Look at the colors and shapes of the people in this room. And as you look around, ask yourself what exactly makes you so individually different from that which you see next to and across the room from you? How meaningful are the differences which you discover? I can tell you what I saw, what I see, and what I hope we all know and understand: *We are the last of the* Homo sapiens.

"In the weeks and days leading up to this speech, I spent a great deal of time imagining this very room and each of the faces that I would see. My imagination ran wild as I thought about seeing faces from places I'd never been and have seen rendered through a map or spinning orb of the globe. As I pictured this very moment, this gift, this present, I realized how the earth is so mighty that she hath brought us together no matter the distance of the lands we represent.

"The earth has a way of reminding us through her treatment that we are all the same to her. And yet, we treat her and each other with such disregard. And even still, the sun continues to rise, minutes roll into hours, hours into weeks, weeks into months, months into years, years into decades, decades into centuries, and so on. So how is it that we continually find ourselves with clocks and calendars that move forward as we continually choose to pretend as though we have done the same? Land and people were stolen, and then at some point while discussing these issues, we are told to stop. Yet each convening of this body is presented with mountains of evidence that the taking of land and people persists, showing not only have we not moved forward, but we have also not moved backward.

"We are stuck. Stuck in sinking sands that beneath them have the bones of our ancestors, skeletons whose flesh was destroyed by false beliefs and manufactured narratives about human hierarchy. We are stuck in a narrative of human history where we continue to choose to turn a blind eye in order to see what we want to see, turn a deaf ear to hear what we want to hear. We are stuck in a set of false beliefs passed down to us by people, many of whom are no longer here in this present. It is my belief that we are left with these narratives so that we have an enhanced purpose. We have explicit directions and instructions of what needs to be done, who needs to be healed, who needs to be acknowledged and recognized, what harms have come to pass. Not so that we will be beleaguered by the weight of it all. Instead, we inherit this earth and this present as a solid foundation to act on purpose with purpose in purpose. And our purpose is to repair and restore the violated covenants. To ensure, as they say here in the United States of America, that everyone's fundamental right to life, liberty, and the pursuit of happiness is not impeded nor blocked because of false value systems that sort humanity, leaving humans to resort to terror, violence, and oppression of one another to secure their fundamental rights.

"I think it is only right that I stand before you in the United States to remind world leaders and this country of its responsibility to be the lighthouse it says it is and beseeches other nations to be. I beseech you to repair and restore the lives and broken hearts of your own people. If you cannot offer reparations and racial healing in this place of only a few hundred years of age, how can we expect to see it happen in places older and longer in their history than here? Reparations happening anywhere, but especially in places like South Africa, Australia, New Zealand, the Caribbean, and the United States of America, are radical moves toward a future where love, justice, and freedom are no longer aspirations but are reality. This radical repair must happen. The future we all need and deserve requires it.

"In closing, I will end by expanding where I began. My name is Fatou, great-great-great granddaughter of Oluwatobi Adeyemi, a Nigerian fisherman stolen and forced into slavery. My name is Fatou, great-great-granddaughter of Ireoluwa Adeyemi, an escaped slave who as a young boy was nearly castrated, made to be a eunuch in a brothel in what is now called Mumbai, and later hid at the bottom of the trunk of fabrics on a ship that sailed across the Indian Ocean until it reached the shores of South Africa. My name is Fatou Mlambo, the great-great-granddaughter of Mlambo, sister of Gugu, of the mighty Xhosa people who met, married, and began a series of successful businesses with her husband Ireoluwa Adeyemi in the heart of Cape Town's District Six. My name is Fatou Mlambo Nkosi, granddaughter of Ife, a fierce and beautiful woman who was made to be called Coloured and evicted from her family's one-hundred-year-old residence and later died of broken-heartedness, her mind left spinning and spiraling from all that had been taken away from her and her family. My name is Fatou Mlambo Nkosi Makeba, the great-niece of Femi Abdullahi, freedom fighter, a friend of Steve Biko, and grandson of Olufemi Abdullahi, an escaped slave who watched his dead father's body float along Nigeria's Oba River as he was forced to travel across an unfamiliar terrain of desert sand and the salt of the Indian Ocean and who was told he would never escape or be safe or free. My name is Fatou Mlambo Nkosi Makeba-Ndungane, daughter of Ireoluwa, the great journalist who investigated and exposed the harms and dangers of apartheid, passing intelligence through codes in his articles.

"My name is Fatou Mlambo Nkosi Makeba-Ndungane, daughter of Nonhle of the Xhosa people, who was made to reside in zones and terrains of forgetting all the while having to watch the land they culti-vated for centuries and the gold reef underneath it be taken by a govern-ment created by people who hadn't lived in Africa until the arrival of the colonizers. My name is Fatou Mlambo Nkosi Makeba-Ndungane, born of the chaotic creation of human subjugation bearing the fertile seeds along the Nile of Kemet turned Egypt, scrolled within the hieroglyphs of the great pyramids and patterned in the mud cloth of West Africa, traced into the grooves of the Baobab and rain staffs of the elders above and below the Sahara Desert, cinched inside the petals of the rooibos bush, carried across the oceans east and west, up rivers north and south, wearing a crown visible only to those with the awareness that we are the last of the *Homo sapiens*, that humanity can only be divided by humans. We, who have been chosen to survive, have the mandate to thrive together and build a world where we create and find love in all things all the time and everywhere. Amandla! Power!"

5

BETTER HAVE MY MONEY

It's been more than eighty-three million minutes, more that five trillion seconds, since the United States abolished slavery in 1865, and
Black people are still waiting on truth and reparations. The year 1865
was both an end and a beginning; it reflected the end of Black people
awaiting slavery's demise while also marking the start of a new waiting
game—that of racial healing, repair, equity, and transformational policies
to mitigate, acknowledge, and prevent the continuance of the horrors and
brutality the slavery regime authorized and permitted. Systemic racism
and systemic inequality are so entrenched in the premise of the United
States of America that even the combination of executive orders, military
orders, and constitutional amendments have proven an inadequate adver-
sary. Taking away or adding ingredients to a lousy recipe is the recipe for
disaster and ongoing crisis. Any meaningful recipe for reparations must
account for the actual, even if unbelievable, losses and injuries occurring
during and following the end of legalized enslavement. For nearly 160
years, Black people have been patiently awaiting repair and restoration.

And so it was that in 2015, 150 years later, I too was waiting. Having
missed the green light that would have allowed me to turn left onto Pico

Boulevard from Motor Avenue, I watched yellow turn red. I waited, increasingly annoyed as other cars moved swiftly and freely up and down
Pico Boulevard. I was anxious that I would be late to my UCLA class
where I was teaching reparations and Derrick Bell's *Faces at the Bottom
of the Well*. I stared at the front of Fox Studios as I searched my reserves
for whatever ounce of patience remained in my near hour-long commute.
As though on a cue set by the ancestors, Rihanna's voice arrived on my
radio, triumphantly declaring "B—Better Have My Money"! Five years
into my exploration and investigation into reparations, I was increasingly
finding myself dubious about its likelihood and needed a sign.

The song, a Kanye West–produced masterwork, arrived just as
my patience and optimism about things happening on time and the
future were wearing thin. After millions of minutes of waiting, a raucous, deliberately profane warning and promise, "B—Better Have My
Money," summarized a global sentiment. Within the sonic and lyrical
landscape of the song, Rihanna crystallized what it means and what it
feels like to be treated as property, to be stolen from, owed, defamed,
and have your dehumanization on public display. The end of waiting
was near, and money, which is due and owed, was everywhere, even
if not in her possession. The green light arrived, and with it, a new
awareness of the purpose of reparations and my exploration of their
essence and import.

My reparations journey began as an outgrowth of a long intellectual
and spiritual tango with Dr. W. E. B. Du Bois. The first Black person to
receive a PhD from Harvard University, Du Bois pioneered in so many
fields of inquiry. A life that began in the small town of Great Barrington,
Massachusetts, would set the world afire. Du Bois's legacy is mighty,
whether it be his penchant for historical and cultural speculation, reframing systemic racism as a disease, or his retelling of the Civil War by
centering Black people's agency and humanity. And while I had never
entirely been taught his work as a student, when I discovered Du Bois, I
knew I had encountered a master teacher. And I certainly was glad to be
his newfound student.

Our relationship is the origin of this book; for it was his first book that became the lighthouse that guided me to reparations and facilitated my very ascension to and arrival in Los Angeles. As was true for Du Bois, Black people's patience and long-suffered waiting serve as a constant source of motivation and inspiration. The research for this book began in earnest in 2009. As I concluded the research process and began writing this book, I understood that I have, like millions of other Black people, within my life's journey, always already been on the quest for and awaiting reparations.

After some years as a high school English teacher, I discovered how little I knew, even as my charge was to educate students about the power of stories, words, poems, plays, language, writing, and communication. Each day as I ventured to Audenreid High School in South Philadelphia, I passed by and through communities and neighborhoods that had raised me and educated me on what it meant to be Black and be to Black in the United States of America. Rather than being "The City of Brotherly Love," Philadelphia was "The City that Don't Love Brothas," as my father Marcus Allan frequently reminded. By the age of nine, I had experienced being called several racial slurs, profiled, chased, and harassed by white adults and their children, especially in the drunken aftermath of Philly's annual New Year's Day Mummers Parade.

By 2003, I found myself instructing high school and AP English in the Philadelphia school district; I had also come to terms with being and being seen as Black and gay, a longtime resident of the outsider space the convergence of those identities created. Over the course of teaching my students, or more accurately being taught by my students, I was compelled to return to school to pursue a PhD in sociology.

Late summer 2005, my family and I were in two packed sedans riding the long route that carried us from Philadelphia, passed Pittsburgh, through Cleveland, on to Gary, and into Chicago. Riding up Lake Shore Drive, I was taken by the spectacular scenery of the ebbs and flows of Great Lake Michigan. And soon enough, my family and I headed around the bends of Sheridan Road to Evanston where Northwestern University

awaited. Five years later, I was offered and accepted a tenure-track
position in the sociology department at Yale University. To get the job,
in my interview lecture, I shared insights from what became my very first
book—a revisit of the Black Seventh Ward neighborhood that was Du
Bois's field site in the 1899 classic *The Philadelphia Negro*.

Landing the job at Yale University in 2011 deepened my connection
to Du Bois, as it meant that a project that revisited the neighborhood of
his very first book helped facilitate me getting a job less than a hundred
miles away from where he was born and raised. To my mind, this was no
coincidence. And though I was excited and proud even, as I packed my
boxes to head to the foggy gray New England climate, the truth was that
I was sad and afraid. My anxious mind was filled with so many memories and thoughts, most of them harkening to the cumulative loneliness
I felt. After twenty-five years of schooling, all I could think about was
all of the people and things that had been lost along the way—friends
and relatives who had died or been murdered. I could only attend family
vacations, birthdays, and homegoings by phone or relive them vicariously
through the recounting of those in attendance. The time I missed with
family members pained me, especially my maternal grandfather and step-
grandmother, who perished from colon cancer just before Yale had come
into my life. To make everything I did at Yale worthy of the losses I had
endured, the sense of loss I felt in my bones, I stepped into my newfound
upward mobility determined.

Even with this seemingly forward momentum, soon after arriving
at Yale, I found myself swarmed and profiled by New Haven police officers. Just outside my apartment and in the middle of the block for all my
neighbors to see, my identification, height, skin color, hairstyle, weight,
and clothing were checked over police dispatch against the culprit of a
reported robbery of a bodega around the corner. Guns in holsters and
side-eyes in tow, the officers looked me over, up and down, with eyes that
seemed convinced that they had found the culprit. Having only left my
home moments earlier to deposit a few items in the mailbox fifty yards
or so from my front door, the fear and sadness that I tried to store and

carry in my subconscious burst forward and held my mouth closed and my tongue still. Although the officers had given me the impression that I was enduring a quick and straightforward check, I felt duped and terrified as I overheard the dispatch and then descriptors about me being used to verify the culprit's identity.

Somehow, I managed to dislodge my tongue and found a split-second pause in the officer's profiling to offer my query. "Please ask the dispatcher if the person was a Yale professor?"

Puzzled, the leading officer looked at me and my relatively plain attire. Before responding, the officer looked around at the near dozen of his surrounding colleagues as though he wondered if they too were stupefied by the question. After a few seconds, which felt like minutes, the officer glanced up from my feet to my face and responded, "Why do you say that?"

"I am a Yale professor." There. I said it. My body was trembling even as I tried to comport myself with the assumed confidence of someone who would be believed to be an Ivy League university professor.

"Really? What proof do you have?" the officer shot back; his increasing anxiety, while evident to me, was also masked by apparent disbelief in the truthfulness of my affirmative statement.

Sensing that there was only a short window available to offer requested proof, I scoured my mind trying to think through what I might have on me that would prove my Yale affiliation. At first, all the items that came to mind were located in my apartment just ten feet away, though obstructed by a semicircle of police officers and police vehicles. Seeing the impatience and disbelief growing in the officer's face, I recalled that my Yale identification was in my back pocket, as I had returned a book for my reparations research to the library just before going home for the day.

"My identification is in my back pocket. May I reach and get it?" I asked hands-up with the savvy born from my days being robbed at bus stops in Philly and stopped by gun-anxious police.

"Go ahead!" the lead officer directed me as the semicircle of surveillance placed their hands in and around their holsters.

As I pulled the card out, I realized for the first time that my Yale identification card did not offer a description or title or affiliation. The white card had just my face within a red border, a bar code, and the date of issuance. Unable to barter any additional time, I swallowed my trepidation and presented the identification with as much confidence as I could muster. Reviewing the identification card, the lead officer sucked his teeth and passed it to a few of his colleagues. Without so much as a word, I was handed back the card, and as suddenly as I had been encircled, I was released. Or at least that's what became apparent as the half dozen police vehicles aimed in my direction backed out in different versions of K-turns and sped off with signals blaring in the distance. Before I felt I could move, I waited for a few seconds. Then I waited a few minutes. Somewhat relieved but even more terrified about venturing further away from my apartment, I decided I would wait another day before attempting to use the mailbox at the opposite side of Wooster Square Park.

After that, and perhaps to cope, I immersed myself further in the quest to recover the experiences and histories embedded in the centuries encompassing and following legalized enslavement and land dispossession in the United States of America. After each query, I kept returning to the year 1865, Abraham Lincoln's 1863 Emancipation Proclamation, and the surrounding and subsequent days and years. This also included Special Field Order No. 15 issued by General Sherman, which famously bequeathed "forty acres and a mule" to free Black people in the South and the Freedmen's Bureau, a congressionally authorized body that would assist and integrate formerly enslaved Black people into the body politic. Of all the deeds, players, and legislation that followed the Emancipation Proclamation, I was most taken with and absorbed by the creation and collapse of the Freedman's Bank.

As Lincoln's last act on behalf of formerly enslaved Black people, Congress created a national savings bank exclusively catered to Black people. The Freedman's Bank had more than twenty branches across the Northeast and South within a few years. All told, Black people deposited more than a billion dollars in today's dollars. Shortly after its rapid success, Congress authorized the bank as a lending institution. And thanks to systemic racism, white people were the exclusive recipients of the money lent or provided as credit by the Freedman's Bank. Even worse, Frederick Douglass was duped and scapegoated as the president of the bank just in time for its abrupt collapse, which blindsided its Black patrons. Douglass, a patron, lost thousands of dollars, taking a major reputational hit to boot. Du Bois and Booker T. Washington each voiced the lasting harm and distrust that the Freedman's Bank collapse caused within Black communities across the United States. At the fall of the Freedman's Bank, all three Black men found a source of agreement, each predicting in his way the lasting impact the sudden loss of wealth would have on the African American community. Douglass, Du Bois, and Washington's difference had fallen away to assess the damage of the Freedman's Bank.

I spent a great deal of time tracking down the bank's records, statements, and newspaper stories, especially Black leaders' insights of the time. This discovery transformed my awareness about the period immediately following the Emancipation Proclamation and became a foundation and launching pad to dig deeper into the history, framework, and reasons for reparations. And I found myself integrating some of these initial insights into my first book. The history of the Black Seventh Ward demonstrated how depriving people and communities of appropriate repair and restoration created a condition whereby those harmed and their descendants were almost always troubleshooting and activating from one preventable racial crisis to the next. As troubling and precise as this pattern seems now, at the time, it rang especially true because intuitively, it resonated with my own life's journey. When I would teach about the War on Drugs and the War on Poverty, I could see in my mind's eye my own family and community transitioning from either prevention or reaction to the dilemmas these policies produced in their lives. Somewhere near the end of the process of producing my first book, I did some family genealogical research and discovered that my great-great-grandmother

Jessie Cannon was a resident of the Black Seventh Ward at the time of Du Bois's research and writing on the neighborhood. It seemed Du Bois was not done with me yet.

I originated #BlackLivesMatter in August 2012, as reparations and the stories of Black people were heavy on my mind and research agenda. By then, I had been bearing witness to the possibilities and problems of America for more than thirty years, born and raised amidst the grueling War on Drugs, the end of the Cold War, the rise and dominance of hip-hop music, and the fulfillment of the prophecy of the Civil Rights Movement as expressed through Barack Obama's historic two terms as the country's first Black president. I had traveled and journeyed a bit myself over those years, from homelessness to a PhD to a job as a professor at Yale University and an author. And despite the real success story it seemed I represented, all I could think about were all the things that had been lost along the way—lost before I began. Black Americans' losses, as they work to build a better life for themselves and their communities, are innumerable. And the stories of Black inventors and Black invention bubbled up from the archives I had researched, the whispers in between the waves crashing along the shores of the Atlantic Ocean, and in the biographies of musicians and scholars I had come to know. The Black people in the ocean have a story to tell, etched into the tides echoing out into the endless sea singing, screaming, crying, laughing, and recalling the long legacy of the Middle Passage, the triangle trade, and slavery in the Americas.

Well into 2013, I was stepping up my exploration and observations of reparations and examining the global enterprise better known as the triangle or transatlantic slave trade. When and if we are taught about slavery, it is in the context of white Europeans exporting an involuntary mass of Black West Africans to the Western Hemisphere or the New World, as it was then called. Yet before this global scheme of human trafficking could prosper, something else had to travel first. What we now commonly refer to as race began as a European narrative export to validate and justify the enslavement of other humans. Systemic racism then is a pyramid scheme of prosperity that manipulates other humans into believing and accepting that humanity is a sliding scale of importance and mattering premised upon skin color.

A global narrative campaign defaming Black people's humanity was foundational to the enterprise's success. Even if an individual slaveholder could not control his captives, there still needed to be a systematic apparatus upholding the premise that enslaved Black people were property, not people at all. Systemic racism operates like gravity, holding people down and in places against their will. Black people everywhere were living in some sort of simulation that at its core was the offspring of the brainchild of the marriage of race and racism.

Four hundred years, more than three trillion minutes, and a thousand months is how long the United States of America has lived with and in the sin of slavery. Abolished yet alive, as many activists and scholars have demonstrated, slavery in one form or another has persisted and lingered like an untreated virus constantly spreading and infecting even as many claim its slow death began as the ink dried on Abraham Lincoln's Emancipation Proclamation. From the prison industrial complex, the Tuskegee experiment, chain gangs, wars on poverty, crime, and drugs, Black people's lives remain vulnerable and unprotected by the very government that abolished the institution and practice of slavery.

As the planter class took its last sips of power and blood at the Civil War's conclusion, they managed to bequeath to us a legacy of debt and devastation that is in our collective advantage and benefit to redress. Slavery is a violation of at least three basic spiritual and moral principles. A person's humanity is not to be owned by another, yet such was the case for enslaved Black people. A person's soul is not to be owned by another, yet such was the case for enslaved Black people. A person's body is not to be owned by anyone other than the individual with whom the soul and humanity that strives within belongs. And yet, this was endemic to American slavery.

American slavery and the broader European slave trade saw to it that these human principles were not only violated but also subverted. The

West African "Door of No Return" carried hundreds of thousands of Black people from their homes in Africa and through the challenging Middle Passage onto lands occupied by Indigenous peoples across the Americas and Caribbean. A passageway born of greed, racism, rape, and colonization carried Black Africans across the many tides and waves of the Atlantic Ocean. Never to be seen again. Or at least that was the intended outcome. Not only were they never to return, the expectation was that they would either die in transport, in the fields of the South, or in basements of the North at an early age, but not before they could procreate the next generation of enslaved Black people.

Black people were owned, their bodies and families were taken from them, and their souls were devastated as a matter of daily life. All the while, their labor was demanded and provided free of charge. This is the landscape of human violation and suffering that we have inherited. And as with any inheritance, we have been bequeathed responsibilities, among them holding the United States government accountable for clearing specific debts. These accumulated and persistent debts, commonly known as *reparations*, remain unpaid and unreconciled. Significantly, though oft ignored, while the etymological root of "reparations" is the word "repair," the term shifts the *I* to *tions*—from individual behavior and action to that of collective responsibility and accountability. Therefore, reparations are always about holding the government accountable for the trauma and harm it knowingly authorized, constitutionalized, and sanctioned. In the interim, Black people have effectively been left to their own devices with little state support and anti-Black state surveillance.

As time passes, it would seem that the ability to calculate damages and appropriately pay affected citizens precisely and their families is impossible and increasingly improbable. Who gets paid? How are they paid? Why are they paid? If all the enslavers died on the Civil War battlefield, who and what parties do we hold accountable? These questions animate the reparations debate and attempt to actualize repair since slavery was abolished in the United States in 1865.

In recent years, persuasive arguments and cases have been made for reparations across the political spectrum. However, with any political differences in these claims and policies, whether from conservative or progressive advocates, in almost every case, reparations are mistakenly conflated with money. To be sure, money matters, especially in a world indelibly impacted and instigated by global racial capitalism. Money-based or *economic reparations* are necessary, though not a holistic reflection of all that is genuinely required to reach some semblance of repair. Through the continued and repeated economic reparations framework, we are led to believe that the death and devastation of slavery can be summed up in and through a blank check awaiting figures delineated by wonks, researchers, and litigators.

But do souls, lives, and human beings have a fixed market rate, an adequate monetary assessment that makes all parties involved whole if reconciled? In my view, the answer is and will always be *no*. Therefore, we must begin with a more radical framing of reparations, an understanding of costs and debts that cannot be neatly monetized. Nor should it be, for there are so many reparations owed, financial and otherwise. For example, a lasting debt of enslavement in any society, especially in the American context, is one of the *intellectual reparations*—the purposeful and public recognition and acknowledgment of the creations, inventions, and ideas of formerly enslaved people and their descendants. Intellectual reparations are precisely their own brand of repair and reconciliation for enslavement, equal if not more important than the money-based pecuniary or economic reparations.

Like their lives, families, and labor, Black ideas were stolen, taken, and attributed to others, usually white people. Black inventions and ideas are still taught and conveyed without proper attribution to their Black creators, inventors, and originators. No origin story provided. No creation story relayed. No Black protagonist to latch on to. Two Black men, a musician and an intellectual, demonstrate this insight well—Charles "Buddy" Bolden, the father of jazz, and W. E. B. Du Bois, the father of American sociology, were born just a few years apart during Reconstruction. Bolden was a child of the South and Du Bois a child of the North.

This expanded reframing of reparations to include other forms alongside financial restoration, like properly acknowledging Black people's intellectual contributions, was swirling especially thunderously as I headed to the theater to see the new film *Bolden* released in Spring 2019. Tackling the history and people that led to the invention of jazz, with the compositions of Wynton Marsalis serving as the score, the film reanimates the world that birthed what is thought to be one of America's most unique contributions to the global community. The rugged and raw Black Storyville, New Orleans, is the protagonist as much as it is the setting. Sepia tones draw us into an America barely reconstructed and baptized in the blood of the Civil War. It was a new world and yet the same one. We learn of Charles "Buddy" Bolden, an unheralded inventor of jazz.

Buddy Bolden has in many ways been lost to history, left to Black collective memory, no proper flowers given. Through film, however, we see the power of representation, as through its attempts, Buddy Bolden gets some due credit, gets overdue recognition, and in the process, gets some form of intellectual reparations. Perhaps inadvertently, the film, in its attempt to acknowledge and call attention to white supremacy and brutality, provides a compelling case for the power of representation as a mechanism for practical and possible repair and reconciliation.

Underneath and atop Buddy Bolden's story is an opportunity to reclaim what has been lost and find people whose contributions should and must be remembered. If America has gifted the world anything of note, it is jazz. And as the film so clearly demonstrates, somewhere between Louis Armstrong's brass section's enticing and bouncing improvisation and the buttons of Bolden's coronet, it is an opportunity to reclaim and repair a significant piece of American history. Jazz as both form and template for intraracial dialogue between Black people is more than a series of riffs and stanzas facilitating the vocal genius of Billie Holiday, Ella Fitzgerald, and Sarah Vaughan and more than an approach scaffolding of the rhetorical genius of Toni Morrison and Amiri Baraka.

Jazz is the musical progeny of the Black church, a kind of gospel foretold in the practice sessions of self-taught musicians as they practiced hymns and spirituals behind the altars of Black churches planted with and across America's chocolate cities. The spiritual striving to the sacred-secular is at the heart of the emergence of the musical genre. Jazz did not just appear. Black people conjured it and summoned it as a new public good. Black people invented it—a powerful, accurate, historical, and current fact. Intellectual reparations never sounded so good or looked so possible.

Buddy's trusty coronet, then, is not simply a musical instrument; it is simultaneously a metaphor for Black industriousness, creativity, and contribution. Bolden's band, lost to history on an unrecovered wax cylinder, is not simply a brave and gifted group; they are always already a metaphor for the unique power of Black collectives to invent using what little Black people have been given in slavery's aftermath. Each chord and tune is wrapped in the mini-freedoms achieved decades following manumission. Like its musical cousins blues, soul, and hip-hop, jazz is quite literally built from the essence of Black people making the most delicious, intoxicating, and libido-moving lemonade from the worst batch of lemons known to humankind.

While recognizing and acknowledging that something as unique and deeply American as jazz emerged from the minds and ingenuity of Black Southerners may not pay the bills or keep the lights on, seeing and hearing Black people's genius properly asserted is beyond value; it's priceless. The film offered one demonstration of the look, feel, and necessity of accomplishing intellectual reparations. To be sure, Buddy Bolden is not an isolated example. For example, the case for intellectual reparations is ever more compelling and more evident if we consider the life and times of W. E. B. Du Bois. Born just a few years after Emancipation in 1868, Du Bois was also Bolden's contemporary.

Fast-forward just a little over a decade from Bolden's death in November 1931. After World War II, Du Bois traveled the globe advocating for nuclear disarmament, sending peacegrams generated from the Stockholm Peace Resolution. On July 13, 1950, just a few months after his eighty-second birthday, W. E. B. Du Bois opened the *New York Times* to find an ominous threat and accusation charged at him and the Peace Information Center organization. Secretary of State Dean Acheson wrote the following: "I am sure that the American people will not be fooled by the so-called 'world peace appeal' or 'Stockholm resolution' now being circulated in this country for signatures. It should be recognized for what it is—a propaganda trick in the spurious 'peace offensive' of the Soviet Union."[1]

Over the next six months, Acheson's attacks on Du Bois reached a fever pitch, upending long-standing plans for a significant bash in honor of Du Bois's eighty-third birthday. Just weeks before his birthday, the Department of Justice formally indicted Du Bois as a foreign agent/spy. "On February 8, I was indicted for an alleged crime," Du Bois intimates in his 1968 autobiography, "on February 14, I was married secretly to Shirley, lest if I were found guilty she might have no right to visit me in jail; February 16 I was arraigned in Washington and on February 19, four days before the dinner, I was released on bail."[2]

Even more, the venue for the birthday bash, the Essex House, canceled his dinner party reservation due to the government's allegations. With the help of his closest supporters, notably sociologist E. Franklin Frazier, Du Bois's eighty-third birthday shindig was moved from Midtown Manhattan to Small's Paradise, a mom-and-pop spot nestled in the chocolate city of Harlem. By November 1951, eighty-three-year-old Du Bois was on trial at a federal courthouse in Washington, DC, with his life and reputation hanging in the balance.

Although over his life he helped found the National Association for the Advancement of Colored People (NAACP), American sociology, and a whole host of ideas and trained many students, as the trial loomed, Du Bois found himself without the full range of friends and associates he had gained over his long career. The toll of the ordeal was evident at the trial, as his jovial nature and youthful spirit had morphed into a worn and hunched posture, and fear and worry etched visible lines in his otherwise smooth, brown face. After a six-day trial, Du Bois was ultimately found innocent. But the damage had been done. Within a few years, he departed the United States for Ghana at the invitation of President Kwame Nkrumah, never to return.

Today, just beyond the shores of Labadi Beach, Ghana, sits Du Bois's final resting place. On a compound several miles from the slave castles, a bust of his face stands beside his final home, House no. 22 First Circular Road, better known as the W. E. B. Du Bois Memorial Centre for Pan African Culture. Du Bois's post-war pivot toward Africa, which led to his fervent interest in ensuring international peace and equity for maligned peoples and nations, had started an intellectual and activist journey that shattered the scholar's faith in the American democratic project. There, in a chocolate city across the Black Atlantic, Du Bois spent his last birthdays reflecting on and imagining a freedom that had not come in the near century he was on earth.

In commemoration of Du Bois's 150th rotation around the sun, in July 2018, I arrived in Ghana and went to the slave castles. And it was there that I realized how there is victory in surviving. I arrived in Accra, went to Du Bois's house, and realized there is sadness in thriving. His work and ideas reflect the tremendous human cost extracted from Black scholars, activists, and regular-smegular-degular folk who dare challenge the status quo. And there are many whose stories we lose, whose lives seem least relevant when the shadow of those who are remembered looms.

We should, of course, use Buddy Bolden and Du Bois's stories as opportunities to revel in the life and work of two of the truest Black inventors and intellectuals the world has known. But we must also remember, as the good sociologist A$AP Rocky reminds in the hook of the popular hip-hop song "No Limit": "It ain't safe. It ain't safe. It ain't safe." Our national security is dependent on cleaning our own house, attending to the piles and piles of dirty laundry replete with stories of slavery, land dispossession, lynching, and the false premise of a hierarchy of human value. Thus, political reparations are necessary. Intellectual reparations are a must. Legal reparations are urgent. Economic reparations are required. Spiritual, spatial, and social reparations are vital. Individually, each has the potential to change the conditions of America for the better. Combined, they are the *radical reparations* that can recalibrate everything and possibly finally address the original sin and its collateral and continuous damage. This we must accept. This we must see. And we are fortunately in a window of opportunity where actionable policies, frameworks, and ideas are available for implementation.

While sipping morning coffee in 2018, my phone rang. I looked away from my cup and at my phone to discover a 202 area code at the front of the number. I confess that when I saw the 202 area code, I was on the verge of not answering, afraid and concerned that any number of governmental offices I had not requested engagement with were on the other line. "The IRS and student loans will just have to leave me a message," I uttered aloud to myself. And then another thought bubbled up inside me, saying, *Answer the call, Marcus! Answer the call.* And so I threw caution to the wind and answered the phone.

On the other end of the line, to my great surprise, was none other than Congresswoman Barbara Lee, and I nearly dropped the phone. Her voice, which I had admired and thus been attuned to for most of my life, reverberated with a palpable, kind seriousness. She graciously informed me that she happened upon the panel on American slavery I moderated at the *LA Times Book Festival* and found it informative. Congresswoman Lee found my moderation and facilitation insightful, fresh, and dynamic. After a long journey from homelessness, this unexpected phone call was affirming and encouraging. She asked that I continue to write and research and follow the path. And as if that wasn't enough to have me on the floor prostrate with gratitude, Congresswoman Lee revealed to me her plan to develop legislation that would authorize the first United States Truth, Racial Healing, and Transformation Commission, aiming to introduce legislation in 2019 as a significant marker and movement toward repair after four hundred years of living with and in the sin of slavery. She asked if I was available and had the time to assist and develop this legislative effort. By this point, I was looking at the phone in disbelief and hadn't realized that we were nestled within the usual pause that comes after a request.

"Most certainly. Congresswoman Lee, it would be my distinct honor to work and do anything I can to assist in this historic effort." I tried to offer a very relaxed and calm tone to hide the fact that inside my body, I was doing handstands, flips, and feeling the call's gravity.

"That is great news. Next week, we will be meeting to kick off the effort, and I hope you will be able to join us." The Congresswoman brought her deputy chief of staff back into the discussion to solidify the details.

"I am there. Count me in."

"Excellent. Thank you, Dr. Hunter." Congresswoman Lee passed the call off to then deputy chief Liz Lee, who kindly gave me the place and time of the planned meeting.

The following week, I was on the first thing smoking to Washington, DC, and looking forward to the meeting. I arrived that morning at Congresswoman Lee's office just as Dr. Gail Christopher was approaching. The visionary behind the reframe from Truth and Reconciliation to Truth, Racial Healing, and Transformation, Gail was ready to get right to work. Having spent many decades studying these issues and working with a host of national and international leaders, Gail's wisdom and clarity were evident and empowering. Former Virginia Representative Tom Perriello also joined us. Together with Congresswoman Lee and several others on the conference call, we discussed the aims and purpose of this proposed legislation. We developed a timeline for drafting and introducing the resolution to establish a United States Truth, Racial Healing, and Transformation Commission. From the beginning, we worked tirelessly and diligently to ensure both in form and practice that this legislation complemented legislative efforts already underway, including the long-championed HR 40 bill to establish a Commission to Study and Develop Reparation Proposals for African Americans, the John Lewis Voting Rights Advancement Act, the GI Repair Bill, the Equal Rights Amendment, Reparations Now, and George Floyd Policing Act.

Over the next few years, there were numerous emails, calls, and meetings to develop thorough-going inclusive legislation that sought to amplify existing calls for repair and racial healing while also emphasizing that now was the time for this nation to do as it has directed other countries—acknowledge the systems of human degradation and human hierarchy that lie at the very premise of its founding. Between government shutdowns, separated families, fake news, and alternative facts, the ambition to introduce the legislation in 2019 did not come to pass. Nevertheless, Congresswoman Lee continued to pursue it and encouraged us that introduction was on the horizon. Remaining steadfast, those who had joined at the inception managed to stay optimistic despite all the evidence suggesting delays were perhaps inevitable.

Then came the reports of a novel virus that had arrived in the United States primarily by way of European visitors. And soon enough, like the virus that is racism, the entire country had been exposed. Then everything shut down. Masks everywhere. Zoom was the new arbiter of meeting space, classroom, and university. Zoom everywhere. Stay-at-home orders everywhere. Overcrowded hospitals everywhere. Death everywhere.

Despite the terrifying pandemic, I began to notice something that gave me great optimism. Public health officials, many of whom had replaced the usual talking heads of cable and national news, were specifying the disproportionate racial impacts of the virus. Centuries and decades of systemic racism were no longer such an amorphous mist. Instead, racism was emerging as a causal explanation for the underlying risk factors for the virus. The pandemic also revealed that the US government had trillions of dollars for an unforeseen crisis. This fact suggested to me that it certainly has the funds and capacity to attend to the known epidemic at its premise, slavery and systemic racism and inequality, which are outgrowths of this crime against humanity.

Two hundred fifty days into the pandemical year of hindsight, my father, Marcus Allan Hunter, died of a sudden heart attack. He was only 33,120 minutes into being age sixty when his heart gave out. Traveling through the South at the time, my father had been on a quest for reparations. Determined to finally leave his birthplace, Philadelphia, my father packed all of his personal effects onto his truck and headed south. Marcus Allan was on his way south in search of his original home or, at the very least, a new home inspired by genealogical investigations he had done on his family. The repair he was searching for was about a material prospect and self-healing long in the making. A fiery Leo, my father was no stranger to cutting all contact with someone, falling outs, and breakups. Over my life, I watched him make and break short and longtime friendships and family relationships. For most of my life, he'd been at odds with his immediate and maternal family. Family holidays had not been gatherings for an extended version of the family. Instead, holiday gatherings were animated just by my immediate family and whatever humor, tensions, and talents we shared.

At the same time, I was also advocating very heavily for congressional cosponsors for the Truth, Racial Healing, and Transformation resolution, Voting Rights Act, and Reparations Study bill. Zoom had taken over my life by that point, so oddly enough, the ability to engage directly with the funeral director in person offered some measure of relief. My dad died in his Savannah, Georgia, hotel room hundreds of miles away from Philly. After speaking with the coroner in Georgia to claim his body, I was told that I needed to arrange with a funeral parlor to get the process in motion to have his body prepared and shipped to Philly.

My father's ascension occurring while he was in the midst of his own reparations quest brought me back to sitting at the red light, this time in Philly, when "B—Better Have My Money" came rumbling across the radio waves. In the wake of his passing, the song returned to me. Soon enough, the song was again on constant replay, blasting through my speaker at a volume that made me sure my neighbors wondered about who exactly was living next door and was I possibly obsessed with Rihanna or Kanye West or profanity or some combination of all of it. In the wake of a pandemic and the deaths of Breonna Taylor, George Floyd, and countless others, the song felt even more prescient. The raucous, deliberately profane warning and promise revealed itself to me as a new age anthem of reparations—a twenty-first-century expansion of "When Will We Be Paid," the Staple Singers' underappreciated 1970s song.

There was a racial reckoning underway, and the ominous sonic progressions underneath Rihanna's melodically commanding alto galloped back into my consciousness. Listened to in one way, the song is a fiercely unapologetic confrontation and reclamation of the sacred though profane means. Listened to in another way—the way that was arriving during the global pandemic in my speakers—is a story of the payoff for waiting. The triumphs awaiting those who have been abused, disrespected, robbed, and cheated are on the horizon with the power to end the waiting game that has been racial equity, healing, and justice. We don't know when Rihanna will encounter those who owe her in the song, but we know she will be victorious when that meeting and collision occur. Rihanna shall take back, receive back, reclaim financial and reputational losses, and win. Six years following the song's release, Rihanna was proven right when *Forbes* declared her a certified billionaire. And the constant replay also allowed me to hear other entities emplacing the pronoun at the front of the song, such as "America," "The United States," "The World," "Europe," "The Future" better have my money—each reflective of institutions and governments that directly benefited, sanctioned, constitutionalized, permitted, and turned a blind eye to the systemic subhuman bondage better known as American chattel slavery.

Yet whenever the word and debates about reparations come up, it is undoubtedly not about the fact of systemic subhuman bondage. Instead, it invariably becomes a debate about money. Questions about who should be paid, why they should be paid, and how much should be paid round out the usual debate. But what if those are the wrong questions centered around a false premise? All reparations do not require direct exchange of monies. Debt relief and credit are such examples. Without direct payment, African Americans could have their debt forgiven and credit repaired overnight. What if Equifax, Experian, and TransUnion began reporting 800+ credit scores? This action alone could allow for systemic access to long overdue banking and entrepreneurial opportunities whereby previously blocked talent and ideas could in short order renew local, state, national, and international economies. Bubbling just beneath the surface of the reparations debate is a real though unspoken combination of worry and fear. A worry that drudging up the past threatens the thinly braided fabric woven to hold all the quilt panels called the United States of America together. Many of the fears tend to emanate from presumed pathologies and dysfunctions believed about Black people. How will they spend the money? What will they buy?

Even when coming from an innocent perspective, these questions treat money as one-dimensional rather than as the multifaceted object it is. Time is money. Currency is money. Wealth is money. Access is money. Energy is money. Memory is money. History is money. Repair is money. Recovery is money. Respect is money. Dignity is money. Truth is money. Healing is money. Restoration is money. Power is money.

We must operate with the understanding and duty that reparations are also about restoring the spiritual damage. On some level, Black people have been attending this part. Despite the wishes of the colonizing Christian missionaries, Black people have globally maintained, sustained, and alchemized cosmologies and religious practices. Black people's global struggle to achieve repair and restoration has required expeditions in their attention to the spirit. Whether it be soul music, soul food, or "soul" as a word in the culture, we are fortunately already amidst an organic though hard-fought era of spiritual reparations.

Until we live in a world where it is safe to advocate for peace without fear of death or defamation while being Black and affirm the Black experience while challenging racial capitalism and white supremacy, we must collectively work together, support, and love on each other to ensure that in our lifetime systemic racism and inequality are counterbalanced by systemic equity, systemic inclusivity, and systemic shared human value and dignity. To achieve that world, we need radical reparations, a dynamically implemented and imagined set of repairs and renovations that by robustly addressing the sins of the past unlock the path to a freer, safer, and more just society. For there are piles of debts to reconcile. There are piles of injuries to repair. And these piles must be sorted to reveal all the forms of reparations needed.

And we have the great fortune to enact policies currently before the United States Congress that could fix America's bottleneck—the massive overlap of systemic poverty and disadvantage and the historically rooted unaddressed needs of Black communities. The problems of poverty, lack of housing and education, and racism are the existing infrastructure for inequity, exclusion, human hierarchy, and hate. Therefore, reparations are an obligation to build a sustainable counterbalancing force, an infrastructure for systemic equity, systemic inclusivity, systemic shared humanity, systemic dignity, and systemic love. Only then will we be able to counter rather than continue to reify the opposing systems of racism, exclusion, and hate that remain alive thanks to centuries of ignorance, band-aid social policies, and refusal to lean into and embrace that slavery helped make America into a nation. It is only by embracing the uncomfortable, painful, and damaging truth that slavery and land dispossession are the twin engines of the premise of America that we can land the plane of destruction that flies overhead, corrupting our very best restitution and repair efforts. Unified with a new imagination about the purpose and power of radical repair, we can proactively build anew. We can collectively unlock restorative transformational alchemy whereby we begin living in a country and world where love, freedom, and equity are not just ideals but the baseline and new premise of our shared reality.

ACKNOWLEDGMENTS

This work is the purest reflection of the places, peoples, and journeys required to make the words that adorn these pages. May these words express my endless gratitude for all that made this possible:

Light for those alongside me.
Optimism for those after me.
Verisimilitude for you, dear reader.
Exaltation for those before me.

NOTES

CHAPTER 2

1. As quoted in Derrick Bell, *Faces at the Bottom of the Well: The Permanence of Racism* (New York: Basic Books, 1992), 55.
2. As quoted in Bell, *Faces at the Bottom*, 55.
3. As quoted in Bell, *Faces at the Bottom*, 60.
4. As quoted in Bell, *Faces at the Bottom*, 61.
5. As quoted in Bell, *Faces at the Bottom*, 61.
6. As quoted in Bell, *Faces at the Bottom*, 61–62.
7. As quoted in Bell, *Faces at the Bottom*, 62.
8. As quoted in Bell, *Faces at the Bottom*, 60.

CHAPTER 5

1. W. E. B. Du Bois, *The Autobiography of W. E. B. Du Bois: A Soliloquy on Viewing My Life from the Last Decade of Its First Century* (New York: International Publishing, 1968), 61; see also "Text of Dean Acheson Statement," *New York Times*, July 13, 1950, 7.
2. W. E. B. Du Bois, *The Autobiography of W. E. B. Du Bois*, 61.

REFERENCES

The following constitute a selected list of resources, scholarship, and works key in the creation and formation of this book. I list these with an abundance of humility and gratitude:

Alroey, Gur. "Journey to New Palestine: The Zionist Expedition to East Africa and the Aftermath of the Uganda Debate." *Jewish Culture and History* 10, no. 1 (2008): 23–58.

Araujo, Ana Lucia. *Reparations for Slavery and the Slave Trade: A Transnational and Comparative History*. London: Bloomsbury Publishing, 2017.

Bell, Derrick. *Faces at the Bottom of the Well: The Permanence of Racism*. New York: Basic Books, 1992.

Beyers, Christiaan. "Reconciling Competing Claims to Justice in Urban South Africa: Cato Manor and District Six." *Journal of Contemporary African Studies* 34, no. 2 (2016): 203–20.

Bittker, Boris I. *The Case for Black Reparations*. Boston: Beacon Press, 2003.

Bogues, Anthony. "C. L. R. James, Pan-Africanism and the Black Radical Tradition." *Critical Arts* 25, no. 4 (2011): 484–99.

Brophy, Alfred L. "Reparations Talk: Reparations for Slavery and the Tort Law Analogy." *Boston College Third World Law Journal* 24, no. 1 (2002): 81.

Butler, Octavia E. *Parable of the Sower* (Parable 1). New York: Open Road Integrated Media, 2012.

Butler, Octavia, Marilyn Mehaffy, and AnaLouise Keating. "'Radio Imagination': Octavia Butler on the Poetics of Narrative Embodiment." *MELUS* 26, no. 1 (Spring 2001): 45–76.

Clegg, Claude A., III. *The Price of Liberty: African Americans and the Making of Liberia*. Chapel Hill: Univ. of North Carolina Press, 2004.

Coates, Ta-Nehisi. "The Case for Reparations." *The Atlantic*, June 2014.

Craemer, Thomas, Trevor Smith, Brianna Harrison, Trevon Logan, Wesley Bellamy, and William Darity Jr. "Wealth Implications of Slavery and Racial Discrimination for African American Descendants of the Enslaved." *The Review of Black Political Economy* 47, no. 3 (2020): 218–54.

Darity, William, Jr. "Forty Acres and a Mule in the Twenty-First Century." *Social Science Quarterly* 89, no. 3 (Sept. 2008): 656–64.

Darity, William, Jr., and Dania Frank. "The Economics of Reparations." *American Economic Review* 93, no. 2 (May 2003): 326–29.

Darity, William, Jr., Darrick Hamilton, Mark Paul, Alan Aja, Anne Price, Antonio Moore, and Caterina Chiopris. *What We Get Wrong about Closing the Racial Wealth Gap*. Samuel DuBois Cook Center on Social Equity and Insight Center for Community Economic Development, 2018.

Darity, William A., Jr., and A. Kirsten Mullen. *From Here to Equality: Reparations for Black Americans in the Twenty-First Century*. Chapel Hill: Univ. of North Carolina Press, 2020.

De Greiff, Pablo, ed. *The Handbook of Reparations*. New York: Oxford Univ. Press, 2008.

Du Bois, W. E. B. *The Autobiography of W.E.B. Du Bois: A Soliloquy on Viewing My Life from the Last Decade of its First Century*. New York: International Publishing, 1968.

———. *Dark Princess*. Jackson: Univ. Press of Mississippi, 1976.

———. *The Souls of Black Folk*. New Haven, CT: Yale Univ. Press, 2015. Originally published in 1903.

Ellis, Stephen. "Liberia 1989–1994: A Study of Ethnic and Spiritual Violence." *African Affairs* 94, no. 375 (April 1995): 165–97.

Fair, Freda L. "'I'm Hard to Catch': Ruth Ellis and Black Queer Longevity in Detroit." *GLQ* 27, no. 4 (2021): 603–27.

Ferreday, Debra. "'Only the Bad Gyal Could Do This': Rihanna, Rape-Revenge Narratives and the Cultural Politics of White Feminism." *Feminist Theory* 18, no. 3 (2017): 263–80.

Foner, Eric. *Gateway to Freedom: The Hidden History of the Underground Railroad*. New York: W. W. Norton, 2015.

Gifford, Paul. *Christianity and Politics in Doe's Liberia*. Cambridge: Cambridge University Press, 2002.

Griffin, Farah Jasmine. "Pearl Primus and the Idea of a Black Radical Tradition." *Small Axe: A Caribbean Journal of Criticism* 17, no. 1 (2013): 40–49.

Haim, Yehoyada. "Zionist Attitudes toward Partition, 1937–1938." *Jewish Social Studies* 40, no. 3/4 (Autumn 1978): 303–20.

Hartman, Saidiya V. *Wayward Lives, Beautiful Experiments: Intimate Histories of Riotous Black Girls, Troublesome Women, and Queer Radicals*. New York: W. W. Norton, 2019.

Horne, Gerald. *The Apocalypse of Settler Colonialism: The Roots of Slavery, White Supremacy, and Capitalism in 17th Century North America and the Caribbean*. New York: New York Univ. Press, 2018.

Horne, Gerald. *The Counter-Revolution of 1776: Slave Resistance and the Origins of the United States of America*. New York: New York Univ. Press, 2014.

Hunter, Marcus Anthony. *Black Citymakers: How the Philadelphia Negro Changed Urban America*. Oxford: Oxford Univ. Press, 2013.

———. "Du Boisian Sociology and Intellectual Reparations: For Coloured Scholars Who Consider Suicide When Our Rainbows Are Not Enuf." *Ethnic and Racial Studies* 39, no. 8 (2016): 1379–84.

———. "Racial Physics or a Theory for Everything That Happened." *Ethnic and Racial Studies* 40, no. 8 (2017): 1173–83.

———. "Seven Billion Reasons for Reparations." *Souls* 20, no. 4 (2018): 420–32.

Hunter, Marcus Anthony, and Zandria F. Robinson. *Chocolate Cities: The Black Map of American Life*. Oakland: Univ. of California Press, 2018.

Johnston, Harry. *Liberia*. New York: Dodd, Mead, 1906.

Kaba, Mariame. *We Do This 'Til We Free Us: Abolitionist Organizing and Transforming Justice*. Chicago: Haymarket Books, 2021.

Kelley, Robin D. G. *Freedom Dreams: The Black Radical Imagination*. Boston: Beacon Press, 2002.

Kendi, Ibram X. *Stamped from the Beginning: The Definitive History of Racist Ideas in America*. New York: Hachette, 2016.

Levmore, Saul. "Changes, Anticipations, and Reparations." *Columbia Law Review* 99, no. 7 (Nov. 1999): 1657.

Marable, Manning. "An Idea Whose Time Has Come . . ." *Newsweek* 138, no. 9 (2001): 22.

———. *How Capitalism Underdeveloped Black America: Problems in Race, Political Economy, and Society*. Chicago: Haymarket Books, 2015.

———. "Reparations and Black Consciousness." *Souls* 5, no. 3 (2003): 33–37.

Martin, Esmond B., and T. C. I. Ryan. "A Quantitative Assessment of the Arab Slave Trade of East Africa, 1770–1896." *Kenya Historical Review* 5, no. 1 (1977): 71–91.

Martin, Michael T., and Marilyn Yaquinto, eds. *Redress for Historical Injustices in the United States: On Reparations for Slavery, Jim Crow, and Their Legacies*. Durham, NC: Duke Univ. Press, 2007.

McCarthy, Thomas. "Coming to Terms with Our Past, Part II: On the Morality and Politics of Reparations for Slavery." *Political Theory* 32, no. 6 (Dec. 2004): 750–72.

McEachern, Charmaine Ruth. "Working with Memory: The District Six Museum in the New South Africa." *Social Analysis: The International Journal of Social and Cultural Practice* 42, no. 2 (1998): 48–72.

Moran, Mary H. *Liberia: The Violence of Democracy*. Philadelphia: Univ. of Pennsylvania Press, 2013.

Moten, Fred. *In the Break: The Aesthetics of the Black Radical Tradition*. Minneapolis: Univ. of Minnesota Press, 2003.

Mutibwa, Phares Mukasa. *Uganda Since Independence: A Story of Unfulfilled Hopes*. Trenton, NJ: Africa World Press, 1992.

Oded, Arye. "Israeli-Ugandan Relations in the Time of Idi Amin." *Jewish Political Studies Review* 18, no. 3–4 (Fall 2006): 65–79.

Patterson, Orlando. *Rituals of Blood: Consequences of Slavery in Two American Centuries*. New York: Basic Books, 1998.

————. *Slavery and Social Death: A Comparative Study*. Cambridge, MA: Harvard Univ. Press, 1982.

Posner, Eric A., and Adrian Vermeule. "Reparations for Slavery and Other Historical Injustices." *Columbia Law Review* 103 (2003): 689.

Quandt, William B. "Camp David and Peacemaking in the Middle East." *Political Science Quarterly* 101, no. 3 (1986): 357–77.

Quandt, William B., ed. *The Middle East: Ten Years after Camp David*. Washington, DC: Brookings Institution Press, 1988.

Rabaka, Reiland. *Africana Critical Theory: Reconstructing the Black Radical Tradition, from W. E. B. Du Bois and C. L. R. James to Frantz Fanon and Amilcar Cabral*. Lanham, MD: Lexington Books, 2009.

Raboteau, Albert J. *Slave Religion: The "Invisible Institution" in the Antebellum South*. Oxford: Oxford Univ. Press, 2004. Updated edition.

Reid, Richard J. *A History of Modern Uganda*. Cambridge: Cambridge Univ. Press, 2017.

Roberts, George. "The Uganda–Tanzania War, the Fall of Idi Amin, and the Failure of African Diplomacy, 1978–1979." *Journal of Eastern African Studies* 8, no. 4 (2014): 692–709.

Robinson, Cedric J. *Black Marxism, Revised and Updated: The Making of the Black Radical Tradition*. 3rd ed. Chapel Hill: Univ. of North Carolina Press, 2021.

Rodney, Walter. *How Europe Underdeveloped Africa*. New York: Verso Trade, 2018. Originally published in 1972 by Bogle-L'Ouverture.

Rowell, Charles H., and Octavia E. Butler. "An Interview with Octavia E. Butler." *Callaloo* 20, no. 1 (1997): 47–66.

Scott, David. "On the Very Idea of a Black Radical Tradition." *Small Axe: A Caribbean Journal of Criticism* 17, no. 1 (March 2013): 1–6.

Smith, Clint. *How the Word Is Passed: A Reckoning with the History of Slavery across America*. New York: Little, Brown and Company, 2021.

Soudien, Crain. "Memory and Critical Education: Approaches in the District Six Museum." *Africa Education Review* 3, no. 1–2: 1–12.

St. Felix, Doreen. "The Prosperity Gospel of Rihanna." *Pitchfork*, April 1, 2015.

Telhami, Shibley. *Power and Leadership in International Bargaining: The Path to the Camp David Accords*. New York: Columbia Univ. Press, 1990.

"Text of the Acheson Statement," *New York Times,* July 13, 1950, 7.

Thomas, Greg. "On Sex/Sexuality & Sylvia Wynter's 'Beyond . . .': Anti-Colonial Ideas in 'Black Radical Tradition.'" *Journal of West Indian Literature,* 10, no. 1–2 (Nov. 2001): 92–118.

Tobin, Jacqueline L., and Raymond G. Dobard. *Hidden in Plain View: A Secret Story of Quilts and the Underground Railroad.* New York: Anchor, 2000.

Torpey, John. *Making Whole What Has Been Smashed: On Reparations Politics.* Cambridge, MA: Harvard Univ. Press, 2006.

Zink, Robert James. "'Uhuru Wa Watumwa' As a Documentary of the Arab Slave Trade in East Africa." Master's thesis, Duquesne University, 1969.